Notions of the Americans

The American Culture

NEIL HARRIS—General Editor

NOTIONS OF THE AMERICANS

1820-1860

Edited,

with Introduction and Notes by

David Grimsted

George Braziller   New York

Published simultaneously in Canada by Doubleday Canada, Limited.
All rights reserved.
For information address the publisher:
George Braziller, Inc.
One Park Avenue
New York, N.Y. 10016

Standard Book Number: 0-8076-0568-9, cloth
0-8076-0567-0, paper

Library of Congress Catalog Card Number: 77–132199
FIRST PRINTING
Printed in the United States of America.

Preface

"Do not tell me only of the magnitude of your industry and commerce," wrote Matthew Arnold during his visit to the United States in the 1890's; "of the beneficence of your institutions, your freedom, your equality: of the great and growing number of your churches and schools, libraries and newspapers; tell me also if your civilization—which is the grand name you give to all this development—tell me if your civilization is *interesting.*"

The various volumes that comprise THE AMERICAN CULTURE series attempt to answer Matthew Arnold's demand. The term "culture," of course, is a critical modern concept. For many historians, as for many laymen, the word has held a limited meaning: the high arts of painting, sculpture, literature, music, architecture; their expression, patronage, and consumption. But in America, where physical mobility and ethnic diversity have been so crucial, this conception of culture is restricting. The "interesting" in our civilization is omitted if we confine ourselves to the formal arts.

The editors of THE AMERICAN CULTURE, therefore, have cast a wider net. They have searched for fresh materials to reconstruct the color and variety of our cultural heritage, spanning a period of more than three hundred years. Forgotten institutions, buried artifacts, and outgrown experiences are included in these books, along with some of the sights and sounds that reflected the changing character of American life.

The raw data alone, however fascinating, are not sufficient for the task of cultural reconstruction. Each editor has organized his material around definitions and assumptions which he explores in the volume introductions. These introductions are essays in their own right; they can be read along with the documents, or they can stand as independent explorations into social history. No one editor presents the same kind of approach; commitments and emphases vary from volume to volume. Together, however, these volumes represent a unified effort to restore to historical study the texture of life as it was lived, without sacrificing theoretical rigor or informed scholarship.

NEIL HARRIS

Contents

III   DEMOCRATIC TRAUMAS

Illustrations

THE FACE OF AMERICA / 297.

An American looking at Cooperstown in 1825:

> There are retrospects of the past, which, brief and familiar as they are, lead the mind insensibly to cheerful anticipations, which may penetrate into a futurity as dim and as fanciful as any fictions the warmest imagination can conceive of the past. . . . Here all that reason allows may be hoped for in behalf of man. . . . We live in the excitement of a rapid and constantly progressive condition. The impetus of society is imparted to all its members, and we advance because we are not accustomed to stand still. . . . I have stood upon this identical hill, and seen nine tenths of its smiling prospect darkened by the shadows of the forest. You observe what it is today. He who comes a century hence, may hear the din of a city rising from that very plain, or find his faculties confused by the number and complexity of its works of art.

> JAMES FENIMORE COOPER
> *Notions of the Americans*

"In the heart of each man there is contrived,
by desperate devices, a magical island. . . . We place
it in the past or future for safety, for we dare
not locate it in the present. . . . We call it memory
or a vision to lend it solidity, but it is neither
really: it is the outcome of our sadness, and of
our disgust with the world that we have made."

E. M. FORSTER

Introduction

DAVID GRIMSTED

1. THE PRETENSIONS OF CULTURAL HISTORY

In 1828 James Fenimore Cooper published *Notions of the Americans* to explain to Europeans the United States where "the institutions, the state of society, and even the impulses of the people, are in some measure new and peculiar." Lafayette's request that he chronicle his 1825 triumphal American tour provided Cooper's excuse for a cultural survey of his native land. His patriotism whetted by a long stay in Europe, his intention was overtly revisionist: to challenge and refute the hostile sketches of the United States drawn by certain English travelers. The result was an honest book with many sharp observations; Cooper, for instance, developed from his European perspective (much as Louis Hartz was to do a century and a quarter later) a "consensus" view of American society:

> People talk of the fluctuations which are necessarily the consequences of a popular government. They do not understand what they say. Every other enlightened nation of the earth is at this moment divided between great opposing principles; whereas here, if we except the trifling collisions of pecuniary interests, everybody is of the same mind, except as to the ordinarily immaterial question of a choice between men. . . . We have ever been reformers rather than revolutionists.

But the book had neither the complexity nor the coherence to make it successful intellectually or financially. It had cost Cooper much more effort than his fiction; he later concluded that it accomplished only an undermining of his literary reputation.

Cooper's efforts—and his problems—are akin to those of cultural historians generally: to winnow from the mass of data those things which would most truly and complexly suggest the stuff of a given society at a particular point of time. Subject matter defines most of the slices into which any national history is carved—labor history is about workers just as diplomatic history concerns foreign policy. So too with those overlapping fields of social or cultural or intellectual history: social history considers institutions and groupings; cultural history centers on the arts or popular culture; intellectual history traces the course and influence of significant ideas.

Yet much cultural (or intellectual) history is not content with a prescribed subject slice of the much-carved historical pie, but seeks the interstices, the explanatory connections between the fields and forms and aspects of a particular historical time and place, just as Cooper tried to tie observations about manners and literature and law and technology into a general picture of American character. All of history's subject areas are, of course, arbitrary divisions that permit deeper consideration of a part by labeling out of existence surrounding multiplicity. The more interesting historical work often does something to re-establish connection between the chosen little historical world and the diverse complexity from which it was wrenched. Cultural history broadly is openly committed to finding those notions which make a unit of the diverse individuals and groups and aspects of a given society. For the cultural historian, no subject matter can be blocked arbitrarily from the field of vision; everything has fascination in itself, and, if one could detect truly, offers clue to, has connection with, everything else.

"Cultural history" is to my mind a more satisfactory designation than "intellectual history" simply because it associates itself with the anthropologic concept of "culture" which includes not just art or legend, but all aspects of one society and especially those beliefs and assumptions that tie together political, economic, familial, social, artistic and religious behavior. Alexis de Tocqueville, the most profound observer of Jacksonian America and of democratic society generally, placed "shared beliefs" at the center of social understanding much as later cultural anthropologists have done. "Obviously without such common belief no society can prosper, say rather no society can exist; for without ideas held in common there is no common action and without common action there may still be men, but there is no social body." Cultural history then is the attempt to find those shared beliefs and assumptions and concerns that hold together the various groups and individuals and activities of a particular society.

The parallel commitment to the potential interest of each bit of data and to the search for the most generalized of social beliefs is what gives to much of cultural history, as it did to Cooper's *Notions*, its uncertainty, the sense of a half-drunken wandering between the quaintly specific and the abstractly portentous. It attempts to describe the mind and the emotions of an age and, in getting at the devious object, nothing is despicable or beside the point. What people wore or ate, their work and their recreations, what excited and what amused them, their gossip and their philosophy, all are telling if one is but a clever listener. The cultural historian takes Emerson seriously when he argues that if one understood deeply "the meal in the firkin; the milk in the pan; the ballad in the street; the news of the boat; the glance of the eye; the form and gait of the body," life becomes "no longer a dull miscellany and lumber-room," but fraught with form and meaning.

Quite obviously, explaining the notions and beliefs and ideas of an individual person, even a highly articulate one who has left copious written explanations of his thought and conduct, is difficult; and as the subject of inquiry expands so do the complexities. When one talks of Jacksonian America, the topic includes so many diverse things, so many hostile groups, so many different people that to speak of shared beliefs, to attempt a conglomerate description is clearly in part pretentious folly.

Particularly is this true for modern societies where the pace of technological change is rapid and the degree of consciousness about social patterns is great, both of which promote intellectual diversity and quicken chronological shifts in ideas and emphases. But there remains human desire to understand man not only individually but conglomerately, and so we talk of groups and periods and nations, or any combination of these things, as if they had some unifiable identity, even when their multiplicity is well recognized. Alfred North Whitehead has made explicit the kind of assumption any historian makes who sets out to describe a period:

> The intellectual strife of an age is mainly concerned with . . . questions of secondary generality which conceal a general agreement upon first principles almost too obvious to need expression, and almost too general to be capable of expression. In each period there is a general form of the forms of thought; and, like the air we breathe, such a form is so translucent, and so pervading, and so seemingly necessary, that only by extreme effort can we become aware of it.

Of course the intellectual strife of an age itself may properly interest an historian, but inasmuch as he pursues that abstraction, an historical age, he grasps for the assumptions and conditions that unite as well as divide contending groups and individuals within it. James Fenimore Cooper's Yankee vernacular term "notions," avoiding the overly intellectual connotation of "ideas" and the aesthetically portentous concept of "myth," is good for the level of perception and conviction suggested here. Cultural history aims at the notions of a given society, the kind of intellectual baggage that everyone peddled or struggled to avoid buying.

The difficulty of capturing the "first principles almost too obvious to need expression, and almost too general to be capable of expression" is clear. Like all questions of historical explanation, the truth depends upon the viewers' angle of vision as much as upon the evidence he looks at. The worth of an historical interpretation dealing with questions of how or why or so what must be judged by aesthetic rather than scientific standards: a particular answer is seldom wholly right or wrong, but is more complex or coherent or convincing or weighty or provocative or probingly honest than a competitor. And in fields like cultural history, where there is less strenuous control of explanation by certain obviously important facts, the aesthetic quality of judgment becomes greater.

Which is not to say that anything goes. For if history is an art, it is a peculiarly classic one that demands not self-indulgence, but a merging of self within the historical form and content. Robert Frost's aphorism that free verse is "like playing tennis with the net down," is even more applicable to history which lacks profound concern for the "reality" being described. Writing free verse may be like playing tennis in blue jeans— sloppy-looking, and a violation of good form to the purist, but obviously the game can be played, and played effectively, that way. A person who writes history without the net of groping toward ideas through pertinent available fact, may be brilliant—ace serves and excellent backhands—but he simply is playing some other sport.

George Santayana held that history lacks the perfectness of form of art and the wholeness of argument of philosophy, but that its tentative and cumbrous movement from incident to meaning, from past to present, possesses a quality that is peculiarly true to life, if never fully satisfying to one's instincts toward perfection of form and system. In some ways history's peculiarities—its sometimes un-idea-ed antiquarian love of the thing itself, its hesitancy to take up either first principles or to round its world into a sonnet, the temerity of its explanations, its stuttering unease in approaching universal meanings or laws—give it special relevance to the modern mind which, in Paul Tillich's words, has had to accept "the world in pieces." History is certainly the most existential of intellectual disciplines where existence not only precedes essence, but insures that no overbearing certainties or truths will impinge on the sovereign complexity of being. Historians generally have a commonsensical wariness about Whitehead's "fallacy of misplaced concreteness," or conclusiveness.

Because of the suggestive tentativeness of the answers cultural history gives, there's particular value in presenting not its conclusions but some of its facts, the documents of cultural history—songs, stories, poems, sermons, philosophy, social criticism, political arguments, broadsides, editorials, diaries, paintings, cartoons, photos—to let the reader search for meanings and connections in their diverse subject matter and varied intimations. My own interests in (and feelings and conclusions about) the United States, 1820 to 1860, have dictated and imposed a rough pattern on the selections, but I think the documents present both a panorama of the types of sources a cultural historian may use and a kind of introduction to the period that doesn't preclude answers and observations different from my own.

Perhaps the best words with which to close these reflections on the pretensions and perplexities of cultural history are those of the early American philosopher Peleg White, who clearly accepted Ralph Waldo Emerson's dictum that the American scholar must be not a "bookworm" but "Man Thinking."

> Larnin in books, with pictars in 'em, is all very well, and ought to be encouraged, but a feller won't know much arter all about human natur, if he don't go around and see folks, and get acquainted with 'em and hear 'em "blow off." Some great writer (I forget his name now, but I kinder think it is Billy Marsh, the poet) has said that there are more things in Haaven and Airth than is dreamed on in the *purtiest kind of books*.

2. NOTIONS OF JACKSONIAN AMERICANS

Tocqueville's *Democracy in America*, written after the Frenchman's visit to this country in 1833, expressed the contrast he saw between a disintegrating aristocratic society in Europe and the democratic society fated to replace it which he had observed in Jacksonian America. A single theme runs through this very complex and wide-ranging book: that democratic society created a new type of man—more independent, energetic, expectant, and lonely than ever before. Man in an aristocracy was born into a class and an occupation and a community and a church and an hereditary family, all of which both controlled and protected him in a net of relatively permanent relationships. In a democratic society all these things became voluntary or transitory so that the individual's potential for improvement might be unleashed. The family controlled only until children reached adulthood; people, especially those of conspicuous ability or ambition, readily changed locale and jobs as opportunity offered; class connections changed as one succeeded or one failed, especially in an economic sense; and one could readily change one's church to match one's new class connections or any new notions one had. Samuel Woodworth's "Dr. Stramonium," moving from place to place and job to job, was a prototype of the potential mobility of American society, though those that succeeded best probably conned less and worked harder than the comic vagabond so prominent in American mythology.

Fully recognizing the advantages of American mobility, Tocqueville also saw its sadness and its dangers. Because few permanent relationships intervened between the individual and the mass, there was a loneliness and unhappiness despite manifold evidence of success and comfort. Cooper felt obliged to deny the charge that Americans were by temperament cold, and foreign observers often commented on the joyless intensity with which Americans pursued even their recreations. Melville's "Bartleby the Scrivener" is the most moving literary evocation of alienation in American life. Bartleby is in some ways the triumphant individualist who perfectly follows his own inclinations in the face of social conventionality. His employer, the story's representative of social truth and expectation, is helpless in the face of Bartleby's quietly relentless "I prefer not." But Melville's man alone finds not the fullness of truth and beauty that Emerson predicted; he starves himself to death because finally he "prefers not" to eat. American society was far from ready to accept such Camus-like heroes as representative men, but the country indeed had many "strangers." Francis Lieber noted how an open and competitive society left few men really at ease and contributed to the "appalling frequency of alienation of mind" in the United States.

Tocqueville saw danger, too, in democratic society's potential for despotism of a kind more repressive than any previously known. Again because little intervened between man and society en masse, he recognized that the pressure to conform to social standards would be powerful, and that this might repress the liberty and integrity of the unique individual. He also foresaw how the alienation of democratic man, which unleashed powerful yearnings for renewed certainties and complete identity with the mass, might lead to totalitarian governments of unprecedented power.

The American angle of vision was very different from Tocqueville's, though many Americans shared his uneasiness about aspects of their society. Tocqueville coined the term "individualism" but used it in a negative way to suggest the pursuit of one's interests in opposition to the pursuit of social well-being and integration. He recognized, however, that most Americans dissented from this sort of distinction and insisted that "self-interest rightly understood" was the opposite of selfishness and indeed the primary friend of social betterment. He also noted how the American notion that one's own betterment and society's were integral led to kindliness and generosity and philanthropy and social concern on a scale unprecedented in Europe.

American confidence that there was no incongruity between individualism and social responsibility was based on certain assumptions carried over from the eighteenth century. To imply any inevitable evil in human society or nature was, the *Democratic Review* pointed out, to suggest "a radical deficiency implanted by its Creator in human society" and the impossibility of human results "analogous to the beautiful and glorious harmony of the rest of his creation." To avoid this kind of sacrilege—this indictment of the goodness of both Nature and Nature's God—it was necessary to see that there need be no conflict between any kind of good: personal, social, or natural. If, indeed, Nature was orderly and benevolent, God beneficent, man at least capable of great goodness and American government and society the best organized in the world—and most Americans assumed these truths—then evil must be some kind of mistake or the result of certain traditional fallacies that encumbered the free workings of men's minds.

P. W. Grayson and Ralph Waldo Emerson were both radicals because they carried the implications of these beliefs further than most Americans wished to go, but their central conviction, modified by common sense, was widely shared: if society and man were to be perfected, the individual must be free to follow the promptings of his own heart and genius. This emphasis on the good inclinations of the individual heart gave intensity to the political and social struggles of Jacksonian America. For eighteenth-century Americans, Nature had been tied to reason, to faith that man's untrammeled intellect could provide answers to social dilemmas. In the nineteenth century the tendency was to substitute Nature and Feeling for Nature and Reason. Part of the problem was similar to that which had led David Hume to make a similar substitution in the eighteenth century: reason could not give sure answers to human problems unless the answers were in essence assumed. It also could give some answers, including such things as Humean skepticism or Francis Wright's plan to substitute communal schools for family training, that frightened society. Feeling offered a surer safeguard to accepted standards if one assumed that true feeling incorporated all important aspects of conventional morality and excluded all else; if one's instincts led one to seduce or rob or murder, this was not the result of feeling, but of its corrupt opposite, passion. Emerson assured his audience that his call for unflinching truth to one's instincts would never allow "the bold sensualist" to "use the name of philosophy to gild his crimes"; something called "the law of consciousness abides"—and this seemingly insured basically moral behavior as surely as any law of conscience.

Feeling not only offered a safer source of knowledge, but also a more democratic one. Some men obviously had more education and intelligence than others, but learning was not necessary for—might even interfere with—the great prompter to truth, the unfettered heart. This indeed made all men equal, and made controversy not simply a matter of disagreement, but of depravity on the other side. If one were sure of the purity of one's own motives, any serious dispute proved the baseness of the other person. This contributed much to the politics of passion in the era with its duels and brawls and violence. It was not only fiery Andrew Jackson making war against a "monster bank" that he believed was trying to kill him. So quiet a man as James K. Polk psychologically had to take himself out of the race for a second term to prove his disinterestedness, in contrast to those who opposed any part of his program, all of whom, Polk confided in his *Diary*, subordinated patriotism to gross personal ambition.

The stress on nature in the sense of pretty scenery and on the supremacy of natural instinct also allowed the United States compensation for cultural inferiority. Americans were bitterly self-conscious about the condescension of Europeans toward their culture, and those who cared for the arts were convinced that the true greatness of a nation must show itself eventually in great art. But until an American Shakespeare or Michelangelo came along, there was comfort in appeal to the country's natural wonders and to its people's natural virtue. Henry Nash Smith and Leo Marx have pointed out how the country pictured its spontaneous virtue as moderating between the overcivilization of Europe and the savagery of Indians, much as "feeling" moderated between overrefinement and passion. Thoreau might say he loved both "the wild and the good"; Thomas Cole might suggest the fascination of wild nature. But more typical were Emerson, who refused to admit any difference between the natural and the good, or Asher Durand, who pictured lovely nature and social man as perfectly "Kindred Spirits."

Despite Nature's loss of most of its passional potential, there remained a peculiar intensity about the American sense of closeness to nature that made Tocqueville warn of the dangers of pantheism in a democracy. It showed up not only in transcendentalism—Thoreau's desire to be neck deep in a swamp and Whitman's inclination to live among the animals—but in such peculiarly homespun technological mysticism, with its note of violent passivity, as that of Peleg White:

And here I am tu the Dodginsville tavern, the winder to my room histed up so that I can look right out upon Law Belly River, not the river of Sticks, but the Ohio filled amost with old logs, a floating on tu Etarnity or some *other* place down South. Sometimes I wish I war a log, a floatin down the Ohio, coolly and comfortably punchin' in the sides of a steamboat now an then, or tu be split up and made inter merlasses hogsheads, or licker barrels, or to be filled with *hard cider*, and drinked around to all the log cabing meetins. It would be amost lappin nice though, that's a fact—and then the idea of bein' well-filled, bunged tight, and hooped so strong as tu be actilly beyond the fear of *bustin' biler*. It would be nigh on as much as human natur could stand—that's a fact.

One wonders how common for Americans might have been the nightmare vision of nature painted by Charles Deas—Indian, white, and trapped animal bent on destroying one another even as they plunge toward emptiness and death. Whatever, neither artist nor society had the technical skill nor moral will to embody the suppressed vision. Deas puts in an Indian observer to make the painting comfortably real rather than psychological, genre rather than expressionist. This inability to accept what he sensed may partly explain why Deas spent most of the remainder of his life in an insane asylum.

Those notions that bind a society together also incorporate the issues that create its conflicts. And both contemporary observers and consequent historians chose to divide their society into "conservatives" and "liberals." Despite the haziness of such designations, usage has wedded, for good and ill, the historian to the job of making some sense of them.

The issue that best separates "liberals" from "conservatives" in the period is the completeness of faith in social improvement if the individual were freed from what Grayson called the "dead weight of the past" so that he might truly seek "in the joyous, genial climate of his own free spirit, for all the rules of his conduct." Ralph Waldo Emerson and Charles Grandison Finney both believed in man's capability for salvation and God's beneficent justice, but Emerson—and, in less emotive form, the Unitarian movement—was liberal in religion because man's natural self was seen as wholly compatible with God's goodness, while Finney more conservatively saw the need for the sacrifice of self to God's will before man could really move toward his own and social perfection. Henry Clay and Andrew Jackson both accepted free enterprise, but the former thought the government could help things along a bit by protective tariffs and internal improvements that would aid the general welfare, while Jackson (as President, at least) saw any governmental action as unwise favoritism and toying with the natural order of things. Joseph Story and Robert Rantoul agreed that the country's inherited English common law should be democratized to American needs; Story conservatively argued that changes be made as problems and defects emerged, but Rantoul wished to demolish the whole system and to erect the few and perfected laws the country needed from whole cloth. Grayson gave the radical view of the question: demolish the legal system and don't bother rebuilding what inevitably will be an imperfect and compulsive structure. The same divisions run through arts and literature: everyone wanted truly American works of art, but conservatives saw these in terms of traditional structures and techniques while liberals called for the individual fancy to invent new forms and new styles to accord with the new world. Washington Irving and James Fenimore Cooper and Nathaniel Hawthorne were conservative writers in that they worked in (and, in Hawthorne's case, played with) traditional forms and language. Thoreau and Melville and Walt Whitman were liberal in the use of idiosyncratic words and forms.

Such a definition allows a rough separation of Democrats and Whigs into liberal and conservative. Certainly the fight over the National Bank, the period's greatest political controversy aside from slavery, fits well. Whigs were dedicated to the institution which offered in important ways both support and control of the country's private economy; for Jacksonians it became the "Monster," the great symbol of governmental interference with the natural order in favor of special interests. The issue was complicated by the political question, that of so much power being put in private hands, but the bank's director, Nicholas Biddle, suggested that the government take over effective control of it, which would have created an incipient Federal Reserve System. The Jacksonians were not interested because of their conviction that the government should not be involved at all. Their solution, after the temporary expedient of farming the funds out to "pet banks," which did encourage grossly speculative capitalism, was the Sub-Treasury Plan, which withdrew government influence on economic growth entirely and is perhaps as close as a modern government could come to keeping its funds in an old mattress.

The trouble with applying "liberal" and "conservative" in this sense is that, in American historiography, the terms have been less descriptive category than moral denominator, even before Arthur Schlesinger's dashingly partial *Age of Jackson* turned all controversy into a proto-New Deal struggle between oppressive capitalists and the people, especially workingmen, bent on correcting the system so that it could continue to operate justly. The definition of liberal and conservative suggested here accords closer to the "classical" or "European" sense of the terms than the meanings they have taken on in the United States since the Populist-Progressive movements. It is European "liberalism," what William Appleman Williams labels "the principles of *laissez nous faire*," much transformed at times by democratic and Utopian connotations into an extreme belief in natural freedom and harmony in all fields, that makes the Jacksonian strengths and failures so perplexing to modern viewers. The Jacksonians took nothing more seriously than the desire for as little government as possible; this stands at the crux of almost all of their arguments—note, for example, how the *Democratic Review* uses it to dissolve any conflict between majoritarian power and minority rights. It was with point that the leading Democratic newspaper took for its motto the slogan: "The world is too much governed."

A lot of Whigs were well-off individuals contented with the status quo and many Democrats were speculative capitalists anxious that the government not interfere with their private economic coups, but the more interesting figures in both parties showed complex, if not very constructive, responsiveness to social needs and problems. The Democrats in their rhetoric were more majoritarian than the Whigs, who coupled their belief in democracy with concern for minority rights, legality, and checks and balances. Given the extent of democratic suffrage, the Whig position in some ways was more courageous and valuable, but the Democratic stance did give them some claim to represent what the *Democratic Review* called the cause of Humanity, "a cheerful creed, a creed of high hope and universal love, noble and ennobling; while all others imply a distrust of mankind, and of the natural moral principles infused into it by its Creator, for its own self-development and self-regulation."

The Democratic position allowed them to take the lead in some social change; their chariness of law, for instance, supported their drive against imprisonment for debt, and their majoritarian convictions led to an elected judiciary's replacing an appointed one in many states. But their confidence in a perfect natural order intervened between sentiment and policy so that they did little to counteract such things as growing inequalities of wealth and opportunity. It was rather conservatives, committed also to democratic progress, who were most prominent in the various reforms and experiments and practical measures, limited as these were, to combat the ills of industrialism and urbanism. Nicholas Biddle more than Andrew Jackson had ideas about how to avoid the worst aspects of untrammeled capitalism; Frederick Grimké more than the *Democratic Review* or John C. Calhoun had practical ideas about ways to protect minority rights in a belligerently majoritarian society; the Whig Horace Greeley much more than Democratic editor William Cullen Bryant turned his paper into an organ for exposing all kinds of social ills and for advocating all kinds of cures. P. W. Grayson was in some ways a more feeling man than Joseph Story, as he was more penetrating in his analysis of the weaknesses of any legal system, but he contributed nothing to the improvement of the American judiciary. Story on the other hand, whose social expectations were modulated by the dense thickets of legal reality, classified and improved judicial concepts and procedures in many ways.

The period's faith in man and God's essential goodness, the nation's success in conquering and filling a continent, its belief in progress, its manifold accomplishments have often led historians to picture it as an age of buoyant, bumptious optimism. More recently several scholars have noted a strange disgust, uneasiness, and even terror with which Americans viewed their society in these years. If this optimism and dread are logically antithetical, they are psychologically perfectly compatible. Indeed, to hold a vision of a perfected or at least constantly improving man and society inspired special responsiveness to the personal tragedies and social failings that honest men saw. Few people were willing to deny their central convictions about man's nature and destiny—too much was staked on them, and besides too much happened to keep alive the hope in human progress—but they nonetheless recognized, dimly or poignantly, the disturbing gap between what ought to be and what they saw about them. Perhaps they even sensed with Hawthorne that evil existed not simply in artifacts that could be burned in the great reform bonfire but in some recess of the human heart itself. There is symbolic significance in one of the institutions developed by the period's revivalists: the anxious seat, where people could go who felt spiritual unrest without any clear calling yet to a better way.

Some of this malaise was the result of purely personal difficulty— professional failure, or familial unhappiness or spiritual emptiness or physical sickness—all of which were hard to reconcile to the genial official ideology. The period's frequent riots and murders and public disasters and divorces awakened deep interest in part because they were so hard to fit to the assumptions about life and man that most people made. And the chief elements of social change stimulated both the period's confidence in man's potential and the uneasiness that accompanied it.

The fruition of political democracy has long been the historical trademark of the Jacksonian period, and rightly so if one interprets democracy not simply in a legalistic sense of the right to vote but in a psychological one of the mass of men's feeling that they are the effective governors. Politics was not simply a governing function, but was (with its slogans and songs and torch-lit parades and treatings) a main source of interest and entertainment for millions of Americans. It developed into a national sport and, like all games, it let people take part in a contest about issues that interested them and offered a clear decision about winning or losing that didn't deeply affect their lives. Mrs. Trollope, the sharp-eared and sharp-tongued Tory gentlewoman, reported this conversation with a Cincinnatian:

> "You spend a good deal of time in reading the newspapers."
> "And I'd like you to tell me how we can spend it better. How should freemen spend their time, but looking after their government, and watching that them fellows as we gives offices to, does their duty, and gives themselves no airs."
> "But I sometimes think, sir, that your fences might be in more thorough repair, and your roads in better order, if less time was spent in politics."
> "The Lord! to see how little you knows of a free country! Why, what's the smoothness of a road, put against the freedom of a free-born American? And what does a broken zig-zag signify, comparable to knowing that the men that we have been pleased to send up to Congress, speaks handsome and straight, as we chooses they should?"
> "It is from a sense of duty, then, that you all go to the liquor store to read the newspapers?"
> "To be sure it is, and he'd be no true born American as didn't. I don't say that the father of a family should always be after liquor, but I do say that I'd rather have my son drunk three times in a week, than not look after the affairs of his country."

European observers were surprised, after the passions of an American political campaign, that the losing side so wholly accepted the result. But Americans knew that not only would any other response sunder society; it would also prevent a renewal of the game next year.

If one accepts the psychological definition of democracy—the individual man's sense of his importance in making political decisions—then there becomes little difference between democracy and demagoguery, or the emotive tricks that draw otherwise disinterested men into the political process. In this sense, American democracy came of age with the election of 1840 when Whigs systematized and expanded such Jacksonian demagogic techniques as song, cider, and slogan, and decisively expanded the American electorate to win the election for "Old Tippecanoe, and Tyler, too." As early as 1837 the *Democratic Review* was lamenting the unseemly clamor for political spoils, the local corruption, and the subordination of issues to emotive claptrap in its own party; in the 1840's almost everyone was appalled by the general quality of American elections and politicians. Few people were against democracy, or even its excesses, but surely democracy deserved something better than gross electoral corruption, hordes of men expecting political jobs and favors in return for their support, and trimming politicians whose deepest convictions were about the importance of their being elected. Andrew Jackson was both the last of the old Presidents who, in retrospect anyway, had pursued what they thought right rather than what they thought popular, and, with his justification of the spoils system and the emotion that surrounded him, the first of the new. If the bleak picture of American political life was overdrawn, it was felt strongly enough to keep the nation's only widely beloved political figure, Henry Clay, out of the Presidency and to create special enthusiasm for the candidacy of nonpoliticians like Generals Harrison and Taylor—and real grief at the death of each man soon after he took office.

Economic change increased psychological perplexity. The accomplishments were great—in communications, in industrialization, in national and individual wealth. There were many cases of poor people becoming fabulously wealthy, and probably most people who worked hard and faithfully lived with some comfort and prospect of progress. But there were the severe depressions of 1819 and 1837 and 1857, and there were the growing discrepancies of wealth and the obvious poverty and degradation of a large group of people in the urban areas, which became especially apparent with the influx of Irish into America in the late 1840's and early 1850's.

Responses to such problems tended to be sentimental rather than practical. Mrs. Mowatt's solution was perfectly typical: somehow the problem of business corruption raised in *Fashion* was solved when fashionable wife and daughter were shipped off to the country to learn "old-fashioned virtues." No one was very clear about what could or should be done, but the concern was profound, especially in the 1850's. Never were urban and working class deprivations more relentlessly exposed by such diverse sources—see Greeley's *Tribune*, the anonymous proletariat pamphlet *The Almighty Dollar!* and even Fanny Fern's *Little Ferns for Fanny's Little Friends*—until the Muckrakers moved the nation toward the Progressive era. There seems reason to believe that the United States might have acted to correct some of these sorriest aspects of laissez-faire industrialism had they not been politically submerged by the slavery controversy.

Unease about economic matters had psychological as well as social stimulation. In the period before the Civil War the businessman, the man who made a lot of money, was not a cultural hero; instead he was looked at something in the way Mrs. Mowatt looks at the businessman in her play *Fashion*—not exactly evil, but morally suspect. Yet, in America, one's comfort and social position were dependent almost wholly on money, and everyone knew this. "Is it the doom of all men in this nineteenth century to be weighed down with the incumbrance of a desire to make money and save money, all their days?" questioned George Templeton Strong. "I suppose if my career is prosperous, it will be spent in the thoughtful, diligent accumulation of dollars, until I suddenly wake up to the sense that the career is ended and the dollars dross. So are we gradually carried into the social currents of our time, whether it be the tenth century, or this cold-blooded, interest calculating age of our own." Mrs. Sigourney's passionate appeal for parents to avoid sullying their children's character by showing a concern for financial distinctions is significant both for its message and its necessity. The ideal of American life, both economic and psychological, had long been that "he that tilleth his land shall be satisfied." The Jacksonian moral psyche was scarred deeply by the obvious dissatisfaction, the constant striving for more, of democratic men already blessed with enough.

Technology also contributed to the confidence-dread syndrome of the period. Each new invention and building project brought forth paeans to the golden age now opened, in tone much like Woodworth's euphoria over the Erie Canal's completion; but Thoreau's tart comment on the telegraph—so far as he knew Maine had nothing to say to Texas— reflected fairly widespread questioning of the overeasy linking of mechanical and human progress. When the Atlantic cable was laid, New York City celebrated the event under a huge sign, "Peace on Earth and Good Will to Men," but on the same night prominent residents of Staten Island, to improve their property values, burned an isolation hospital in their midst and left its diseased inmates without shelter. Strong noted in his *Diary*, "I fear that this millennium over which we've been braying is made of gutta-percha and copper wire and is not the real thing after all."

The numerous public catastrophes caused by faulty workmanship or handling in buildings, steamboats, and railroads further awakened doubts about this kind of progress. When Hawthorne showed the traveler on his "Celestial Railroad" swaying uneasily over the Slough of Despond on a questionably constructed bridge, he spoke both mechanical and metaphorical truth. And Ralph Waldo Emerson foresaw in his *Journal* the dilemma that haunts twentieth-century man:

Don't trust children with edged tools. Don't trust man, great God, with more power than he has, until he has learned to use that little better. What a hell should we make of the world if we could do what we would! Put a button on the foil till the young fencers have learned not to put each other's eyes out.

Technology also threatened man's sense of controlling his own destiny by making him servant rather than master of the world around him. Emerson's lament that "things are in the saddle and ride mankind" was widely felt. The poignancy of the John Henry ballad and the fireboys' decade-long struggle against the steam engine grew from man's sense of loss of position and importance in the face of the more efficient machine.

Economic and political and technological fears were combated in many ways. Perhaps most important were religion and the home as protective devices to bridge distinctions between glowing ideal and disturbing fact. Religion at least gave some solace and explanation for the personal tragedy of death and disease and failure, so frequently a part of life and so hard to handle in the optimistic context. And both institutions, without challenging the hopeful creed, were capable of suggesting modifications of it and of instilling moral guidelines in life, which made them peculiarly important to those conservatives who had the strongest latent reservations about the goodness of man's natural self. Particularly the home, the most basic of social units, could be a refuge for those social ideals so rudely buffeted in the outer world of politics and finance. William R. Taylor has shown how Sarah J. Hale, the editress of *Godey's Lady's Book,* saw the family as antidote to social disintegration; Heman Humphrey, in his advice to parents, made clear that only proper family structure could prevent political collapse. It was this idealized "Home, Sweet Home," outside of competitive strife and peculiarly the domain of gentle woman, that supposedly offered real happiness to man and the best hope of protection against those social pressures most threatening to what he ought to be. People played out their dreams in the 1840's and 1850's in board games like the Ives Company's "The Reward of Virtue" and "The Mansion of Happiness"; it was still a long way to "Monopoly" as social enthusiasm.

Religious and familial safeguards couldn't really counteract those standards of conduct and those results that created uneasiness, but neither could such things be allowed to impugn the central optimistic faith. Hence devices were invented to give fears expression and at the same time to subordinate them to faith in man, America, and God's order. Simplest was the device of villainy, used most obviously in the period's melodramas, where these human monsters provided real terror but where their eventual failure supposedly restored a perfectly ordered moral universe. Rather similar was the Jacksonian attack on "stock-jobbers" and "speculators," and common attacks on the follies of fashion. Not that Americans didn't speculate or ape foreign foolishness, but these qualities were so exaggerated in the rhetoric, its exemplars were so much more wicked or foolish than any normal human being, that all tie to meaningful social criticism was cut.

Even more common was the escape through nostalgia, the tacit condemnation of the present generation by idealizing the preceding one. Fears and uneasiness could be shifted to this short-term contrast seemingly without denying convictions about long-range improvement. Marvin Meyers has argued persuasively that the Jacksonians' uneasiness about their own period revealed itself particularly in their nostalgic idealization of Jeffersonian agrarianism. The same pattern can be seen at least as clearly in Whig oratory, and even more pronouncedly in that of third-party movements such as the Anti-Masons and Know-Nothings, where nostalgia was crystallized around the pursuit of specific social villains. The nicknames given to leading politicians—Old Hickory, Old Kentucky, Old Granite, Old Rough and Ready, Old Fuss and Feathers—expressed not only popularization of national politics, but yearning for the just-lost good old days. How else explain how William Henry Harrison could be elected President while being affectionately called not only "Old Tippecanoe," but "Old Granny" to boot?

Yearnings after the "Old Oaken Bucket" and the rest of the paraphernalia of a simple, rural existence were a large part of the sentimental baggage of the period. Mrs. Mowatt's contrast between the weak and dishonest businessman and Adam Trueman, who had stayed strong of mind and pure of heart (and incidentally fairly rich) back on the farm in Catteraugus County expressed a profound social conviction:

> Heigh-ho, I grieve, I grieve
> For the good old days of Adam and Eve.

Augustus Longstreet's story "The Dance" is moving because it captures the nostalgia for an older style of life given up for no very good reason, but also because Longstreet has the honesty to wonder if his retrospective Utopia ever really existed at all.

Indeed, the sense of perfection recently lost was reconcilable to man's constant progress only by a tacit recognition that it was part dream. Jackson's advisers might pine for Jeffersonian agrarianism, but most of them would go on, as Bray Hammond has shown, to be highly successful capitalists, none of them to be "yeoman farmers." Woodworth's affection for "The Old Oaken Bucket" back on his father's farm was real—indeed life there probably was better than his New York City poverty—but he had no intention of returning. This separation of truths according to different spheres of reality was used in complex ways to keep joined the ideal expectations of what life must be if this were a good and morally ordered world, and the actual way it worked out.

Emerson's intellectual distinction between "reason" and "understanding," between an intuitive faculty that perceived a higher truth and the practical or mechanical mental processes that solved everyday problems, was similar to mental mechanisms commonly used in society. If one segregated the workaday world from the realm of higher truth, it was possible to act effectively in one and, despite apparent contradictions, retain belief in the other. This distinction was partially embodied in the social roles allotted to the sexes: the man was to embody the practical sphere which involved questions of power and money-getting and sexual impulse, while woman was, in Cooper's words, not to come "in any manner in contact with the world" so that she might be guardian of the higher sphere where resided morality, religion, and culture. Hence the great preponderance of women in American church services (Thomas Hart Benton argued that Andrew Jackson was quite religious, on the grounds that he was always kind to the ministers his wife invited to their home), and the excessive female pretensions of modesty which so annoyed Mrs. Trollope. When the Philadelphia Museum displayed plaster casts of classical statues, separate hours were set up for male and female viewing.

The heart of the "genteel tradition" came to be this separation of life into two spheres, and the cherished notion that the higher sphere was at least as real, and certainly more to be talked about, than any nasty reality about sex or money-getting. It's easy to laugh at this—George Bernard Shaw and others have so delightfully taught us how—but there was frequently poignancy, and nobility too, in the efforts to hold together the notion of a morally orderly universe with the messy business of living.

Most of the serious writing of the period felt obliged to uphold the higher values, and this does much to explain the convoluted diction, the elaborate formalism of so much oratory and writing. What was being talked about were higher truths, and colloquial simplicity was reserved for the workaday world. John Kouwenhoven has made a distinction between the "vernacular" in American art—that is, the everyday things like carpets and tools and house-building where the country displayed its real genius—and "formalism" in such areas of official culture as painting, statuary, and architecture where it produced poor duplicates of European impulses. The terms are at least equally useful when applied to language and used to illumine the period's desire to uphold the ideal and yet take into consideration reality. Formalistic was the language of the transcendent sphere, the vernacular was the voice of the workaday world: as Henry James said, a nation's language always reflects its spirit. Part of the greatness of men like Thoreau and Lincoln was that, more than others, they combined both formal and popular language into a recognizable American idiom. F. O. Matthiessen has pointed out how Thoreau's writing benefited from his knowledge of Greek and Latin word roots; he also knew and loved American slang. It's his ability to write and pun in both verbal worlds that gives such texture and life to his prose.

If one could talk home-truths in the vernacular, it was still wise to present them in humorous guise; it was safer to let in worldly wisdom only under the pretense of not being fully serious. Samuel Woodworth's poems show the dualism perfectly; seriously he presents the notion that only a monster could toy with the affections of a woman, but Dr. Stramonium can travel from town to town leaving most of the eligible women pregnant without any moral condemnation because he's comic; formal characters scorn acquisition and pine for a little cottage near the wood, but Jonathan, as vernacular character, can be both lovable and sharp at trade. The American comic tradition, often written in vernacular, was a way of giving expression to worldly wisdom about sex and money and man's dilemma without giving way to it. Mrs. Trollope thought American liking for jokes featuring the Yankee's sharpness in trade proved the country's tendencies to amoral acquisitiveness. They did, but the joke form also revealed that they were embarrassed about it.

Another romantic handling of covert fears about the country's character was the development of the cavalier myth. William R. Taylor has shown how there existed in American culture a contrast between Yankee qualities—acquisitiveness, selfishness, drivingness—and the gracious, cultivated benevolence of the cavalier. The South cultivated the notion—William Gilmore Simms's *Woodcraft* gives perhaps its most complete expression—but the North believed in it, too. The Jacksonian publicist Francis Grund, in a book bitterly lampooning people with aristocratic pretensions in the North, was ecstatic in praise of a "real" aristocracy like that of the South. This idealization of the South to give voice covertly to their own disgust at gross acquisition faded in the 1850's in face of Southern belligerence.

The Southern attitude was understandable: moral attacks against their peculiar institution had always stung deeply, in part because slavery was impossible to defend without impugning the American democratic beliefs which also meant much to them. And the inferiority of their society in all measurable ways daily increased: in population, in wealth, in improvements, in comfort, in education, in art, and, finally in their last citadel of equality, the United States Senate. But Northern reaction was also certain. When the South treated as hero the man who came up behind Charles Sumner with a club in the Senate chamber and beat him senseless, it was not only George Templeton Strong who decided the South was less chivalric than barbaric. Frederick Law Olmsted's brilliant observational reports on the South also helped in these years to change the South's image from that of *Gone With the Wind* to *Tobacco Road* with a few (in Strong's words) "woman-beating, baby-selling bully-aristocrats" thrown in. It was this deterioration of the Southern myth, along with the moral-religious stand against slavery that abolitionists, black and white, had long fostered and which Grierson describes so powerfully in *The Valley of the Shadows*, that terminated the period in Civil War.

PART ONE

THE DEMOCRATIC
EGO

1. Favorite Songs

SAMUEL WOODWORTH

Woodworth was born in Scituate, Massachusetts, in 1784, the son of poor farming parents. The local parson, recognizing his intellectual quickness, tutored him, but was unable to get his parishioners to send Woodworth to college as he had led the boy to hope. Woodworth instead apprenticed himself to a printer in Boston; some unsuccessful business and literary speculations caused him to flee first to New Haven, and in 1808 to New York City, to avoid imprisonment for debt. He remained there for the rest of his life, supporting a large family by editing ephemeral magazines and writing popular verses and musical comedies. In 1818, when his poems were first collected in book form, the editors wrote what remains the most touching biographical notice of Woodworth (and indeed of any early American poet): he was at that time editing a Swedenborgian journal, *The New Jerusalem,* and writing verse on the glories of America and the old oaken bucket while living in "a sphere of life but one degree removed from penury and want" in New York City. In the 1820's, his fortunes improved a bit and the popularity of his writings greatly. He wrote several comic operas, one of which, *The Forest Rose* or *American Farmers* (1825), was the first truly American play to be successful abroad; in London it was given over 100 performances. Many of his poems— "The Bucket," "The Hunters of Kentucky," "The Needle," "Cottage Near the Wood"—won their way into the hearts of Americans—and incidentally into McGuffey's *Readers* when they appeared in 1836. Most of Woodworth's poems were set to music, and it is really as popular lyricist that he is significant. He was the George M. Cohan, the Oscar Hammerstein II of the 1820's.

Samuel Woodworth, *Melodies, Duets, Trios, Songs, and Ballads, Pastoral, Amatory, Sentimental, Patriotic, Religious, and Miscellaneous* (New York, 1830).

COLUMBIA, THE PRIDE OF THE WORLD

Oh, there is a region, a realm in the West,
   To Tyranny's shackles unknown,
A country with union and liberty blest,
   That fairest of lands is our own.
Where commerce has opened her richest of marts,
   Where freedom's bright flag is unfurled,
The garden of science, the seat of the arts,
   Columbia, the pride of the world.
Her clime is a refuge for all the oppressed,
   Whom tyranny urges to roam;
And every exile we greet as a guest,
   Soon feels like a brother at home.
Then hail to our country, the land of our birth,
   Where freedom's bright flag is unfurled;
The rays of whose glory have lighted the earth,
   Columbia, the pride of the world.

OUR NATIVE LAND

In this vast rising empire of the west,
With freedom, science, fame, and plenty blest,
Where earthly comforts in profusion flow,
Each virtuous bosom must with rapture glow;
For here, where Liberty her fane has built,
No grief is found, but in the path of guilt;
No pains, nor fears, the good man's heart annoy,
No tears are shed but those of sympathy or joy.

THE HUNTERS OF KENTUCKY

Air—"Miss Bailey"

Ye gentlemen and ladies fair,
   Who grace this famous city,
Just listen, if ye've time to spare,
   While I rehearse a ditty;
And for the opportunity,
   Conceive yourselves quite lucky,
For 'tis not often that you see,
   A hunter from Kentucky.
Oh! Kentucky, the hunters of Kentucky,
   The hunters of Kentucky.

We are a hardy free-born race,
   Each man to fear a stranger,

Whate'er the game, we join in chase,
    Despising toil and danger;
And if a daring foe annoys,
    Whate'er his strength and forces,
We'll show him that Kentucky boys
    Are "alligator horses."
Oh! Kentucky, the hunters of Kentucky,
    The hunters of Kentucky.

I s'pose you've read it in the prints,
    How Packenham attempted
To make Old Hickory JACKSON wince,
    But soon his scheme repented;
For we with rifles ready cock'd,
    Thought such occasion lucky,
And soon around the General flock'd
    The hunters of Kentucky.
        Oh! Kentucky, &c.

You've heard, I s'pose, how New-Orleans
    Is famed for wealth and beauty—
There's girls of every hue, it seems,
    From snowy white to sooty;
So Packenham he made his brags,
    If he in fight was lucky,
He'd have their girls and cotton bags,
    In spite of Old Kentucky.
        Oh! Kentucky, &c.

But JACKSON, he was wide awake,
    And wasn't scared at trifles;
For well he knew what aim we take,
    With our Kentucky rifles;
So he led us down to Cypress swamp,
    The ground was low and mucky;
There stood John Bull, in martial pomp,
    And here was Old Kentucky.
        Oh! Kentucky, &c.

A bank was raised to hide our breast,
    Not that we thought of dying,
But then we always like to rest,
    Unless the game is flying;
Behind it stood our little force—
    None wished it to be greater,
For every man was half a horse,
    And half an alligator.
        Oh! Kentucky, &c.

They did not let our patience tire,
    Before they showed their faces—
We did not choose to waste our fire,
    So snugly kept our places;
But when so near we saw them wink,
    We thought it time to stop them;
And 'twould have done you good, I think,
    To see Kentucky pop them.
        Oh! Kentucky, &c.

They found at last 'twas vain to fight
    Where lead was all their booty,
And so they wisely took to flight,
    And left us all the beauty.
And now, if danger e'er annoys,
    Remember what our trade is,
Just send for us Kentucky boys,
    And we'll protect you, Ladies.
        Oh! Kentucky, &c.

THE GRAND CANAL

While millions awaken to Freedom the chorus,
    In wreathing for valor the blood-sprinkled bay,
The new brilliant era which opens before us,
    Demands the rich tribute of gratitude's lay;
For ours is a boast unexampled in story,
    Unequalled in splendor, unrivalled in grace,
A conquest that gains us a permanent glory,
    The triumph of science o'er matter and space!
For realms that were dreary, are now smiling cheery,
Since Hudson and Erie like sisters embrace.

From heroes whose wisdom and chivalrous bearing
    Secured us the rights which no power can repeal,
Have spirits descended as brilliantly daring,
    To fix on the charter Eternity's seal.
Behold them consummate the giant conception,
    Unwearied in honor's beneficent race,
While nature submits to the daring surreption,
    And envy and ignorance shrink in disgrace.
For realms that were dreary, are now smiling cheery,
Since Hudson and Erie like sisters embrace.

The nymphs of our rivers, our lakes, and our fountains,
    Are now by the monarch of ocean caressed;

While spurning the barriers of forests and mountains,
    Bold Commerce enriches the wilds of the West.
Then hail to the sages, whose wisdom and labors
    Conceived and perfected the brilliant design;
Converting the remotest strangers to neighbors,
    By weaving a ligament nought can disjoin;
For regions once dreary, are now smiling cheery,
Since Hudson and Erie like their waters combine.

THE BUCKET

Air—"The Flower of Dumblane"

How dear to this heart are the scenes of my childhood,
    When fond recollection presents them to view!
The orchard, the meadow, the deep-tangled wild-wood,
    And every loved spot which my infancy knew!
The wide-spreading pond and the mill that stood by it,
    The bridge, and the rock where the cataract fell,
The cot of my father, the dairy-house nigh it,
    And e'en the rude bucket that hung in the well—
The old oaken bucket, the iron-bound bucket,
The moss-covered bucket which hung in the well.

That moss-covered vessel I hail'd as a treasure,
    For often at noon, when return'd from the field,
I found it the source of an exquisite pleasure,
    The purest and sweetest that nature can yield.
How ardent I seized it, with hands that were glowing,
    And quick to the white-pebbled bottom it fell;
Then soon, with the emblem of truth overflowing,
    And dripping with coolness, it rose from the well—
The old oaken bucket, the iron-bound bucket,
The moss-covered bucket, arose from the well.

How sweet from the green mossy brim to receive it,
    As poised on the curb it inclined to my lips!
Not a full blushing goblet could tempt me to leave it,
    The brightest that beauty or revelry sips.
And now, far removed from the loved habitation,
    The tear of regret will intrusively swell,
As fancy reverts to my father's plantation,
    And sighs for the bucket that hangs in the well—
The old oaken bucket, the iron-bound bucket,
The moss-covered bucket that hangs in the well!

THE WATERMELON

Air—"Away with Contention"

'Twas noon, and the reapers reposed on the bank
    Where our rural repast had been spread,
Beside us meandered the rill where we drank,
    And the green willows waved overhead.
Lucinda, the queen of our rustical treat,
    With smiles, like the season, auspicious,
Had rendered the season and banquet more sweet,
    But, oh! the dessert was delicious!

A melon, the richest that loaded the vine,
    The kind-hearted damsel had brought,
Its crimson core teem'd with the sweetest of wine,
    "How much like her kisses!" I thought.
And I said, as its nectarous juices I quaff'd,
    "How vain are the joys of the vicious!
No tropical fruit ever furnish'd a draught
    So innocent, pure, and delicious.

"In the seeds which embellish this red juicy core
    An emblem of life we may view,
For human enjoyments are thus sprinkled o'er
    With specks of an ebony hue.
But if we are wise to discard from the mind
    Every thought and affection that's vicious,
Like the seed-speckled core of the melon, we'll find
    Each innocent pleasure delicious."

BANKRUPTCY OF THE HEART

Air—"Erin go Bragh"

Let infamy cover the dastard, that meanly
    Can sport with the peace of an innocent maid,
For there is no pang which the heart feels so keenly
    As finding its confidence basely betray'd.
No power can retrieve such a wide desolation,
As spreads o'er the face of the mental creation,
When once a sincere trusting heart's adoration
    Has been with a cold-blooded treason repaid.

For woman, dear woman, ne'er traffics by measure,
    But risks her whole heart, without counting the cost;
And if the dear youth whom she trusts with the treasure
    Be shipwreck'd, or faithless, her capital's lost.
For all she was worth, was her stock of affection,

And bankruptcy follows, with sad retrospection,
And nothing can ever remove the dejection
   That preys on a bosom whose prospects are cross'd.

VARIETY

The noblest talent love can claim,
Is never to appear the same;
For 'tis variety alone,
That props the urchin-tyrant's throne.
So do the seasons, as they range,
Afford new pleasure when they change:
The sweetest flower would cease to cheer,
Should fragrant spring bloom all the year.

THE NEEDLE

The gay belles of fashion may boast of excelling
   In waltz or cotillion—at whist or quadrille;
And seek admiration by vauntingly telling,
   Of drawing, and painting, and musical skill;
But give me the fair one, in country or city,
   Whose home and its duties are dear to her heart,
Who cheerfully warbles some rustical ditty,
   While plying the needle with exquisite art.
The bright little needle—the swift-flying needle,
   The needle directed by beauty and art.

If Love have a potent, a magical token,
   A talisman, ever resistless and true—
A charm that is never evaded or broken,
   A witchery certain the heart to subdue—
'Tis this—and his armory never has furnished
   So keen and unerring, or polished a dart;
Let Beauty direct it, so pointed and burnished,
   And oh! it is certain of touching the heart.

Be wise then, ye maidens, nor seek admiration
   By dressing for conquest, and flirting with all;
You never, whate'er be your fortune or station,
   Appear half so lovely at rout or at ball,
As gayly convened at a work-covered table
   Each cheerfully active and playing her part,
Beguiling the task with a song or a fable,
   And plying the needle with exquisite art.

OH, WOMEN ARE ANGELS

Oh, women are angels, in limbs,
   In person, and manners, and features,
But what shall we say of the whims,
   That govern these comical creatures?

By turns they will fondle and tease—
   With what would you have me compare them?
Though buzzing and stinging like bees,
   For the sake of the honey we bear them.
     Yet women are angels, you see,
       There's something so charming about them,
     Whatever their oddities be,
       Oh, we never could manage without them.

There are some that resemble ice-cream,
   Which coldly forbids you to sip, sir;
But however frosty it seem,
   It will melt with the warmth of your lip, sir.
While others, like counterfeit grapes,
   The best imitations are hollow,
With beautiful colors and shapes,
   But oh, they're the devil to swallow.
         Yet women are angels, &c.

What strange contradictions they show,
   In matters of conjugal bliss, sir,
While frowning and crying "no, no!"
   They wish you to take it for "yes, sir."
Pursue, and how swift they will fly,
   All panting with fears and alarms, sir,
Retreat—and I'll bet you my eye,
   They'll pant, by-and-by, in your arms, sir.
         Yet women are angels, &c.

JONATHAN'S COURTING

JONATHAN:

I cannot tell the reason, but I really want a wife,
And every body tells me 'tis the sweetest thing in life;
But as for cheeks like roses, with pouting lips, and such,
I know no more about them, than Ponto does of Dutch.
         Tol de rol lol, &c.

HARRIET [*Imitating*]:

If you expect to please me and win me for your bride,
You'll have to lie and flatter, and swear, my lad, beside—
So now begin to practice, and if you'd have me wed,
Declare you even love, sir, the ground on which I tread.
                                        Tol de rol lol, &c.

JONATHAN:

I'll tell you that sincerely, nor think it any harm,
I love the ground you walk on, for 'tis your father's farm,
Could that be mine without you, I'd be a happy man,
But since you go together, I will love you if I can.
                                        Tol de rol lol, &c.

HARRIET:

If I consent to have you, we must reside in town,
And sport a coach and horses, to travel up and down—
With footmen all in livery, to make a splendid show,
And when you don't attend me, I will get another beau.
                                        Tol de rol lol, &c.

JONATHAN:

If that's your calculation, we never can agree,
For such a mode of living will never do for me—
And as for beaux and lovers, though you may like the fun,
I guess the deacon's Sally will be content with one.
                                        Tol de rol lol, &c.

KATE ROMPWELL

Kate Rompwell is a funny lass, with lips as sweet as treacle,
And for a partner in a jig, I never know'd her equal,
She'll run, and jump, and wrestle, too, although she's fat and weighty,
And many a time upon the green I've tripped the heels of Katy.
    O, my Katy! my pretty bouncing Katy.

Her eyes are blue as indigo, or high-bush huckle-berry,
Her cheek and lips are red as beets, or like a full ripe cherry;
Her teeth are white, her hair is brown as a rusty-coat petate,
And like two dumplins are the breasts of pretty buxom Katy.
    O, my Katy! my pretty buxom Katy.

One 'lection night, the candle out, perhaps a little tipsy,
I caught a female in my arms, and thought it was the gipsy.
But zounds, it prov'd her maiden aunt, a little short of eighty,
That I'd mistaken in the dark for pretty buxom Katy.
    O, my Katy, my pretty buxom Katy.

COTTAGE NEAR THE WOOD

The fortune I crave, and I sigh for no more,
   Is health and contentment, apparel and food,
The smile of affection from one I adore,
   And a neat little cottage that stands near a wood.

While the slaves of ambition sell comfort for fame,
   Be mine the applause of the wise and the good,
A conscience that daily acquits me of blame,
   And a neat little cottage that stands near a wood.

Let others for grandeur and opulence toil,
   I'd share not their turbulent joys if I could,
The treasure I seek is affection's sweet smile,
   And a neat little cottage that stands near a wood.

AMERICAN FARMERS

MILLER:

And now relieved from day's turmoil,
   Let festive pleasures fill each breast,
And no intruding sorrows spoil,
   The song or mirthful jest.
For lords of the soil, and fed by our toil,
   American farmers are blest, my boys,
   American farmers are blest.

CHORUS:

For lords of the soil, &c.

LYDIA:

Ye fair, who seek a splendid lot,
   Behold content, a richer prize,
Within the humblest ploughman's cot,
   That rank and pride despise.
And palace or cot, whatever your lot,
   The farmer your table supplies, my dear,
   The farmer your table supplies.

CHORUS:

For lords of the soil, &c.

WILLIAM:

> If some gay rival gain a smile
>> From her who holds your plighted vow,
> Whatever pangs you feel the while,
>> Let smiles adorn your brow;
> For nought can annoy a husbandman's joy,
>> If Heaven but prosper the plough, my boys,
>> If Heaven but prosper the plough.

CHORUS:

> For lords of the soil, &c.

JONATHAN:

> By girls we may be thus cajoled,
>> But not by any dandy blade:
> A Yankee's honour can't be sold,
>> Whatever price be paid.
> But tempters are told, as we pocket the gold,
>> 'Tis all in the way of trade, my boys,
>> 'Tis all in the way of trade.

CHORUS:

> For lords of the soil, &c.

BELLAMY:

> Would you a maiden's heart assail,
>> Be careful or you'll miss the mark,
> For Hymen's torch with some prevail,
>> While others choose a spark;
> But modest or frail, peep under her veil,
>> Before you make love in the dark, my boy
>> Before you make love in the dark.

CHORUS:

> For lords of the soil, &c.

DOCTOR STRAMONIUM

Air—"Nothing at All"

1

A last and a lapstone, were once my delight,
And I sung while I hammered, from morning till night;
But all the day's earnings, at eve, I would spend,
Till the *thread* of my credit was brought to an *end*.

Spoken

For I was up to a thing or two, and loved fun, passed the night in reciting Shakespeare at the ale-house, and kept myself awake the next day, by beating time with the hammer, while I sung—

Make a death, cut a stick, high time I tramp'd,
Rise again, tick again, credit new vamp'd.

2

I next taught the gamut, the sharps, and the flats,
To a nasal-twang'd bass, and a treble of cats;
Till my *private* duet with a miss, got abroad,
Which chang'd the *key note*, and produced a *discord*.

Spoken

A little love affair, that ran *counter* to my wishes, and induced some slanderous tongues to pronounce the whole *tenor* of my conduct to be thorough *bass*. . . .

Fa, sol, la; fa, sol, la; fa, sol, la, me;
Hop a twig, such a rig ought not to be.

3

A travelling merchant I quickly became,
With a new stock in trade, a new dress, and new name;
And I bartered my goods with such exquisite grace,
That I left a fair mourner in every place.

Spoken

"O Tabitha, what will become of me! The dear sweet Mr. Rover, (for that was my travelling name,) my dear sweet Mr. Rover, the pedler, is gone, and perhaps I shall never see him again. O dear!" "*Your* dear sweet Mr. Rover, indeed! I'd have you to know, cousin Keziah, that he is *my* dear sweet Mr. Rover, and he has left me something to remember him by."—"O the base, wicked deceiver! He has left me something too." Thus would they sympathize with each other, or tear caps for poor Rover, while I was unconsciously preparing a similar mine to spring in the next village, or jogging quietly along the road, inviting every one to buy my

Dutch ovens, cullenders, dippers and pans,
Broaches and buckles, with ear-rings and fans.

4

A schoolmaster, next, with a visage severe,
Board, lodging and washing, and twelve pounds a year,
For teaching the rustics to spell, and to read
The New-England Primer, the Psalter and Creed.

Spoken

You must know, that I undertook to hammer a little learning through the calfskin'd pates of seventy or eighty square-toed, leather-headed numskulls. But after vainly trying the experiment at both ends of the patients, I lost my own patience, and my school into the bargain, and was glad to make a precipitate retreat with a whole skin: and this so forcibly reminded me of my musical scrape, that I struck up the old chorus of

Fa, sol, la; fa, sol, la; fa, sol, la, me;
Hop a twig, such a rig ought not to be.

5

I then became preacher without any call,
When a sweet village lass came to hear brother Paul;
And told her experience o'er with such grace,
That I gave the dear creature an ardent embrace.

Spoken

There was the devil to pay, and poor I once more in the vocative. But, I made my escape to the back-woods, singing my old Crispin ditty—

Make a death, cut a stick, high time I tram'd,
Rise again, tick again, credit new vamp'd.

6

And now a physician, with cock'd hat and wig,
I can feel ladies' pulses, look wise, and talk big;
With a fine ruffled shirt, and good coat to my back,
I pluck the poor *geese*, while the ducks exclaim *quack!*

Spoken

. . . "Let me see your tongue, Miss."—"My tongue! Law souls, Doctor, what in the world has the tongue to do with the heart?" "In general, Miss, not much; but your case is an exception." "An exception! O goody gracious! now, you don't say so; is an exception a dangerous disorder, Doctor?" "Not at all dangerous, Miss. An application of stramonium externally, and copious draughts of catnip tea internally, will soon restore you."—The lady's heart becomes composed, I pocket my fee, and make my exit, singing—

Feel the pulse, smell the cane, look at the tongue,
Touch the gold, praise the old, flatter the young.

2. From Classic to Gothic

Illustrations

1. *Philadelphia from Girard College, Thomas V. Walter, arch., 1833.*

40

2. *The Hermitage of Andrew Jackson, rebuilt in 1835, possibly from Robert Mills'
plans.*

3. *Capital on the columns of
the Litchfield mansion in
Brooklyn, Andrew Jack-
son Davis, arch., 1854.*

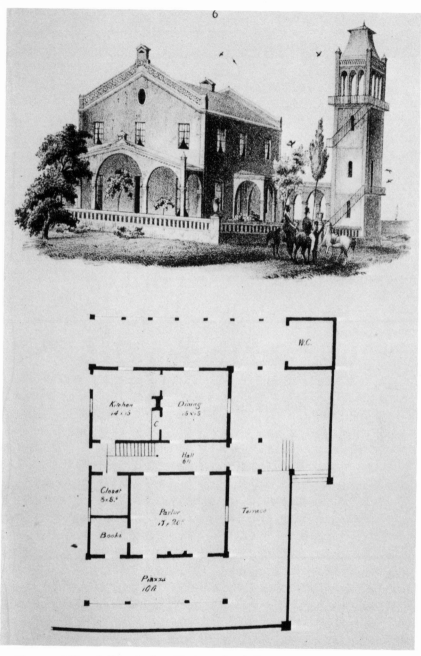

4. *House and Plan, Andrew Jackson Davis, arch., 1848.*

5. *Trinity Church, New York City, Richard Upjohn, arch., 1846.*

6. *Wedding Cake House, Kennebunk, Maine, c. 1850.*

7. *Church of the Holy Trinity, Grahamville, South Carolina.*

8. *Alterations on a house, 1854.*

3. Vice Unmasked

P. W. GRAYSON

Little is known about Grayson's life; in his book he mentions only that he has good right to criticize lawyers, having been one himself before he repented. His connections at the time of publication (1830) were with The New York City Workingmen's movement. George Henry Evans published the essay, and the *Workingmen's Advocate* touted it as a highly important work, if a little "enthusiastic." The *Advocate* said that Grayson came from Kentucky, where he'd served in the state legislature at one time.

Many early-nineteenth-century notions—particularly those concerning the natural goodness of man and the perfect structure of nature—tended toward anarchism, and Grayson's argument, combining as it does Enlightenment ideas drawn notably from Tom Paine with transcendental and radical Jacksonian sentiment, is precursor of Josiah Warren's more systematic theory of the "sovereignty of the individual." In exposing the inevitable chasm between any legal system and the ideal of justice it supposedly serves, Grayson reveals much of the reason for popular skepticism about the law and its practitioners in America.

There is a halo which settles upon the *uses* of antiquity, which, consigning them to sanctuaries of senseless veneration, protects them forever from the scrutiny of reason.

If, however, there be a spot on the face of the globe where the light of liberal intelligence and just opinions is beginning to show itself, through the clouds of prejudice, custom, and superstition, it is the land we are all standing on here in these free states of America.

P. W. Grayson, *Vice Unmasked, an Essay: Being a Consideration of the Influence of Law Upon the Moral Essence of Man* (New York, 1830), vii–viii, 11–19, 28–29, 35–45, 60–67, 73–75, 81, 90–95, 98–99, 137–138, 159–162, 168.

The light is as yet, indeed, but a feeble ray, struggling with darkness of immeasurable depth, extent, and intensity. But if it be, as there is hope it is, the light of truth, it must and will, in time, *show in*, to bless the eyes of men, the radiant suns of science—freedom—virtue, that shall banish cloud and darkness from the earth, and light the heart of man—purely, truly—to his long sought happiness. . . .

Blessed, as we are, with all advantages, we shall indeed be no better than traitors to ourselves and unborn millions, if we fail to exert every faculty which the God of nature has given us in our endeavors to explore every recess of society—to scrutinize the whole economy of its structure, all its regulations from the highest of them all, down to the minutest prescription of authority, and the pettiest observance of custom. To this task, we should bring the most benevolent, unbiased, and fearless intelligence. Wherever we find evil, no matter how venerable it may seem from the sanctity of its origin, or reputable from the customary regards of men, we should not scruple, even for an instant, to tear off the disguises which conceal its enormity, and, exposing the viciousness of its essence, strike for its extinction!

> Together let us beat this ample field;
> Try what the open—what the covert yield."—Pope

Arduous, indeed, is the task before us; yet how unworthy shall we be if we do not perform it with fidelity—enthusiasm. . . .

The truth is, we have only removed the great evil of slavery; but, as yet, have comparatively done no good with our liberty. We have shivered the chains which bound us, as it were, to the dungeon floor of despotism—burst open the prisons in which we had been immured, and emerged into liberty and light. But that is all. To this hour we are stunned with the unexpected good which so strangely broke in upon us; and, instead of flying upon untiring wings far up into the heaven of virtuous liberty, we have scarce left the thresholds of the frightful dungeons of tyranny, from which we have escaped. We know nothing of the superfluous mass of evil that is incorporated with our conditions, civil, political, and moral; for we have not even opened our eyes upon it; or, if we have, custom has so far sanctified it to our acceptance and use, that we are even worse than ignorant of it for that. We are, indeed, as I think, tainted to the core of our social relations, even of our very hearts, too, with the most subtle hues of folly and vice, with which we have become insensibly imbued, from the unscrutinized inheritance of custom and of thought fallen upon us from past ages and generations. How solemn, I repeat, is the duty incumbent upon us to search out all this pollution; and, confessing its hideousness, to wash our souls clean of all of it.

Till this be faithfully done, we shall scarce be worthy of either liberty or life! . . .

The great principle of human action is *self love*. But the wisdom of providence has so organized the human heart, that, to a certain extent, the good of *others* is, oftentimes, an object of that very self love. Whatever degree of contradiction there may seem to be in this idea, must, nevertheless, vanish before the light of every one's experience, which will, unequivocally, assure him, that to promote the good or happiness of others is, at once, to advance his own. That, then, would plainly appear to be the happiest temperature and disposition of the passions, in which, while we effectually serve ourselves, we, at the same time, promote, by our actions, the greatest amount of felicity to others.

It is the duty, and must for a long time continue to be the greatest labor, of men, to look so narrowly into the human character, as to ascertain those causes which conspire to seduce, to corrupt, and lead the passions out into malignant extravagancies of indulgence, over ways that are intricate and perplexing, to objects that are foul and unworthy; and, exposing those causes, then to unfold the genuine influences upon the characters and conduct of men; such as might appear suited to compose *all* the incentives of human action, and fix them fast in that easy equilibrium of enjoyment and operation, which could not fail to bring up the greatest amount of pure and unadulterated happiness, of which our nature is susceptible.

The great desideratum of man is, that he should both comprehend and practise the *true mode* of gratifying this supreme passion of his nature— this controlling, sovereign principle of his existence—his self love. It is pitiable to observe how far removed he has ever been from an acquaintance with this precious science. An infinite number of causes have conspired to keep him so far profoundly ignorant *even of himself*, and of the simple mode of reaching the happiness which nature certainly intended him. Those causes have done no less than struck him blind to the glorious light which this Nature, his mother, has been ever ready to pour upon all eyes that would but open to receive it,—teeming with the revelation of her mysteries, and full of instruction to this wayward child of her bosom, in all the arts of life,—the precious secret of his happiness. But

> "Dark—dark—dark—amid the blaze of noon
> Irrecoverably dark—total eclipse
> Without all hope of day,"

hath ever been the race of men, wherever they have been heard of on
the earth, through all its long, uncounted ages. . . .

The complaint is that the motives which impel the great mass of men,
and the means they employ to reach these objects, are, in the main, to
the last degree execrable. The ways they are treading are traced out to
them by a serpent policy, which gives to every impulse the taint of pollution, and stamps every action with obliquity.

How often, in time past, have these ways, which the million have
trodden, been even mired with blood! while they have led to an abyss of
disappointment and desolation—more hideous than the grave, wild as
primeval chaos, and terrible as the blackest dream of hell.

When THIS *man shall strike up in his soul the light of justice and humanity, and in his heart shall open the sleeping fountains of benevolence—
then will his self love revel in its fullest enjoyments—the purest, most
enduring ecstacies;—then will he be as happy as all which the earth
contains can make him, poor worm as he is, ephemera of a day, and almost
viewless atom of the universe!* . . .

A system of jurisprudence acting upon those engagements of men,
which are the offspring of trust and confidence, more especially in its
application to the free states of America, instead of being, as it seems generally thought to be, wholly indispensable to the interests of society, is
nothing better than a tax, and a grievous tax, too, upon its substantial
happiness; that it actually abridges and encumbers, instead of extending
and relieving, the sphere of human enjoyment; or in other words still, that
the whole compulsory agency of law, (in regard to the class of engagements just described,) which certain plausible views of its drift and
tendency may seem quite well to justify, does nevertheless fall so far
short of its benignant aim, as actually to produce consequences in the
highest degree mischievous to the best interests of society. . . .

The sun of heaven is scarcely deemed in ordinary apprehensions more
necessary to the day, than tribunals of justice to the very existence of
civilized society. The truth is, that the minds of men have never yet, for
a moment, contemplated them apart. We have all taken it for granted,
that they must be joined together, just as we have them among ourselves
and behold them everywhere else, for no other reason, perhaps, than
because they have never yet been discovered asunder.

Is it, indeed, certain, that there cannot be justice among men, without
coercive means to enforce the observance of it? And must they, of necessity, keep in employment, and subject themselves to the tax of, all this
cumbrous machinery of law, to supply them, from abroad, with justice,

as though it were a precious commodity, only indigenous in certain favored parts of the mass of mankind, and wholly in the hands of gifted monopolizers?

Are we never to think better of ourselves, than that it is necessary we should be driven, lashed into the practice of the plain principles of right? Is even this mode of *lashing* likely to prove more successful in time to come, than it has been in time past? Has it yet succeeded at all? Is there, I demand, no mode of engaging men voluntarily to comply with their duties and engagements to one another, by motives which are *wholly natural* to them, and of most adequate sufficiency, too, if properly cultivated and allowed to spring into action? . . .

In regard to the business of government and laws among a people who might be placed in a political condition like that of those of the United States, my reflections have brought me to this plain conclusion—that it should be confined, as nearly as might be, to the simple purpose of protecting the life, liberty, and property of the citizen from positive violation. Scarce any further than this, does there seem to be the least necessity for government, or any of its appendages, ever to interfere with the affairs and intercourse of men.

How simple would such a government be! How simple, too, would man himself be! Freed from the tortures of endless prescriptions—the maddening harassments and insolence of authority, and secure in all that is dear to him, his nature, for the first time on earth, would begin to unfold its beauties and exert its energies. How surely would this unfettered, unpolluted creature find out the true sources of his happiness, and, fixing his whole heart upon them, yield them up but with his life!

Whatever amount of good it might be shown, could be brought to the enjoyment of a people, by means of authority exercised for their advantage, still nothing seems more certain than that this good, great as it might be, could never fully compensate for the evil that would spring from the mere action of this authority upon them. It would not matter how beneficially it might be employed—it could not fail to make essential inroads upon the artless virtue, the essential dignity and glorious sovereignty, of man. Let these but be preserved unimpaired and unpolluted, and there is much reason for believing that they will cheerfully of themselves yield, in time, infinitely more good to the general condition of the species than any sort of authority, that could be *reckoned on as likely to accede to the control of its affairs,* would ever succeed in forcing it to procure to itself. If we should add to the consideration just presented, that of the highly mischievous abuses of all authority that was ever either usurped or delegated, that but too often, under pretence of doing great good, is found to be only plotting mischief and sowing the seeds of general evil, in the husbandry of partial and corrupt interests, and there would appear to be but little ground left for any one to stand on, who would advocate any interference of what is called government with the interests of men, beyond the limits which have just been suggested.

A very capital reason why the idea so prevails in the world, that mankind requires severe government—such watchful supervision and dogmatical direction, seems to me to be, that they never yet have been fairly favored with circumstances which might enable them to evince the contrary. . . .

What has authority, which has been at work these thousands of years, done for the condition of human nature? Absolutely nothing. Has it produced justice among men? No one will have the hardihood to say that it has. On the contrary, it has produced injustice of endless complexity. All we can boast to have been achieved by it is a reluctant forbearance of violence and wrong that sometimes shows itself in what we call civilized society. In the mass of evil it has produced, it has, indeed, only been bounded by impossibilities. It has banished the practice of justice from the earth, and has only spared the spirit of it, because it could not be reached by any power, however desolating and destructive. There are those, I know, who think this spirit, in any thing like purity, is but a chimera—a phantom of the imagination—that it is not in nature.

As well might they urge, methinks, that in the moist day of the deluge the pure element of fire was wholly extinct on the earth, because there was so little appearance of any, and so much water to quench all there might be. But though all the actual fire was *out*, its spirit was indestructible—partly did it reside even in the very waves that weltered over its ashes.

The great boon of government, its liberty and security from outrage—these two blessings fully guaranteed, man wants nothing more than a field in which to exert his powers. Whether he be poor or rich, humble or exalted, let him but be *free* and *uninjured,* and his life cannot be a burthen to him. It must yield him gratification, and be positively worthy of his care. After sufficient checks are imposed, to prevent the liberty of men from running out into licentiousness, there is *nothing* which can compensate for the least subtraction from all that remains.

The power even to refuse a good, that arrogance would impose, confers unspeakable satisfaction, and is essential to freedom. Even the simple consciousness in the bosom of a freeman, that he is absolutely one—that he is the untrammelled artificer of his own destiny, is in its very self a fund of happiness, richer, purer, and more precious than could be purchased by all the wealth of the world.

What luxury is the very breathing of the humblest freeman, compared with the suffocated respirations of one bound up in the fetters of even benignant authority, and goaded on through life with ceaseless prescriptions? No matter what outward advantages this last may reach, he wears a humiliated, martyred, and debauched spirit, unworthy of a man, and degrading to his nature. . . .

There is no opinion which has ever occurred with more force to my mind, than that the *System of Law*, merely, employed to the extravagant extent we behold it everywhere in civilized society, must ever prevent the ascent of human beings to any condition that should at all approach, or in the lowest degree even resemble, such a one as has just been imagined.

For my own part I find it impossible to conceive of force and coercion exercised upon man, in any way whatever, that shall not degrade his character, and poison the springs of his nature. If we would suppose him ready, even rapturously disposed to enter upon a measure of any kind, in obedience to his own voluntary impulses, and at this moment would imagine an order assailing him from some imperious superior, peremptorily requiring him to proceed even in the very line of his inclinations, we would, I am persuaded, find the certain result to be, that he would suddenly revolt, in heart at least, from all thought of bestowing his action accordingly, whatever the dire necessity of his condition might oblige him to do. . . .

Were it, indeed, within the scope of human wisdom and penetration, to anticipate every conceivable inflexion of cunning; to foresee all the hidings, every resort, shift, and device of legal chicanery; to paint, beforehand, the infinite variety of hues and colors it can bring itself to assume, and provide against them, in terms of unequivocal description and application: why, then, indeed, the good which seems to be hoped for, from law, might be, perhaps, in some degree realized. But this task would not seem more easy of execution, than a delineation of the leaves of the next year's forest, or of the special colors of the clouds that are to float on the bosom of the air tomorrow!

It is something easier for any one to conceive, than specially to set forth the contrivances, by which the most circumspect, well guarded, and well intended provisions of a law may be wrenched from their true aim, and actually prostituted to the ends of injustice; how fraud may manage to bring itself within the *mere letter*, by the adduction to its aid, of certain nominal features of a transaction, which might be demanded by the requisitions of a statute, (features that it may be quite easy to fabricate) and thus obtain the full benefit and protection of a legal provision, at the very moment its whole spirit is wickedly outraged.

This is what every one familiarly knows—has actually seen and experienced with his own eyes, and is, indeed, a kind of exploit, which is of no less than daily occurrence. It were needless to adduce special instances of this species of management.

For such abuses as these, there can in the nature of things, be *no remedy;* for they spring from the absolute and irremediable imperfections of the laws themselves—their pitiable inaptitude to the affairs of men. The terms of all laws must, to some extent, be general. They must needs take for their guide, certain standards, which are commonly considered as the least fallacious, many of which are at best but treacherous reliances. For example, in fixing the character of those transactions among men, to which they will lend their sanction, reliance must be placed upon the *customary* signals of honest, bona fide intentions on the one hand, and of dishonest, or mala fide, on the other; declaring those valid which are characterized by the former; those void, which are marked by the latter. But what in many cases appears so easy as for knavery to counterfeit all the first, and sedulously to avoid the last, and by these means clothe itself in benefits which were never intended for it.

Who is there that ever expects to behold the phenomenon of a man, turning over the pages of a law book, for the mere purpose of enlightening himself in the principles of justice, that he may, without fee or reward, conform to them in practice?

The earth will never, I dare say, produce such a simpleton, as he would be, who should expect to realize this imagination. It is, on the other hand, melancholy to observe the kind of spirit, with which a provision of law is commonly looked into, by those whose interest leads them to acquaint themselves with its character. It is, indeed, with the greatest solicitude they hunt out the page, but who does see that it is anything but a pure concern for justice, that prompts and hurries on the examination. Manifestly, in all cases, they are only eager to see how far the law will be found to favor their interests, that may be at the moment in jeopardy, or to what extent it may lean against them; and then, in this last contingency, there can be little doubt, they study it with more intensity and minuteness, for the purpose of inventing some device, by which they may elude its force. . . .

One of the effects of law, then, seems to be, instead of teaching men justice, and inspiring them with a love for it, but to animate their craft, deepen their duplicity, lengthen out the labyrinths of their contrivances, and supply them with a practical villany, of which they had, perhaps, never dreamed themselves capable. . . .

There is, indeed, no such thing as limiting their subtlety and pitiable resorts, when they go in quest of arguments to help out their lame pretensions, and vindicate their unjust assumptions. Now it is certain, that *whatever is law*—no matter how dry, hard, and unjust it may be in special instances, passes through the great body of society, at least as an excusable rule of conduct for every one. All the injustice which is produced by so venerable a cause, there seems a very general willingness to consent to and allow of.

Whoever will reflect, however, upon the mass of injustice, which is the inevitable fruit of laws founded on mere policy, will be able to form some proper conception of the *reputable pollution* of principle and knavery of practice engendered by them, through all classes of society.

To expand the circle of our observation here, what immeasurable evil discovers itself, as we contemplate how large a part of all our innate notions of right, our purest, noblest conceptions of natural equity, are given up in spite of ourselves, and sacrificed to the superior authority of legal prescriptions. Everyone knows that his own ideas of justice, with whatever care he may form them, are not for that reason law. Well is he aware that let him reflect and determine, no matter how wisely, upon any question where the principles of justice are involved, that in most cases, they are all inveterately settled beforehand, some way or other, and will certainly prevail, in utter disregard of either his opposition or consent, and that, in respect to them, his wisdom or folly are alike impertinent and indifferent.

Anticipated and disheartened by authority, which it is vain to oppose, mankind, in general, wholly forego both the pleasures and labors of speculation, upon subjects that most nearly concern them.

They soon learn that they are commanded to look elsewhere for their rules of action, in matters of the highest moment, than in their own bosoms, where, though they may find justice, they may by no means find the rule to which authority is about to constrain them to conform. Thus are they, as it were, hurried *out* of themselves, and made impatiently to look abroad for foreign criterions of right, which they well know they are bound to respect, indeed, implicitly obey, whether they approve them or not. It is, surely, an influence of no slight malignity, which thus fatally checks the career of investigation, even suffocates in the bosoms of men that joyous spirit of free enquiry and discussion, upon all subjects affecting their interests and their happiness, which is so essential to their improvement and amelioration. But this we have seen is but little of the evil. Would men but faithfully yield even a mechanical sort of obedience to authority, which is imposed on them for their government, we should have nothing more to lament than a general inaction, or rather inanity, of intellect—we should see them nothing better or worse than a herd of ignorant, innocent slaves, ready to be driven, without thought or remonstrance, whithersoever their superiors might direct. . . .

These judicial results seem, indeed, to wear, oftentimes, about the same resemblance to the healthy, genuine conceptions of right, that the mangled carcase of an animal, prostrate in death, would be acknowledged to be like one of the same species actually alive, upon its feet, in all the luxury of bounding health and roving liberty. . . .

First, we see they take no account in the general, and cannot, of the infinite variety of human conditions, feelings, circumstances, and characters. These, it is plain, should be specially considered for the purposes of clear, unclouded justice. This very inaptitude in them, has had the strange good fortune, however, to procure to the system the credit of pure inflexibility! There is nothing more required than certain *nominal* features in a case, to exact the application of a legal rule, which attaches at once, as it does ever, in all cases alike, with the very same energy, however substantially different in a thousand other particulars the cases may be, notwithstanding the mere nominal similitude. For example, a man of overflowing wealth stands indebted to a poor fellow being in some amount, which the severe necessities of the latter make it the extremest injustice in the former to withhold. Yet he does withhold. The consequence is, that resource is had to the law, and it may be supposed, redress actually obtained. This is as it should be. But again: some honest creature, whose wretched hovel is the picture of poverty and distress, happens to be indebted to one of immeasurable wealth; no matter in what amount. In reply to a demand of the due, for which he stands obliged, he pleads poverty and impossibility. But this plea, touching and conclusive as it is, has the ill fortune to be scoffed at by his lordly unfeeling creditor, as utterly idle and impertinent. Without the least touch of compassion or humanity, this man of wealth flies to the law, and demands its speediest action upon his victim. The consequence is, we do not fail to see the law apply itself with precisely the same promptness and force, in the latter case here, as in the other, that has just been supposed—pronouncing the same sentence, and inflicting the same execution of that sentence.

But can there be conceived two cases more unlike in every essential particular. In the one justice is really attained—in the other grossly and inhumanly violated. I do not of course here mean, when I employ the word justice, that technical legal justice, which knaves, fools, and hirelings affect to *revere;* but that pure, enlarged, liberal, informal justice, which both faithfully recognizes and warmly embraces all the essential interests and duties of humanity, as far as they can be possibly perceived.

How ridiculous is it to talk of any other kind! The hapless creature I have just supposed, is stripped of his earthly substance, and exposed, with his wretched family, to all the horrors of want—houseless, homeless, penniless. An hour before, they had a shelter, and some few of the necessaries of life; now the beasts of the field are far more blessed than they. What has produced such bitter, unmixed distress? Legal justice. . . .

There are thousands who would cry out, there is nothing perfect under the sun—that whatever evils may be shown to exist in jurisprudence, are necessary evils, and will somehow or other have to be borne—that human affairs admit of no change that can by any possible means succeed in relieving us of them. *That is, indeed, the question.* . . .

I have already sufficiently considered the demoralizing influence of law, as far as respects its own unaided operation, on the temper and principles of men. But I have yet to unfold another influence, of an entirely congenial stamp with the former, that operates, as I think, with wonderful force, to inflame its mischievous power. It is that of a certain class of men, who are professionally concerned in the administration of what is called justice. A class of men, in short, we know by the name of lawyers, whom we find swarming in every hole and corner of society. I fear I shall present in them a picture of the seeds of depravity, at which philanthropy may fold her arms, in utter despair, and weep as though the cause of mankind were indeed irredeemably lost forever!

We have seen that men in general, of their own accord, without any advice or incitement from others, feeling themselves bound up by arbitrary prescriptions, and depraved by their malign influence, would be apt enough to exert all their craft in turning the laws to their own advantage, with but little regard to the whispers of conscience, or to the dictates of justice. But who can set bounds to their iniquity, when these natural impulses come to be instructed and fomented by the learned and licensed jugglers in legal chicanery, creatures who are *ever at hand,* and ready the moment they are *roused* by a suitable *douceur* to point out the sinuous labyrinths which lead to gain, while *themselves* heroically lead the way. How can mankind resist such council and such temptations!

These men are, in truth, the lights of all the land! The very sun, moon, and stars of all intelligence. Bright bodies it must be owned they seem to the stupid gaze of innocent ignorance—the lustful admiration of congenial knavery. Yet how malignant are the beams they shoot over the whole surface of society, shedding upon it the pestilence of discord, strife, and injustice! It is, indeed, the result of inevitable necessity—the very fiat of nature, that these men should be, as we find the most of them are under the present constitution of things. That is to say, that *knaves* they must be in practice, however upright in principle. To be sure, indeed, custom and the laws, which can do anything, sanctify their conduct and loudly proclaim their indemnity. But in the meanwhile, what have become of conscience, and of right, that existed before written laws had either shape or name, and before the introduction among men of all this multitudinous machinery, in the shape of judges and justices, counsellors and attorneys, bailiffs and bumbailiffs, with the long train of congenial agents, blood suckers, and caterpillars of the state? At the very onset of this mighty corps of undertakers—these slippery factors of justice—their doom, the doom of conscience and of right, was sealed forever; that doom has been a hopeless and eternal banishment from almost every bosom into which its victims have been hurled, as dangerous pests, as *paltry things*, which enlightened experience had found too *inconvenient* to suit the newly invented, highly improved condition of society. . . .

Their business is with statutes, dictates, decisions, and authority. They go on, emptying volume after volume, of all their heterogeneous contents, till they become so laden with other men's thoughts, as scarce to have any of their own. Seldom do their sad eyes look beyond the musty walls of authority, in which their souls are all perpetually immured. And now, as soon as their minds have come to be duly instructed, first, in the antique sophistries, substantial fictions, wise absurdities, and profound dogmas of buried sages, and then fairly liberalized by all the light of modern innovation, and of precious salutary change, do we see them step forward into the world, blown with the most triumphant pretensions, to deal out blessings to mankind. Now, indeed, are they ready to execute any prescription of either justice or injustice—to lend themselves to any side—to advocate any doctrine, for they are well provided with the means in venerable print. Eager for employment, they pry into the business of men, with snakish smoothness slip into the secrets of their affairs, discern the ingredients of litigation, and blow them up into strife. *This is, indeed, but laboring in their vocation.*

Abject slaves of authority themselves, these counterfeits of men are now to be the proud dictators of human destiny, and withal the glittering favorites of fortune! . . .

This order of men certainly come from the hands of nature, with as fair susceptibilities of virtue as any other creatures of mortality. But a malignant destiny overtakes them in time to turn them far off from all the benign purposes of nature, to serve the corrupt contrivances of men; and here, in this devious devotion of their powers, we see them under the tutelage of custom, and the provocations of cupidity, in proportion as they are conspicuous, depraved—and, with the power to be useful, inclined only to be vicious. . . .

Can there be a more pitiable sight than that we are here constrained to behold? Quite certain it is, that the law, if it do not absorb all the talents and genius of the country, attracts, at least, the choice of it all, and leaves but little more than the refuse for other callings. What then is this sight?—*genius putting itself to sale*—the brightest intelligence of the land offering itself a loose prostitute to the capricious use of all men alike, for gold!

We shudder at the hapless female, who yields her person, indiscriminately, to the lust of libertines, for hire.

Though there is even a total wreck of virtue in these creatures, yet, in no given instance of prostitution in them, is there involved any thing like the pollution of spirit, which we must observe in your talking hireling of justice. . . .

Surely the system, which involves such a spectacle as this, through all its parts, to its deepest depths, must be *rotten!* Let us consider for a moment how genius should be employed. Certainly in the great cause of philanthropy and morals. What should be its reward? The pure *light of nature* which it would woo to its heart, the indestructible treasure of inward satisfaction with itself—an unquenchable ray of brightness, that a conscience, pure and unsullied, would shed on the soul, and the whole face of visible creation!

But this genius, we have seen, instead of flying heavenward, with the whole race of man, is *meanly sold* to knaves, for that which procures the assassin, to plunge his dagger into the bosom of innocence—its best and faithfulest service, actually bought like the meanest commodity, anywhere to be found in the filthiest market, even as it were tainted meat for the epicure, or base confectionary slimed into color and shape, for greedy brats, or silly women. . . .

I would fain *hope*, at least, for something better than this, as long as I am a breather myself, and die with the fond delusion in my bosom.

When we come to consider the moral condition of the people of our own country, who, in a political point of view, are doubtless more favored than any other under the sun, we shall, I think, be somewhat pained to

find that that condition is to the last degree depraved and imperfect—
that it answers but little to the hopes that might have been entertained
from the establishment of those great principles of natural liberty and
equality, without which, indeed, it must be owned that human nature can
do little more than vegetate or live on, in the stain of every species of
depravity. All essential as the enjoyment of pure liberty has at last come
on all sides to be allowed as a mean to the end of exalting man to his true
dignity, yet experience, it seems, is beginning pretty clearly to show that
that great boon, albeit it is the *foundation* of all other blessings, compre-
hends *not* within itself *all* that is necessary to fix the true condition of
mankind. Because it has been for a time so long—well nigh all that has
past—the great desideratum of this degraded earth, men seem to have
been drawn into an impression, even a sort of conviction, that now it is
achieved, there can be *nothing more* wanting to sweeten or enrich the
cup of their felicity.

How great is the oversight here—how deep the delusion!

Still will we hope that the time is coming when we shall all see, and,
seeing, confess, how little we have gained—in fact, how much we hold
of illusion—how poor we are in every thing that's good—how rich in all
that is evil. . . .

Having touched upon a few of the capital evils and errors, that have
seemed to me inherent in all of the world's civilized societies, I come at
once to suggest the measure I have to propose, as a mere start to their
improvement and amelioration.

The *repeal of all law,* as far as it has been treated on in this essay as
matter of evil, I have brought myself to believe, would be at once the
beginning of human prosperity.

There is, however, no part of the world in which such a measure as
this were at all possible, except where the people are free. They must
have the power to do as they *please,* if they would throw off abuse and
strike for their happiness.

We should see, as the striking result of even this change, that the self
love of men would be everywhere set on the *side of their virtue.* In so far
would this be the case, that the interests of all, of whatever kind they
might be, could not fail to be found obviously harmonizing with their
open integrity, and as plainly at war with their knavery.

In short, there could be no one so stupid as not clearly to see that *good
faith* would bring up, by means of infallible certainty, the highest results
of thrift and prosperity to all who should practice it; while bad faith
would as surely be seen to entail on its votaries every form of affliction.

It would have to be received as a truth; that even in societies the most depraved we could conceive of, perfect integrity, or, in other words, fair and sound dealing, would produce more genuine fruits of prosperity, than would be found to proceed from any other species of action whatever.

But, unluckily, in most societies, which we find at the mercy of laws, whose influence, we have seen, is to deprave and corrupt, this *truth* is by no means a self evident one; so numerous are the circumstances to set it at a distance, to cloud the medium through which it is its fate to be seen, if not wholly to shut out its light. . . .

The old adage, that honesty is the best policy, is constantly rung in our ears, even by knaves!

While they speak it from their mouths, they laugh at it in their hearts, as a sort of Utopian silliness, a kind of conceit that exclusively belongs to the closet gentry of philosophers, moralists, and the like, but is wholly abroad and out of its climate, in the *cutting* affairs of the world—the general scramble for gain.

However given over to knavery any people may be, we should have to admit that if they are stirring, industrious, and enterprizing, their affairs may be brought to present *an air* of thrift and prosperity, engaging enough. They may ravish the eye with scenes of beauty and sights of splendor, that would serve at last no other end, if rightly considered, than only to sicken the heart.

For what were the face of the earth, though dressed in the bloom of Elysium, if man, in the midst of it all, to the *guile of the snake*, add the *rage of the vulture.*

How well do all of us know that glittering houses hold breaking hearts, and the rudest huts joyous ones!

What does this prove, but that *outside show* is but a cheat. Yet, whatever it be, we see it has power to turn the whole earth we inhabit into something deserving no better name than an open, brawling, furious bedlam.

He who would gaze upon a city, its gaudy colors of persons and things, might probably fancy that all he saw was real. There, might he say, at last my eyes behold unclouded happiness. There, is not a man he sees, but seems the glass of fashion—the pampered favorite of wealth; nor a woman, who might not play the angel upon earth, to his deluded eyes, in all but wings. To feed their dainty senses, the land and sea seem but to emulate each other, in pouring into the laps of all the luxuries of the world.

Still, do we know, that this is all but miserable illusion.

We cannot be too cautious, then, lest we take the *pompous shine of things* for the pure *happiness of human hearts*.

The truth is this, there is no prosperity for man, but what is found in innocence and virtue—all else is trash. . . .

CONCLUSION

Man will never be virtuous, until his interests instruct him to be so. So long as these shall even so much as *seem* opposed to his virtue, he will inevitably pursue the former and renounce the latter.

That which must be done, is to clear from his mind the horrible mists and fogs of prejudice—to bid him no longer worship the *cold prescriptions* of policy, for the *warm principles* of justice—to free his soul from the fetters of authority—to remit and exalt him to himself—to let him seek, by the light of his conscience alone, in the joyous, genial climate of his own free spirit, for all the rules of his conduct. Then, and not till then, will he be virtuous and happy.

4. Self-Reliance

RALPH WALDO EMERSON

While Grayson argued man's need for absolute freedom on a social level, Ralph Waldo Emerson was the great theoretician of the idea applied to the individual. The descendant of a long line of New England ministers, Emerson served as a Unitarian minister before becoming disillusioned with what he considered the coldly rational nature of that faith. To think of Christ simply as Divinity, Emerson came to think, was folly; he was God, but only in the sense that he was the one man who had been totally true to himself. Man's potential divinity through self-reliance and openness to the intuitive impulses of nature was the constant theme of Emerson's writing and his Lyceum circuit lectures. He gave much the most thoughtful defense of the cardinal tenet of democratic America—the dignity and potential greatness of the individual—and one of its major corollaries—the superiority of natural to highly cultivated human responsiveness. He even condemned reliance on books as an encumbrance to "man thinking" but recognized that some things like history could be acquired only by "laborious reading."

Despite early condemnations of his social radicalism ("the view taken of Transcendentalism in State Street is that it threatens to invalidate contracts," he noted in his journal in 1841), he, like Grayson, had a strong American sense of the essential compatibility of total individualism with social responsibility.

There is a time in every man's education when he arrives at the conviction that envy is ignorance; that imitation is suicide; that he must take himself for better, for worse, as his portion; that though the wide universe is full of good, no kernel of nourishing corn can come to him but through his toil bestowed on that plot of ground which is given to him to till. The power which resides in him is new in nature, and none but he knows what

Ralph Waldo Emerson, "Self-Reliance," in *Essays* (Boston, 1841), 37–73.

that is which he can do nor does he know until he has tried. Not for nothing one face, one character, one fact, makes much impression on him, and another none. This sculpture in the memory is not without pre-estab-lished harmony. The eye was placed where one ray should fall, that it might testify of that particular ray. We but half express ourselves, and are ashamed of that divine idea which each of us represents. It may be safely trusted as proportionate and of good issues, so it be faithfully im-parted, but God will not have his work made manifest by cowards. A man is relieved and gay when he has put his heart into his work and done his best; but what he has said or done otherwise, shall give him no peace. It is a deliverance which does not deliver. In the attempt his genius deserts him; no muse befriends; no invention, no hope.

Trust thyself: every heart vibrates to that iron string. Accept the place the divine providence has found for you, the society of your contempo-raries, the connection of events. Great men have always done so, and confided themselves childlike to the genius of their age, betraying their perception that the absolutely trustworthy was seated at their heart, working through their hands, predominating in all their being. And we are now men, and must accept in the highest mind the same transcendent destiny; and not minors and invalids in a protected corner, not cowards fleeing before a revolution, but guides, redeemers, and benefactors, obey-ing the Almighty effort, and advancing on Chaos and the Dark.

What pretty oracles nature yields us on this text, in the face and behavior of children, babes, and even brutes! That divided and rebel mind, that distrust of a sentiment because our arithmetic has computed the strength and means opposed to our purpose, these have not. Their mind being whole, their eye is as yet unconquered, and when we look in their faces we are disconcerted. Infancy conforms to nobody: all conform to it, so that one babe commonly makes four or five out of the adults who prattle and play to it. So God has armed youth and puberty and manhood no less with its own piquancy and charm, and made it enviable and gracious and its claims not to be put by, if it will stand by itself. Do not think the youth has no force, because he cannot speak to you and me. Hark! in the next room his voice is sufficiently clear and emphatic. It seems he knows how to speak to his contemporaries. Bashful or bold, then, he will know how to make us seniors very unnecessary.

The nonchalance of boys who are sure of a dinner, and would disdain as much as a lord to do or say aught to conciliate one, is the healthy attitude of human nature. A boy is in the parlor what the pit is in the playhouse; independent, irresponsible, looking out from his corner on such people and facts as pass by, he tries and sentences them on their merits, in the swift, summary way of boys, as good, bad, interesting, silly, eloquent, troublesome. He cumbers himself never about consequences, about interests: he gives an independent, genuine verdict. You must court him: he does not court you. But the man is, as it were, clapped into jail by his consciousness. As soon as he has once acted or spoken with eclat, he is a committed person, watched by the sympathy or the hatred of hundreds, whose affections must now enter into his account. There is no Lethe for this. Ah, that he could pass again into his neutrality! Who can thus avoid all pledges, and having observed, observe again from the same unaffected, unbiased, unbribable, unaffrighted innocence, must always be formidable. He would utter opinions on all passing affairs, which being seen to be not private, but necessary, would sink like darts into the ear of men, and put them in fear.

These are the voices which we hear in solitude, but they grow faint and inaudible as we enter into the world. Society everywhere is in conspiracy against the manhood of every one of its members. Society is a joint-stock company, in which the members agree, for the better securing of his bread to each shareholder, to surrender the liberty and culture of the eater. The virtue in most request is conformity. Self-reliance is its aversion. It loves not realities and creators, but names and customs.

Whoso would be a man must be a nonconformist. He who would gather immortal palms must not be hindered by the name of goodness, but must explore if it be goodness. Nothing is at last sacred but the integrity of your own mind. Absolve you to yourself, and you shall have the suffrage of the world. I remember an answer which when quite young I was prompted to make a valued adviser, who was wont to importune me with the dear old doctrines of the church. On my saying, What have I to do with the sacredness of traditions, if I live wholly from within? my friend suggested: "But these impulses may be from below, not from above." I replied: "They do not seem to me to be such; but if I am the Devil's child, I will live then from the Devil." No law can be sacred to me but that of my nature. Good and bad are but names very readily transferable to that or this; the only right is what is after my constitution, the only wrong what is against it. A man is to carry himself in the presence of all opposition, as if everything were titular and ephemeral but he. I am ashamed to think how easily we capitulate to badges and names, to large societies and dead institutions. Every decent and well-spoken individual affects and sways me more than is right. I ought to go upright and vital, and speak the rude truth in all ways. If malice and vanity wear the coat of philanthropy, shall that pass?

If an angry bigot assumes this bountiful cause of Abolition, and comes to me with his last news from Barbadoes, why should I not say to him: "Go love thy infant; love thy woodchopper: be good-natured and modest: have that grace; and never varnish your hard, uncharitable ambition with this incredible tenderness for black folk a thousand miles off. Thy love afar is spite at home." Rough and graceless would be such greeting, but truth is handsomer than the affectation of love. Your goodness must have some edge to it,—else it is none. The doctrine of hatred must be preached as the counteraction of the doctrine of love when that pules and whines. I shun father and mother and wife and brother, when my genius calls me. I would write on the lintels of the door-post, *Whim.* I hope it is somewhat better than whim at last, but we cannot spend the day in explanation. Expect me not to show cause why I seek or why I exclude company. Then, again, do not tell me, as a good man did to-day, of my obligation to put all poor men in good situations. Are they *my* poor? I tell thee, thou foolish philanthropist, that I grudge the dollar, the dime, the cent, I give to such men as do not belong to me and to whom I do not belong. There is a class of persons to whom by all spiritual affinity I am bought and sold; for them I will go to prison, if need be; but your miscellaneous popular charities; the education at college of fools; the building of meeting-houses to the vain end to which many now stand; alms to sots; and the thousand-fold Relief Societies;—though I confess with shame I sometimes succumb and give the dollar, it is a wicked dollar which by and by I shall have the manhood to withhold.

Virtues are, in the popular estimate, rather the exception than the rule. There is the man *and* his virtues. Men do what is called a good action, as some piece of courage or charity, much as they would pay a fine in expiation of daily non-appearance on parade. Their works are done as an apology or extenuation of their living in the world—as invalids and the insane pay a high board. Their virtues are penances. I do not wish to expiate, but to live. My life is for itself and not for a spectacle. I much prefer that it should be of a lower strain, so it be genuine and equal, than that it should be glittering and unsteady. I wish it to be sound and sweet, and not to need diet and bleeding. I ask primary evidence that you are a man, and refuse this appeal from the man to his actions. I know that for myself it makes no difference whether I do or forbear those actions which are reckoned excellent. I cannot consent to pay for a privilege where I have intrinsic right. Few and mean as my gifts may be, I actually am, and do not need for my own assurance or the assurance of my fellows any secondary testimony.

What I must do is all that concerns me, not what the people think. This rule, equally arduous in actual and in intellectual life, may serve for the whole distinction between greatness and meanness. It is the harder, because you will always find those who think they know what is your duty better than you know it. It is easy in the world to live after the world's opinion; it is easy in solitude to live after our own; but the great man is he who in the midst of the crowd keeps with perfect sweetness the independence of solitude. . . .

For non-conformity the world whips you with its displeasure. And therefore a man must know how to estimate a sour face. The bystanders look askance on him in the public street or in the friend's parlor. If this aversation had its origin in contempt and resistance like his own, he might well go home with a sad countenance; but the sour faces of the multitude, like their sweet faces, have no deep cause, but are put on and off as the wind blows and a newspaper directs. Yet is the discontent of the multitude more formidable than that of the senate and the college? It is easy enough for a firm man who knows the world to brook the rage of the cultivated classes. Their rage is decorous and prudent, for they are timid as being very vulnerable themselves. But when to their feminine rage the indignation of the people is added, when the ignorant and the poor are aroused, when the unintelligent brute force that lies at the bottom of society is made to growl and mow, it needs the habit of magnanimity and religion to treat it godlike as a trifle of no concernment.

The other terror that scares us from self-trust is our consistency; a reverence for our past act or word, because the eyes of others have no other data for computing our orbit than our past acts, and we are loath to disappoint them.

But why should you keep your head over your shoulder? Why drag about this corpse of your memory, lest you contradict somewhat you have stated in this or that public place? Suppose you should contradict yourself; what then? It seems to be a rule of wisdom never to rely on your memory alone, scarcely even in acts of pure memory, but to bring the past for judgment into the thousand-eyed present, and live ever in a new day. In your metaphysics you have denied personality to the Deity: yet when the devout motions of the soul come, yield to them heart and life, though they should clothe God with shape and color. Leave your theory, as Joseph his coat in the hand of the harlot, and flee.

A foolish consistency is the hobgoblin of little minds, adored by little statesmen and philosophers and divines. With consistency a great soul has simply nothing to do. He may as well concern himself with his shadow on the wall. Speak what you think now in hard words and to-morrow speak what to-morrow thinks in hard words again, though it contradict everything you said to-day.—"Ah, so you shall be sure to be misunderstood?"—Is it so bad, then, to be misunderstood? Pythagoras was misunderstood, and Socrates, and Jesus, and Luther, and Copernicus, and Galileo, and Newton, and every pure and wise spirit that ever took flesh. To be great is to be misunderstood.

I suppose no man can violate his nature. All the sallies of his will are rounded in by the law of his being, as the inequalities of Andes and Himmaleh are insignificant in the curve of the sphere. Nor does it matter how you gauge and try him. A character is like an acrostic or Alexandrian stanza;—read it forward, backward, or across, it still spells the same thing. In this pleasing, contrite wood-life which God allows me, let me record day by day my honest thought without prospect or retrospect, and, I cannot doubt, it will be found symmetrical, though I mean it not and see it not. My book should smell of pines and resound with the hum of insects. The swallow over my window should interweave that thread or straw he carries in his bill into my web also. We pass for what we are. Character teaches above our wills. Men imagine that they communicate their virtue or vice only by overt actions, and do not see that virtue or vice emit a breath every moment.

There will be an agreement in whatever variety of actions, so they be each honest and natural in their hour. . . .

The relations of the soul to the divine spirit are so pure, that it is profane to seek to interpose helps. It must be that when God speaketh he should communicate, not one thing, but all things; should fill the world with his voice; should scatter forth light, nature, time, souls, from the centre of the present thought; and new date and new create the whole. Whenever a mind is simple, and receives a divine wisdom, old things pass away,—means, teachers, texts, temples fall; it lives now, and absorbs past and future into the present hour. All things are made sacred by relation to it,—one as much as another. All things are dissolved to their centre by their cause, and, in the universal miracle, petty and particular miracles disappear. If, therefore, a man claims to know and speak of God, and carries you backward to the phraseology of some old mouldered nation in another country, in another world, believe him not. Is the acorn better than the oak which is its fulness and completion? Is the parent better than the child into whom he has cast his ripened being? Whence, then, this worship of the past? The centuries are conspirators against the sanity and authority of the soul. Time and space are but physiological colors which the eye makes, but the soul is light; where it is, is day; where it was, is night; and history is an impertinence and an injury, if it be anything more than a cheerful apologue or parable of my being and becoming.

Man is timid and apologetic; he is no longer upright; he dares not say "I think," "I am," but quotes some saint or sage. He is ashamed before the blade of grass or the blowing rose. These roses under my window make no reference to former roses or to better ones; they are for what they are; they exist with God to-day. There is no time to them. There is simply the rose; it is perfect in every moment of its existence. Before a leaf-bud has burst, its whole life acts; in the full-blown flower there is no more; in the leafless root there is no less. Its nature is satisfied, and it satisfies nature, in all moments alike. But man postpones or remembers; he does not live in the present, but with reverted eye laments the past, or, heedless of the riches that surround him, stands on tiptoe to foresee the future. He cannot be happy and strong until he too lives with nature in the present, above time.

This should be plain enough. Yet see what strong intellects dare not yet hear God himself, unless he speak the phraseology of I know not what David, or Jeremiah, or Paul. We shall not always set so great a price on a few texts, on a few lives. We are like children who repeat by rote the sentences of grandames and tutors, and, as they grow older, of the men of talents and character they chance to see,—painfully recollecting the exact words they spoke; afterwards, when they come into the point of view which those had who uttered these sayings, they understand them, and are willing to let the words go; for, at any time, they can use words as good when occasion comes. If we live truly, we shall see truly. It is as easy for the strong man to be strong, as it is for the weak to be weak. When we have new perception, we shall gladly disburden the memory of its hoarded treasures as old rubbish. When a man lives with God, his voice shall be as sweet as the murmur of the brook and the rustle of the corn. . . .

If we cannot at once rise to the sanctities of obedience and faith, let us at least resist our temptations; let us enter into the state of war, and wake Thor and Woden, courage and constancy in our Saxon breasts. This is to be done in our smooth times by speaking the truth. Check this lying hospitality and lying affection. Live no longer to the expectation of these deceived and deceiving people with whom we converse. Say to them, "O father, O mother, O wife, O brother, O friend, I have lived with you after appearances hitherto. Henceforward I am the truth's. Be it known unto you that henceforward I obey no law less than the eternal law. I will have no convenants but proximities. I shall endeavor to nourish my parents, to support my family, to be the chaste husband of one wife,—but these relations I must fill after a new and unprecedented way. I appeal from your customs. I must be myself. I cannot break myself any longer for you, or you. If you can love me for what I am, we shall be the happier. If you cannot, I will still seek to deserve that you should. I will not hide my tastes or aversions. I will so trust that what is deep is holy, that I will do strongly before the sun and moon whatever inly rejoices me, and the heart appoints. If you are noble, I will love you; if you are not, I will not hurt you and myself by hypocritical attentions. If you are true, but not in the same truth with me, cleave to your companions; I will seek my own. I do this not selfishly, but humbly and truly. It is alike your interest, and mine, and all men's, however long we have dwelt in lies, to live in truth. Does this sound harsh to-day? You will soon love what is dictated by your nature as well as mine, and, if we follow the truth, it will bring us out safe at last." But so you may give these friends pain. Yes, but I cannot sell my liberty and my power, to save their sensibility. Besides, all persons have their moments of reason, when they look out into the region of absolute truth; then will they justify me, and do the same thing.

The populace think that your rejection of popular standards is a rejection of all standard, and mere antinomianism; and the bold sensualist will use the name of philosophy to gild his crimes. But the law of consciousness abides. There are two confessionals, in one or the other of which we must be shriven. You may fulfil your round of duties by clearing yourself in the *direct,* or in the *reflex* way. Consider whether you have satisfied your relations to father, mother, cousin, neighbor, town, cat, and dog; whether any of these can upbraid you. But I may also neglect this reflex standard, and absolve me to myself. I have my own stern claims and perfect circle. It denies the name of duty to many offices that are called duties. But if I can discharge its debts, it enables me to dispense with the popular code. If any one imagines that this law is lax, let him keep its commandment one day.

And truly it demands something godlike in him who has cast off the common motives of humanity, and has ventured to trust himself for a taskmaster. High be his heart, faithful his will, clear his sight, that he may in good earnest be doctrine, society, law, to himself, that a simple purpose may be to him as strong as iron necessity is to others! . . .

Society is a wave. The wave moves onward, but the water of which it is composed does not. The same particle does not rise from the valley to the ridge. Its unity is only phenomenal. The persons who make up a nation to-day, next year die, and their experience with them.

And so the reliance on Property, including the reliance on governments which protect it, is the want of self-reliance. Men have looked away from themselves and at things so long, that they have come to esteem the religious, learned, and civil institutions as guards of property, and they deprecate assaults on these, because they feel them to be assaults on property. They measure their esteem of each other by what each has, and not by what each is. But a cultivated man becomes ashamed of his property, out of new respect for his nature. Especially he hates what he has, if he see that it is accidental,—came to him by inheritance, or gift, or crime; then he feels that it is not having; it does not belong to him, has no root in him, and merely lies there, because no revolution or no robber takes it away. But that which a man is does always by necessity acquire, and what the man acquires is living property, which does not wait the beck of rulers, or mobs, or revolutions, or fire, or storm, or bankruptcies, but perpetually renews itself wherever the man breathes. "Thy lot or portion of life," said the Caliph Ali, "is seeking after thee; therefore be at rest from seeking after it." Our dependence on these foreign goods leads us to our slavish respect for numbers. The political parties meet in numerous conventions; the greater the concourse, and with each new uproar of announcement, The delegation from Essex! The Democrats from New Hampshire! The Whigs of Maine! the young patriot feels himself stronger than before by a new thousand of eyes and arms. In like manner the reformers summon conventions, and vote and resolve in multitude. Not so, O friends, will the God deign to enter and inhabit you, but by a method precisely the reverse. It is only as a man puts off all foreign support, and stands alone, that I see him to be strong and to prevail. He is weaker by every recruit to his banner. Is not a man better than a town? Ask nothing of men, and in the endless mutation, thou only firm column must presently appear the upholder of all that surrounds thee. He who knows that power is inborn, that he is weak because he has looked for good out of him and elsewhere, and so perceiving, throws himself unhesitatingly on his thought, instantly rights himself, stands in the erect position, commands his limbs, works miracles; just as a man who stands on his feet is stronger than a man who stands on his head. . . .

5. Man in Nature

Illustrations

1. *"Kindred Spirits," by Asher B. Durand, 1849.*

2. *"He That Tilleth His Land Shall Be Satisfied," c. 1850.*

3. *"Lackawanna Valley," by George Innes, 1855.*

4. *"Fur Traders Descending the Mississippi," by George Caleb Bingham, 1845.*

5. *"Meditation by the Sea," c. 1855*

6. *"Picking Flowers,"* 1845.

7. *"View Near Ticonderoga," by Thomas Cole, 1826.*

8. *"The Death Struggle," by Charles Deas, 1845.*

6. Sinners Bound to Change Their Own Hearts

CHARLES GRANDISON FINNEY

Giving up his legal profession in 1824 to become a minister, Finney was to be the country's great revivalist for almost a decade. His success was unprecedented, especially in the "burned over district" of upstate New York, which was the seedbed of such varied religious enthusiasms, and in Yankee-settled sections of the Midwest. Finney in 1837 began teaching theology at Oberlin, where he remained until his death; he was president of that college from 1851 to 1866.

Unlike Emerson, Finney argued that man must desert self for God before he could act with true freedom, but his faith was based on generally genial assumptions: that God was just and benevolent, that any man could be saved if he wanted to be, and that once salvation was accepted man had responsibility for perfecting society. Hence reform movements, especially abolition, followed in the wake of the Finney revivals; one of his converts, Theodore Dwight Weld, was one of the most successful of early abolitionists. Not emotionalism, but a kind of tough-minded intensity, often dotted with metaphors and similes drawn from the political and legal life his audience knew well, characterized Finney's rhetoric.

> *Ezek. xviii, 31: Make you a new heart and a new spirit, for why will ye die?*

The command here addressed to the Israelites is binding upon every impenitent sinner to whom the gospel shall be addressed. He is required to perform the same duty, upon the same penalty. It becomes, therefore, a matter of infinite importance that we should well understand, and fully

Charles Grandison Finney, "Sinners Bound to Change Their Own Hearts," in *Sermons on Important Subjects* (New York, 1836), 3–4, 8–10, 13–15, 17, 25, 28, 31–32, 35–38, 40; parts of sermon and prayer quoted in Thomas Low Nichols. *Forty Years of American Life* (London, 1864), I, 373–374.

and immediately obey, the requirement. The questions that would naturally arise to a reflecting mind on reading this text, are the following:

1. What are we to understand by the requirement to make a new heart and a new spirit?

2. Is it reasonable to require the performance of this duty on pain of eternal death?

3. How is this requirement, that we should make to us a new heart and a new spirit, consistent with the often repeated declarations of the Bible, that a new heart is the gift and work of God?

Does God require of us the performance of this duty, without expecting its fulfilment only, merely to show us our impotency and dependence upon him? Does he require us to make to ourselves a new heart, on pain of eternal death, when at the same time he knows we have no power to obey; and that if ever the work is done, he must himself do the very thing which he requires of us?

It should here be observed, that although the Bible was not given to teach us mental philosophy, yet we may rest assured that all its declarations are in accordance with the true philosophy of mind. . . .

The term *heart*, as applied to mind, is figurative, and recognizes an analogy between the heart of the body, and the heart of the soul. The fleshly organ of the body called the *heart*, is the seat and fountain of animal life, and by its constant action, diffuses life through the animal system. *The spiritual heart is the fountain of spiritual life, is that deep seated but voluntary preference of the mind, which lies back of all its other voluntary affections and emotions, and from which they take their character.* In this sense I understand the term heart to be used in the text. It is evidently something over which we have control; something voluntary; something for which we are to blame, and which we are bound to alter. Now if the requirement is, that we are to make some constitutional change in the substance of the body or mind, it is evidently unjust, and enforced by a penalty no less than infinite, as obedience is impossible, the requirement is infinite tyranny. It is evident, that the requirement here is to change our *moral character;* our *moral disposition;* in other words, to change that abiding preference of our minds, which prefers sin to holiness; self-gratification to the glory of God. I understand a change of heart, as the term is here used, to be just what we mean by a change of mind in regard to the supreme object of pursuit; a change in the choice of an *end*, not merely in the choice of *means*. . . .

A change of heart, then, consists in changing the controlling preference of the mind in regard to the *end* of pursuit. The selfish heart is a preference of self-interest to the glory of God and the interests of his kingdom. A new heart consists in a preference of the glory of God and the interests of his kingdom to one's own happiness. In other words, it is a change from selfishness to benevolence, from having a supreme regard to one's own interest to an absorbing and controlling choice of the happiness and glory of God and his kingdom.

It is a change in the choice of a *Supreme Ruler.* The conduct of impenitent sinners demonstrates that they prefer Satan as the ruler of the world, they obey his laws, electioneer for him, and are zealous for his interests, even to martyrdom. They carry their attachment to him and his government so far as to sacrifice both body and soul to promote his interest and establish his dominion. A new heart is the choice of JEHOVAH as the supreme ruler; a deep-seated and abiding preference of his laws, and government, and character, and person, as the supreme Legislator and Governor of the universe.

Thus the world is divided into two great political parties; the difference between them is, that one party choose Satan as the god of this world, yield obedience to his laws, and are devoted to his interest. Selfishness is the law of Satan's empire, and all impenitent sinners yield it a willing obedience. The other party choose Jehovah for their governor, and consecrate themselves, with all their interests, to his service and glory. Nor does this change imply a constitutional alteration of the powers of body or mind, any more than a change of mind in regard to the form or administration of a human government. . . .

Suppose a human sovereign should establish a government, and propose as the great end of pursuit, to produce the greatest amount of happiness possible within his kingdom. He enacts wise and benevolent laws, calculated to promote this object to which he conforms all his own conduct; in the administration of which, he employs all his wisdom and energies, and requires all his subjects to sympathize with him; to aim at the same object; to be governed by the same principles; to aim supremely and constantly at the same end; the promotion of the highest interests of the community. Suppose these laws to be so framed, that universal obedience would necessarily result in universal happiness. Now suppose that one individual, after a season of obedience and devotion to the interest of the government and the glory of his sovereign, should be induced to withdraw his influence and energies from promoting the public good, and set up for himself; suppose him to say, I will no longer be governed by the principles of good will to the community, and find my own happiness in promoting the public interest; but will aim at promoting my own happiness and glory, in my own way, and let the sovereign and the subjects take care for themselves. "Charity begins at home." Now suppose him thus to set up for himself; to propose his own happiness and aggrandizement as the supreme object of his pursuit, and should not hesitate to trample upon the laws and encroach upon the rights, both of his sovereign and the subjects, wherever those laws or rights lay in the way of the accomplishment of his designs. It is easy to see, that he has become a rebel; has changed his *heart*, and consequently his conduct; has set up an interest not only separate from, but opposed to the interest of his rightful sovereign. He has changed his heart from good to bad; from being an obedient subject he has become a rebel; from obeying his sovereign, he has set up an independent sovereignty; from trying to influence all men to obey the government, from seeking supremely the prosperity and the glory of his sovereign, he becomes himself a little sovereign; and as Absalom caught the men of Israel and kissed them, and thus stole away their hearts; so he now endeavors to engross the affections, to enlist the sympathies, to command the respect and obedience of all around him. Now what would constitute a change of heart in this man towards his sovereign? I answer, for him to go back, to change his mind in regard to the supreme object of pursuit;—to prefer the glory of his sovereign and the good of the public to his own separate interest, would constitute a change of heart.

Now this is the case with the sinner; God has established a government, and proposed by the exhibition of his own character, to produce the greatest practicable amount of happiness in the universe. He has enacted laws wisely calculated to promote this object, to which he conforms all his own conduct, and to which he requires all his subjects perfectly and undeviatingly to conform theirs. After a season of obedience, Adam changed his heart, and set up for himself. So with every sinner, although he *does not first obey, as Adam did;* yet his wicked heart consists in setting up his own interest in opposition to the interest and government of God. In aiming to promote his own private happiness, in a way that is opposed to the general good. Self-gratification becomes the law to which he conforms his conduct. It is that minding of the flesh, which is enmity against God. A change of heart, therefore, is to prefer a different *end*. To prefer supremely the glory of God and the public good, to the promotion of his own interest; and whenever this preference is changed, we see of course a corresponding change of conduct. If a man change sides in politics, you will see him meeting with those that entertain the same views and feelings with himself; devising plans and using his influence to elect the candidate which he has now chosen. He has new political friends on the one side, and new political enemies on the other. So with a sinner; if his heart is changed, you will see that Christians become his friends—Christ his candidate. He aims at honoring him and promoting his interest in all his ways. Before, the language of his conduct was, "Let Satan govern the world." Now, the language of his heart and of his life is, "Let Christ rule King of nations, as he is King of saints." Before, his conduct said, "O Satan, let thy kingdom come, and let thy will be done." Now, his heart, his life, his lips cry out, "O Jesus, let thy kingdom come, let thy will be done on earth as it is in heaven." . . .

The second inquiry is, whether the requirement of the text is reasonable and equitable. The answer to this question must depend upon the nature of the duty to be performed. If the change be a physical one, a change in the constitution or substance of the soul, it is clearly not within the scope of our ability, and the answer to the question must be, No, it is not reasonable nor equitable. To maintain that we are under obligation to do what we have no power to do, is absurd. If we are under an obligation to do a thing, and do it not, we sin. For the blame-worthiness of sin consists in its being the violation of an obligation. But if we are under an obligation to do what we have no power to do, then sin is unavoidable; we are forced to sin by a natural necessity. But this is contrary to right reason, to make sin to consist in any thing that is forced upon us by the necessity of nature. Besides, if it is sin, we are bound to repent of it, heartily to blame ourselves, and justify the requirement of God; but it is plainly impossible for us to blame ourselves for not doing what we are conscious we never had any power to do. Suppose God should command a man to fly; would the command impose upon him any obligation, until he was furnished with wings? Certainly not. But suppose, on his failing to obey, God should require him to repent of his disobedience, and threaten to send him to hell if he did not heartily blame himself, and justify the requirement of God. He must cease to be a reasonable being before he can do this. He knows that God never gave him power to fly, and therefore he had no right to require it of him. His natural sense of justice, and of the foundation of obligation, is outraged, and he indignantly and conscientiously throws back the requirement into his Maker's face. Repentance, in this case, is a natural impossibility; while he is a reasonable being, he knows that he is not to blame for not flying without wings; and however much he may regret his not being able to obey the requirement, and however great may be his fear of the wrath of God, still to blame himself and justify God is a natural impossibility. As, therefore, God requires men to make to themselves a new heart, on pain of eternal death, it is the strongest possible evidence that they are able to do it. To say that he has commanded them to do it, without telling them they are able, is consummate trifling. Their ability is implied as strongly as it can be, in the command itself. . . .

This giving the sinner *power*, by the aid of the Holy Spirit, to obey God, is what the Arminians call a *gracious* ability, which terms are a manifest absurdity. What is grace? It is undeserved favor; something to which we have no claim in justice. That which may be withheld without injustice. If this is a true definition, it is plain that a *gracious ability to do our duty* is absurd. It is a dictate of reason, of conscience, of common sense, and of our natural sense of justice, that if God require of us the performance of any duty or act, he is bound in justice to give us *power* to obey; i.e., he must give us the faculties and strength to perform the act. But if *justice* require this, why call it a *gracious* ability. Natural ability to do our duty cannot be a *gracious* ability. To call it so, is to confound grace and justice as meaning the same thing. The sin of disobedience then must lie, not in his having broken the law of God, but solely in his not having complied with the strivings of the spirit. Accordingly the definition of sin should be, upon these principles, not that "sin is a transgression of the law," but that it consists in not yielding to the influence of the Spirit. . . .

The very terms used by our Savior in the promise of the Spirit to reprove the world of sin, of righteousness, and of a judgment to come, strongly imply the mode of his agency. The term rendered *Comforter* in our translation of the Bible, is Parakletos; it is the same term which, in one of the epistles of John, is rendered *Advocate*. The term is there applied to Jesus Christ. It is there said, "If any man sin, we have a *Parakletos,* or an Advocate with the Father, even Jesus Christ the righteous." In this passage Jesus Christ is spoken of as the Advocate of men with God. The Parakletos, or Comforter, promised by our Savior, is represented as God's Advocate, to plead His cause with men. The term rendered *reprove* or *convince* in our translation is a law term, and signifies the summing up of an argument, and establishing or demonstrating the sinner's guilt. Thus the strivings of the Spirit of God with men, is not a physical scuffling, but a debate; a strife not of body with body, but of mind with mind; and that in the action and reaction of vehement argumentation. From these remarks, it is easy to answer the question sometimes put by individuals who seem to be entirely in the dark upon this subject, whether in converting the soul the Spirit acts directly on the mind, or on the truth. This is the same nonsense as if you should ask, whether an earthly advocate who had gained his cause, did it by acting directly and physically on the jury, or on his argument. . . .

You see from this subject that a sinner, under the influence of the Spirit of God, is just as free as a jury under the arguments of an advocate.

Here also you may see the importance of right views on this point. Suppose a lawyer, in addressing a jury, should not expect to change their minds by any thing he could say, but should wait for an invisible, and physical agency, to be exerted by the Holy Ghost upon them. And suppose, on the other hand, that the jury thought that in making up their verdict, they must be passive, and wait for a direct physical agency to be exerted upon them. In vain might the lawyer plead, and in vain might the jury hear, for until he pressed his arguments as if he was determined to bow their hearts, and until they make up their minds, and decide the question, and thus act like rational beings, both his pleading, and their hearing is in vain. So if a minister goes into a desk to preach to sinners, believing that they have no power to obey the truth, and under the impression that a direct physical influence must be exerted upon them before they *can* believe, and if his audience be of the same opinion, in vain does he preach, and in vain do they hear, "for they are yet in their sins;" they sit and quietly wait for some invisible hand to be stretched down from heaven, and perform some surgical operation, infuse some new principle, or implant some constitutional taste; *after* which they suppose they shall be *able* to obey God. Ministers should labor with sinners, as a lawyer does with a jury, and upon the same principles of mental philosophy; and the sinner should weigh his arguments, and make up his mind as upon oath and for his life, and give a verdict upon the spot, according to law and evidence. . . .

But here perhaps another objection may arise—*If the sinner is able to convert himself, why does he need the Spirit of God?*

Suppose a man owed you one hundred dollars, was abundantly able, but wholly unwilling to pay you; you obtain a writ, and prepare, by instituting a suit against him, to ply him with a motive that will constrain him to be honest and pay his debts. Now suppose that he should say, I am perfectly able to pay this hundred dollars, of what use then is this writ, and a sheriff, and a lawsuit? The answer is, It is to make him willing —to be sure, he is able, but he is unwilling. Just so with the sinner—he is able to do his duty, but is unwilling, therefore the Spirit of God plies him with motives to make him willing. . . .

Sinner! instead of waiting and praying for God to change your heart, you should at once summon up your powers, put forth the effort, and change the governing preference of your mind. But here some one may ask, Can the carnal mind, which is enmity against God, change itself? I have already said that this text in the original reads, "The minding of the flesh is enmity against God." This minding of the flesh, then, is a choice or preference to gratify the flesh. Now it is indeed absurd to say, that a choice can change itself; but it is not absurd to say, that the agent who exercises this choice, can change it. The sinner that minds the flesh, can change his mind, and mind God.

From this subject it is manifest that the sinner's obligation to make to himself a new heart, is infinite.

Sinner! your obligation to love God is equal to the excellence of his character, and your guilt in not obeying him is of course equal to your obligation. You cannot therefore for an hour or a moment defer obedience to the commandment in the text, without deserving eternal damnation. . . .

If men would act as wisely and as philosophically in attempting to make men Christians, as they do in attempting to sway mind upon other subjects; if they would suit their subject to the state of mind, conform "the action to the word and the word to the action," and press their subject with as much address, and warmth, and perseverance, as lawyers and statesmen do their addresses; the result would be the conversion of hundreds of thousands, and converts would be added to the Lord "like drops of the morning dew." Were the whole church and the whole ministry right upon this subject; had they right views, were they imbued with a right spirit, and would they "go forth with tears, bearing precious seed, they would soon reap the harvest of the whole earth, and return bearing their sheaves with them."

From this subject you may see the importance of pressing every argument, and every consideration, that can have any weight.

And now, sinner, while the subject is before you, will you yield? To keep yourself away from under the motives of the gospel, by neglecting church, and neglecting your Bible, will prove fatal to your soul. And to be careless when you do attend, or to hear with attention and refuse to make up your mind and yield, will be equally fatal. And now, "I beseech you, by the mercies of God, that you at *this time* render your body and soul, a living sacrifice to God, which is your reasonable service." Let the truth take hold upon your conscience—throw down your rebellious weapons—give up your refuges of lies—fix your mind steadfastly upon the world of considerations that should instantly decide you to close in with the offer of reconciliation while it now lies before you. Another moment's delay, and it may be too late forever. The Spirit of God may depart from you—the offer of life may be made no more, and this one more slighted offer of mercy may close up your account, and seal you over to all the horrors of eternal death. Hear, then, O sinner, I beseech you, and obey the word of the Lord—"Make you a new heart and a new spirit, for why will ye die?"

The importance of rightly understanding that God converts souls by motives, is inconceivably great. Those who do not recognize this truth in their *practice* at least, are more likely to hinder than to aid the Spirit in his work. Some have denied this truth in theory, but have happily admitted it in practice. They have prayed, and preached, and talked, as if they expected the Holy Spirit to convert sinners by the truth. In such cases, notwithstanding their theory, their practice was owned and blessed of God. But a want of attention to this truth in practice has been the source of much and ruinous error in the management of revivals, and in dealing with anxious souls. Much of the preaching, conversation and exhortation have been irrelevant, perplexing and mystical. Sufficient pains have not been taken to avoid a diversion of public and individual attention. Sinners have been kept long under conviction, because their spiritual guides withheld those particular truths which at the time above all others they needed to know. They have been perplexed and confounded by abstract doctrines, metaphysical subtleties, absurd exhibitions of the sovereignty of God, inability, physical regeneration, and constitutional depravity, until the agonized mind, discouraged and mad with contradiction from the pulpit, and absurdity in conversation, dismissed the subject as altogether incomprehensible, and postponed the performance of duty as impossible.

FROM A FINNEY SERMON:

"A thing is not right or good because God commands it. The principles of right are as eternal as God, and He is good because His being is in accordance with them. God cannot make anything right any more than He can make the three angles of a triangle equal to two right angles."

FROM A FINNEY PRAYER:

"O Lord, I have been walking down Broadway today, and I have seen a good many of my friends and Thy friends, and I wondered, O Lord! if they seemed as poor, and vapid, and empty, and worldly to Thee as they did to me."

7. The Democratic Principle

No more concise statement of the convictions of Andrew Jackson's democracy exists than this introductory essay to the intellectual organ of Jacksonianism. Edited by John L. O'Sullivan, the periodical was the most able one devoted to a purely partisan task that America has known. Nathaniel Hawthorne, William Cullen Bryant, Orestes Brownson, James Kirke Paulding, George Bancroft, and Walt Whitman all were contributors to it.

The essay shows particularly well the way in which faith in individual capacity and benevolent natural law led the party to its insistence on unhampered majoritarian democracy linked to a theory of negative government. It is Grayson's social anarchism modulated by party practicality. The essay reveals as well how quickly Jacksonians became disturbed by the tendencies toward political pondering and profiteering that were tied to the full flowering of American democracy they fostered. Hardly had the bud opened, before it became blowsy.

The character and design of the work of which the first number is here offered to the public, are intended to be shadowed forth in its name, the "United States Magazine and *Democratic Review.*" It has had its origin in a deep conviction of the necessity of such a work, at the present critical stage of our national progress, for the advocacy of that high and holy DEMOCRATIC PRINCIPLE which was designed to be the fundamental element of the new social and political system created by the "American experiment;" for the vindication of that principle from the charges daily brought against it, of responsibility for every evil result growing out, in truth, of adventitious circumstances, and the adverse elements unhappily com-

John L. O'Sullivan, editor, *United States Magazine and Democratic Review* (October–December, 1837), I, 1–15.

bined with it in our institutions; for its purification from those corruptions and those hostile influences, by which we see its beneficent and glorious tendencies, to no slight extent, perverted and paralysed; for the illustration of truth, which we see perpetually darkened and confused by the arts of wily error; for the protection of those great interests, not alone of our country, but of humanity, looking forward through countless ages of the future, which we believe to be vitally committed with the cause of American Democracy. This is, in broad terms, the main motive in which this undertaking has had its origin: this is the object towards which, in all its departments, more or less directly, its efforts will tend.

There is a great deal of mutual misunderstanding between our parties; but in truth, there does not exist in the people, with reference to its great masses, that irreconcileable hostility of opinions and leading principles which would be the natural inference from the violence of the party warfare in which we are perpetually engaged. There does exist, it is true, an essential opposition of principles, proceeding from opposite points of departure, between the respective political creeds or systems of our two great parties, the Democratic and the Whig;* but we feel well assured that the great body of the latter party, those who supply their leaders and leading interests with their votes, do not rightly understand the questions at issue, in their true popular bearings; and that, if these could but be exhibited in their proper lights, to their sound minds and honest hearts, they would soon be found ranged, by the hundreds of thousands, under the broad and bright folds of our democratic banner.

So many false ideas have insensibly attached themselves to the term "democracy," as connected with our party politics, that we deem it necessary here, at the outset, to make a full and free profession of the cardinal principles of political faith on which we take our stand; principles to which we are devoted with an unwavering force of conviction and earnestness of enthusiasm which, ever since they were first presented to our minds, have constantly grown and strengthened by contemplation of them, and of the incalculable capabilities of social improvement of which they contain the germs.

We believe, then, in the principle of *democratic republicanism*, in its strongest and purest sense. We have an abiding confidence in the virtue, intelligence, and full capacity for self-government, of the great mass of our people—our industrious, honest, manly, intelligent millions of freemen.

* We concede to all the privilege of exercising their own fancy in the choice of their own names.

We are opposed to all self-styled "wholesome restraints" on the free action of the popular opinion and will, other than those which have for their sole object the prevention of precipitate legislation. This latter object is to be attained by the expedient of the division of power, and by causing all legislation to pass through the ordeal of successive forms; to be sifted through the discussions of co-ordinate legislative branches, with mutual suspensive veto powers. Yet all should be dependant with equal directness and promptness on the influence of public opinion; the popular will should be equally the animating and moving spirit of them all, and ought never to find in any of its own creatures a self-imposed power, capable (when misused either by corrupt ambition or honest error) of resisting itself, and defeating its own determined object. We cannot, therefore, look with an eye of favor on any such forms of representation as, by length of tenure of delegated power, tend to weaken that universal and unrelaxing responsibility to the vigilance of public opinion, which is the true conservative principle of our institutions.

The great question here occurs, which is of vast importance to this country, (was it not once near dissolving the Union, and plunging it into the abyss of civil war?)—of the relative rights of majorities and minorities. Though we go for the republican principle of the supremacy of the will of the majority, we acknowledge, in general, a strong sympathy with minorities, and consider that their rights have a high moral claim on the respect and justice of majorities; a claim not always fairly recognised in practice by the latter, in the full sway of power, when flushed with triumph, and impelled by strong interests. This has ever been the point of the democratic cause most open to assault, and most difficult to defend. This difficulty does not arise from any intrinsic weakness. The democratic theory is perfect and harmonious in all its parts; and if this point is not so self-evidently clear as the rest is generally, in all candid discussion, conceded to be, it is because of certain false principles of government, which have, in all practical experiments of the theory, been interwoven with the democratic portions of the system, being borrowed from the example of anti-democratic systems of government. We shall always be willing to meet this question frankly and fairly. The great argument against pure democracy, drawn from this source, is this:

Though the main object with reference to which all social institutions ought to be modelled is undeniably, as stated by the democrat, "the greatest good of the greatest number," yet it by no means follows that the greatest number always rightly understands its own greatest good.

Highly pernicious error has often possessed the minds of nearly a whole nation; while the philosopher in his closet, and an enlightened few about him, powerless against the overwhelming current of popular prejudice and excitement, have alone possessed the truth, which the next generation may perhaps recognise and practice, though its author, now sainted, has probably, in his own time, been its martyr. The original adoption of the truth would have saved perhaps oceans of blood, and mountains of misery and crime. How much stronger, then, the case against the absolute supremacy of the opinion and will of the majority, when its numerical preponderance is, as often happens, comparatively small. And if the larger proportion of the more wealthy and cultivated classes of the society are found on the side of the minority, the disinterested observer may well be excused if he hesitate long before he awards the judgment, in a difficult and complicated question, in favor of the mere numerical argument. Majorities are often as liable to error of opinion, and not always free from a similar proneness to selfish abuse of power, as minorities; and a vast amount of injustice may often be perpetrated, and consequent general social injury be done, before the evil reaches that extreme at which it rights itself by revolution, moral or physical.

We have here, we believe, correctly stated the anti-democratic side of the argument on this point. It is not to be denied that it possesses something more than plausibility. It has certainly been the instrument of more injury to the cause of the democratic principle than all the bayonets and cannon that have ever been arrayed in support of it against that principle. The inference from it is, that the popular opinion and will must not be trusted with the supreme and absolute direction of the general interests; that it must be subjected to the "conservative checks" of minority interests, and to the regulation of the "more enlightened wisdom" of the "better classes," and those to whom the possession of a property "test of merit" gives what they term "a stake in the community." And here we find ourselves in the face of the great stronghold of the anti-democratic, or *aristocratic,** principle.

It is not our purpose, in this place, to carry out the discussion of this question. The general scope and tendency of the present work are designed to be directed towards the refutation of this sophistical reasoning and inference. It will be sufficient here to allude to the leading ideas by which they are met by the advocate of the pure democratic cause.

* Ἀριστοχρατία, the government of the best.

In the first place, the greatest number are *more likely*, at least, as a general rule, to understand and follow their own greatest good, than is the minority.

In the second, a minority is much more likely to abuse power for the promotion of its own selfish interests, at the expense of the majority of numbers—the substantial and producing mass of the nation—than the latter is to oppress unjustly the former. The social evil is also, in that case, proportionately greater. This is abundantly proved by the history of all aristocratic interests that have existed, in various degrees and modifications, in the world. A majority cannot subsist upon a minority; while the natural, and in fact uniform, tendency of a minority entrusted with governmental authority is, to surround itself with wealth, splendor, and power, at the expense of the producing mass, creating and perpetuating those artificial social distinctions which violate the natural equality of rights of the human race, and at the same time offend and degrade the true dignity of human nature.

In the third place, there does not naturally exist any such original superiority of a minority class above the great mass of a community, in intelligence and competence for the duties of government—even putting out of view its constant tendency to abuse from selfish motives, and the safer honesty of the mass. The general diffusion of education; the facility of access to every species of knowledge important to the great interests of the community; the freedom of the press, whose very licentiousness cannot materially impair its permanent value, in this country at least, make the pretensions of those self-styled "better classes" to the sole possession of the requisite intelligence for the management of public affairs, too absurd to be entitled to any other treatment than an honest, manly contempt. As far as superior knowledge and talent confer on their possessor a natural charter of privilege to control his associates, and exert an influence on the direction of the general affairs of the community, the free and natural action of that privilege is best secured by a perfectly free democratic system, which will abolish all artificial distinctions, and, preventing the accumulation of any social obstacles to advancement, will permit the free development of every germ of talent, wherever it may chance to exist, whether on the proud mountain summit, in the humble valley, or by the wayside of common life.

But the question is not yet satisfactorily answered, how the relation between majorities and minorities, in the frequent case of a collision of sentiments and particular interests, is to be so adjusted as to secure a mutual respect of rights, to preserve harmony and good will, and save society from the *malum extremum discordia,* from being as a house divided against itself—and thus to afford free scope to that competition, discussion, and mutual moral influence, which cannot but result, in the end, in the ascendency of the truth, and in "the greatest good of the greatest number." On the one side, it has only been shown that the absolute government of the majority does not always afford a perfect guarantee against the misuse of its numerical power over the weakness of the minority. On the other, it has been shown that this chance of misuse is, as a general rule, far less than in the opposite relation of the ascendency of a minority; and that the evils attendant upon it are infinitely less, in every point of view, in the one case than the other. But this is not yet a complete or satisfactory solution of the problem. Have we but a choice of evils? Is there, then, such a radical deficiency in the moral elements implanted by its Creator in human society, that no other alternative can be devised by which both evils shall be avoided, and a result attained more analogous to the beautiful and glorious harmony of the rest of his creation?

It were scarcely consistent with a true and living faith in the existence and attributes of that Creator, so to believe; and such is not the democratic belief. The reason of the plausibility with which appeal may be made to the experience of so many republics, to sustain this argument against democratic institutions, is, that the true theory of national self-government has been hitherto but imperfectly understood; bad principles have been mixed up with the good; and the republican government has been administered on ideas and in a spirit borrowed from the strong governments of the other forms; and to the corruptions and manifold evils which have never failed, in the course of time, to evolve themselves out of these seeds of destruction, is ascribable the eventual failure of those experiments, and the consequent doubt and discredit which have attached themselves to the democratic principles on which they were, in the outset, mainly based.

It is under the word *government,* that the subtle danger lurks. Understood as a central consolidated power, managing and directing the various general interests of the society, all government is evil, and the parent of evil. A strong and active democratic *government,* in the common sense of the term, is an evil, differing only in degree and mode of operation, and not in nature, from a strong despotism. This difference is certainly vast, yet, inasmuch as these strong governmental powers must be wielded by human agents, even as the powers of the despotism, it is, after all, only a difference in degree; and the tendency to demoralization and tyranny is the same, though the development of the evil results is much more gradual and slow in the one case than in the other. Hence the demagogue—hence the faction—hence the mob—hence the violence, licentiousness, and instability—hence the ambitious struggles of parties and their leaders for power—hence the abuses of that power by majorities and their leaders—hence the indirect oppressions of the general by partial interests—hence (fearful symptom) the demoralization of the great men of the nation, and of the nation itself, proceeding (unless checked in time by the more healthy and patriotic portion of the mind of the nation rallying itself to reform the principles and sources of the evil) gradually to that point of maturity at which relief from the tumult of moral and physical confusion is to be found only under the shelter of an energetic armed despotism.

The best government is that which governs least. No human depositories can, with safety, be trusted with the power of legislation upon the general interests of society so as to operate directly or indirectly on the industry and property of the community. Such power must be perpetually liable to the most pernicious abuse, from the natural imperfection, both in wisdom of judgment and purity of purpose, of all human legislation, exposed constantly to the pressure of partial interests; interests which, at the same time that they are essentially selfish and tyrannical, are ever vigilant, persevering, and subtle in all the arts of deception and corruption. In fact, the whole history of human society and government may be safely appealed to, in evidence that the abuse of such power a thousand fold more than overbalances its beneficial use. Legislation has been the fruitful parent of nine-tenths of all the evil, moral and physical, by which mankind has been afflicted since the creation of the world, and by which human nature has been self-degraded, fettered, and oppressed. Government should have as little as possible to do with the general business and interests of the people. If it once undertake these functions as its rightful province of action, it is impossible to say to it "thus far shalt thou go, and no farther." It will be impossible to confine it to the public interests of the *commonwealth*. It will be perpetually tampering with private interests, and sending forth seeds of corruption which will result in the demoralization of the society. Its domestic action should be confined to the administration of justice, for the protection of the natural equal rights of the citizen, and the preservation of social order. In all other respects, the VOLUNTARY PRINCIPLE, the principle of FREEDOM, suggested to us by the analogy of the divine government of the Creator, and already recognised by us with perfect success in the great social interest of Religion, affords the true "golden rule" which is alone abundantly competent to work out the best possible general result of order and happiness from that chaos of characters, ideas, motives, and interests—human society. Afford but the single nucleus of a system of administration of justice between man and man, and, under the sure operation of this principle, the floating atoms will distribute and combine themselves, as we see in the beautiful natural process of crystallization, into a far more perfect and harmonious result than if government, with its "fostering hand," undertake to disturb, under the plea of directing, the process. The natural laws which will establish themselves and find their own level are the best laws. The same hand was the Author of the moral, as of the physical world; and we feel clear and strong in the assurance that we cannot err in trusting, in the former, to the same fundamental principles of spontaneous action and self-regulation which produce the beautiful order of the latter.

This is then, we consider, the true theory of government, the one simple result towards which the political science of the world is gradually tending, after all the long and varied experience by which it will have dearly earned the great secret—the elixir of political life. This is the fundamental principle of the philosophy of democracy, to furnish a system of administration of justice, and then leave all the business and interests of society to themselves, to free competition and association—in a word, to the VOLUNTARY PRINCIPLE—

> Let man be fettered by no duty, save
> His brother's right—like his, inviolable.

It is borrowed from the example of the perfect self-government of the physical universe, being written in letters of light on every page of the great bible of Nature. It contains the idea of full and fearless faith in the providence of the Creator. It is essentially involved in Christianity, of which it has been well said that its pervading spirit of democratic equality among men is its highest fact, and one of its most radiant internal evidences of the divinity of its origin. It is the essence and the one general result of the science of political economy. And this principle alone, we will add, affords a satisfactory and perfect solution of the great problem, otherwise unsolved, of the relative rights of majorities and minorities.

This principle, therefore, constitutes our "point of departure." It has never yet received any other than a very partial and imperfect application to practice among men, all human society having been hitherto perpetually chained down to the ground by myriads of lilliputian fetters of artificial government and prescription. Nor are we yet prepared for its full adoption in this country. Far, very far indeed, from it; yet is our gradual tendency toward it clear and sure. How many generations may yet be required before our theory and practice of government shall be sifted and analysed down to the lowest point of simplicity consistent with the preservation of some degree of national organization, no one can presume to prophecy. But that we are on the path toward that great result, to which mankind is to be guided down the long vista of future years by the democratic principle,—walking hand in hand with the sister spirit of Christianity,—we feel a faith as implicit as that with which we believe in any other great moral truth.

This is all generalization, and therefore, though necessary, probably dull. We have endeavored to state the theory of the Jeffersonian democracy, to which we profess allegiance, in its abstract essence. . . .

But having done so, we will not be further misunderstood, and we hope not misrepresented, as to immediate practical views. We deem it scarcely necessary to say that we are opposed to all precipitate radical changes in social institutions. Adopting "Nature as the best guide," we cannot disregard the lesson which she teaches, when she accomplishes her most mighty results of the good and beautiful by the silent and slow operation of great principles, without the convulsions of too rapid action. *Festina lente* is an invaluable precept, if it be not abused. On the other hand, that specious sophistry ought to be no less watchfully guarded against, by which old evils always struggle to perpetuate themselves by appealing to our veneration for "the wisdom of our fathers," to our inert love of present tranquillity, and our natural apprehension of possible danger from the untried and unknown—

> Better to bear the present ills we know,
> Than fly to others that we know not of.

We are not afraid of that much dreaded phrase, "untried experiment," which looms so fearfully before the eyes of some of our most worthy and valued friends. The whole history of the progress hitherto made by humanity, in every respect of social amelioration, records but a series of *"experiments."* The American revolution was the greatest of "experiments," and one of which it is not easy at this day to appreciate the gigantic boldness. Every step in the onward march of improvement by the human race is an "experiment;" and the present is most emphatically an age of "experiments." The eye of man looks naturally *forward;* and as he is carried onward by the progress of time and truth, he is far more likely to stumble and stray if he turn his face backward, and keep his looks fixed on the thoughts and things of the past. We feel safe under the banner of the democratic principle, which is borne onward by an unseen hand of Providence, to lead our race toward the high destinies of which every human soul contains the God-implanted germ; and of the advent of which—certain, however distant—a dim prophetic presentiment has existed, in one form or another, among all nations in all ages. . . .

For Democracy is the cause of Humanity. It has faith in human nature. It believes in its essential equality and fundamental goodness. It respects, with a solemn reverence to which the proudest artificial institutions and distinctions of society have no claim, the human soul. It is the cause of philanthropy. Its object is to emancipate the mind of the mass of men from the degrading and disheartening fetters of social distinctions and advantages; to bid it walk abroad through the free creation "in its own majesty;" to war against all fraud, oppression, and violence; by striking at their root, to reform all the infinitely varied human misery which has grown out of the old and false ideas by which the world has been so long misgoverned; to dismiss the hireling soldier; to spike the cannon, and bury the bayonet; to burn the gibbet, and open the debtor's dungeon; to substitute harmony and mutual respect for the jealousies and discord now subsisting between different classes of society, as the consequence of their artificial classification. It is the cause of Christianity, to which a slight allusion has been already made, to be more fully developed hereafter. And that portion of the peculiar friends and ministers of religion who now, we regret to say, cast the weight of their social influence against the cause of democracy, under the false prejudice of an affinity between it and infidelity, (no longer, in this century, the case, and which, in the last, was but a consequence of the overgrown abuses of religion found, by the reforming spirit that then awakened in Europe, in league with despotism,) understand but little either its true spirit, or that of their own faith. It is, moreover, a cheerful creed, a creed of high hope and universal love, noble and ennobling; while all others, which imply a distrust of mankind, and of the natural moral principles infused into it by its Creator, for its own self-development and self-regulation, are as gloomy and selfish, in the tone of moral sentiment which pervades them, as they are degrading in their practical tendency, and absurd in theory, when examined by the light of original principles.

Then whence this remarkable phenomenon, of the young mind of our country so deeply tainted with anti-democratic sentiment—a state of things lamentable in itself, and portentous of incalculable future evil?

Various partial causes may be enumerated in explanation of it; among which we may refer to the following: In the first place, the possession of the executive power (as it exists in our system) is, in one point of view, a great disadvantage to the principles of that ascendant party. The Administration occupies a position of defence; the Opposition, of attack. The former is by far the more arduous task. The lines of fortification to be maintained against the never relaxing onsets from every direction, are so extensive and exposed, that a perpetual vigilance and devotion to duty barely suffice to keep the enemy at bay. The attacking cause, ardent, restless, ingenious, is far more attractive to the imagination of youth than that of the defence. It is, moreover, difficult, if not impossible, to preserve a perfect purity from abuse and corruption throughout all the countless ramifications of the action of such an executive system as ours, however stern may be the integrity, and high the patriotism, of the presiding spirit which, from its head, animates the whole. Local abuses in the management of party affairs are the necessary consequence of the long possession of the ascendancy. The vast official patronage of the executive department is a weight and clog under which it is not easy to bear up. . . .

In the second place, we may refer to a cause which we look upon with deep pain, as one of the worst fruits of the evil principles to which allusion has already been made above as existing in our system—the demoralization of many of the great men of the nation. How many of these master-spirits of their day, to whom their country had long been accustomed to look with generous affection as her hope and pride, have we not seen seduced from the path of their early promise by the intrigues of party and the allurements of ambition, in the pursuit of that too dazzling prize, and too corrupting both in the prospect and the possession—the presidential office! . . .

The influence of such men, (especially on the minds of the young,) commanding by their intellectual power, misleading by their eloquence, and fascinating by the natural sympathy which attaches itself to greatness still proud in its "fallen estate," produces certainly a powerful effect in our party contests.

We might also refer to the fact, that the anti-democratic cause possesses at least two-thirds of the press of the country, and that portion of it which is best supported by talent and the resources of capital, under the commercial patronage of our cities. To the strong influence that cities,—where wealth accumulates, where luxury gradually unfolds its corrupting tendencies, where aristocratic habits and social classifications form and strengthen themselves, where the congregation of men stimulates and exaggerates all ideas,—to the influence that cities exert upon the country, no inconsiderable effect is to be ascribed. From the influence of the mercantile classes, too, (extensively anti-democratic) on the young men of the professions, especially that of the law, creating an insensible bias, from the dependence of the latter mainly on the patronage of the former, these young men becoming again each the centre of a small sphere of social influence; from that of the religious ministry, silently and insensibly exerted, from the false prejudice slightly touched upon above; from these and some other minor influences, on which we cannot here pause, a vast and active power on public opinion is perpetually in operation. And it is only astonishing that the democratic party should be able to bear up against them all so successfully as we in fact witness. This is to be ascribed (under that Providence whose unseen hand we recognise in all human affairs) only to the sterling honesty and good sense of the great industrious mass of our people, its instinctive perception of, and yearning after, the democratic truth, and the unwavering generosity of its support of those public servants whom it has once tried well and long, and with whom it has once acknowledged the genuine sympathy of common senti-ments and a common cause. Yet still the democratic principle can do little more than hold its own. The moral energies of the national mind are, to a great extent, paralyzed by division; and instead of bearing forward the ark of democratic truth, entrusted to us as a chosen people, towards the glorious destiny of its future, we must fain be content, if we can but stem with it the perpetual tide of attack which would bear it backward towards the ideas and habits of past dark ages.

But a more potent influence than any yet noticed, is that of our national literature. Or rather we have no national literature. We depend almost wholly on Europe, and particularly England, to think and write for us, or at least to furnish materials and models after which we shall mould our own humble attempts. We have a considerable number of writers; but not in that consists a national literature. The vital principle of an American national literature must be democracy. Our mind is enslaved to the past and present literature of England. . . . But we should not follow in her wake; a radiant path invites us forward in another direction. We have a principle—an informing soul—of our own, our democracy, though we allow it to languish uncultivated; this must be the animating spirit of our literature, if, indeed, we would have a national American literature. There is an immense field open to us, if we would but enter it boldly and cultivate it as our own. All history has to be re-written; political science and the whole scope of all moral truth have to be considered and illus-trated in the light of the democratic principle. All old subjects of thought and all new questions arising, connected more or less directly with human existence, have to be taken up again and re-examined in this point of view. We *ought* to exert a powerful moral influence on Europe, and yet we are entirely unfelt; and as it is only by its literature that one nation can utter itself and make itself known to the rest of the world, we are really entirely unknown. In the present general fermentation of popular ideas in Europe, turning the public thoughts naturally to the great democracy across the Atlantic, the voice of America might be made to produce a powerful and beneficial effect on the development of truth; but as it is, American writings are never translated, because they almost always prove to be a diluted and tardy second edition of English thought.

8. Majorities and Minorities

Illustrations

1. *"Politics in an Oyster House,"* lithograph from painting by Richard Caton Wood-
   ville, *1851.*

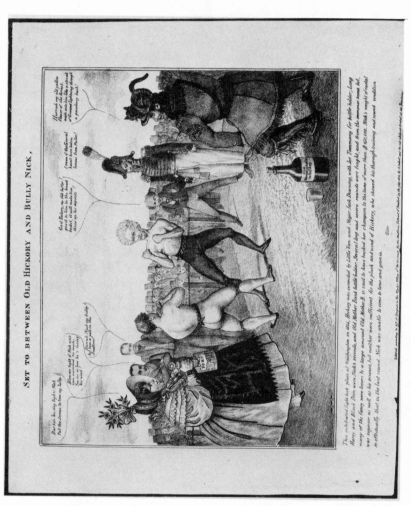

2. *"Set-To between Old Hickory and Bully Nick,"* 1834.

102

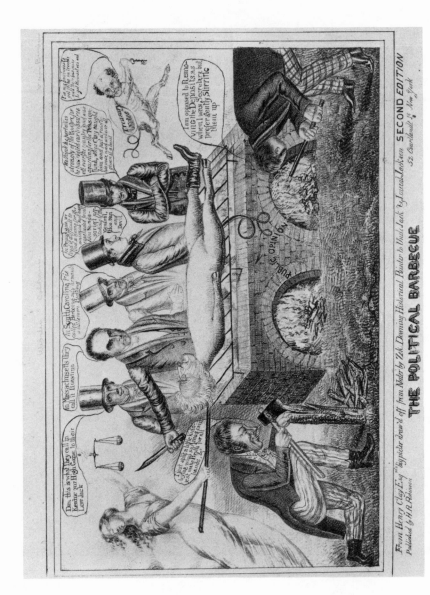

3. *"The Political Barbecue,"* 1835.

4. "Acts for Better Maintaining the Purity of Elections."

104

5. *"The Fruits of Amalgamation,"* 1839.

6. *"The Verdict of the People," by George Caleb Bingham, 1855.*

PART TWO

SUBLIMATION THROUGH HUMOR AND NOSTALGIA

9. Georgia Scenes

AUGUSTUS B. LONGSTREET

The first American literary group to adapt and develop an oral tradition to their purposes were the "Southwestern humorists," whose first significant production was Longstreet's *Georgia Scenes*. A Georgian who graduated from Yale and Litchfield Law School, Longstreet began his sketches of his native state in 1827. Influenced by the death of a favorite son, Longstreet gave up law and politics in 1838 to become a Methodist minister and president of Emory College (1839–1848) and of the University of South Carolina (1857–1865).

The sketches are twofold: one batch, signed "Hall," deals with frontier existence; the other, signed "Baldwin," attacks pseudo-aristocratic affectation and weakness. The frontier sketches are rightly best-known because in them Longstreet shows both observational shrewdness and restrained affection toward his subject within the bounds of his moralism; his scorn of aristocratic pretension makes his other sketches less satire than diatribe or soap opera. Longstreet's diction lacks the naturalness and vigor of later practitioners of the tradition, in part because he uses a "framing" device so heavily to separate himself from the life he describes; he even felt obliged to explain to his readers that "the coarse, inelegant, and sometimes ungrammatical language" in the stories was simply adapted to the level of life he wrote about. Yet, in *The Dance,* which describes the kind of life between barbarism and refinement that Longstreet idealized, he created a touching myth of America's yearning for a retroactive yeoman Utopia that perhaps had never existed.

GEORGIA THEATRICS

If my memory fail me not, the 10th of June, 1809 found me, at about 11 o'clock in the forenoon, ascending a long and gentle slope in what

Augustus B. Longstreet, *Georgia Scenes, Characters, Incidents, Etc.* (Augusta, Ga., 1835), 5–20.

was called "The Dark Corner" of Lincoln. I believe it took its name from the moral darkness which reigned over that portion of the county at the time of which I am speaking. If in this point of view it was but a shade darker than the rest of the county, it was inconceivably dark. If any man can name a trick or sin which had not been committed at the time of which I am speaking, in the very focus of all the county's illumination (Lincolnton), he must himself be the most inventive of the tricky, and the very Judas of sinners. Since that time, however (all humour aside), Lincoln has become a living proof "that light shineth in darkness." Could I venture to mingle the solemn with the ludicrous, even for the purposes of honourable contrast, I could adduce from this county instances of the most numerous and wonderful transitions, from vice and folly to virtue and holiness, which have ever, perhaps, been witnessed since the days of the apostolic ministry. So much, lest it should be thought by some that what I am about to relate is characteristic of the county in which it occurred.

Whatever may be said of the *moral* condition of the Dark Corner at the time just mentioned, its *natural* condition was anything but dark. It smiled in all the charms of spring; and spring borrowed a new charm from its undulating grounds, its luxuriant woodlands, its sportive streams, its vocal birds, and its blushing flowers.

Rapt with the enchantment of the season and the scenery around me, I was slowly rising the slope, when I was startled by loud, profane, and boisterous voices, which seemed to proceed from a thick covert of undergrowth about two hundred yards in the advance of me, and about one hundred to the right of my road.

"You kin, kin you?"

"Yes, I kin, and am able to do it! Boo-oo-oo! Oh, wake snakes, and walk your chalks! Brimstone and —— fire! Don't hold me, Nick Stoval! The fight's made up, and let's go at it. —— my soul if I don't jump down his throat, and gallop every chitterling out of him before you can say 'quit!' "

"Now, Nick, don't hold him! Jist let the wild-cat come, and I'll tame him. Ned'll see me a fair fight, won't you, Ned?"

"Oh, yes; I'll see you a fair fight, blast my old shoes if I don't."

"That's sufficient, as Tom Haynes said when he saw the elephant. Now let him come."

Thus they went on, with countless oaths interspersed, which I dare not even hint at, and with much that I could not distinctly hear.

In Mercy's name! thought I, what band of ruffians has selected this holy season and this heavenly retreat for such Pandæmonian riots! I quickened my gait, and had come nearly opposite to the thick grove whence the noise proceeded, when my eye caught indistinctly, and at intervals, through the foliage of the dwarf-oaks and hickories which intervened, glimpses of a man or men, who seemed to be in a violent struggle; and I could occasionally catch those deep-drawn, emphatic oaths which men in conflict utter when they deal blows. I dismounted, and hurried to the spot with all speed. I had overcome about half the space which separated it from me, when I saw the combatants come to the ground, and, after a short struggle, I saw the uppermost one (for I could not see the other) make a heavy plunge with both his thumbs, and at the same instant I heard a cry in the accent of keenest torture, "Enough! My eye's out!"

I was so completely horrorstruck, that I stood transfixed for a moment to the spot where the cry met me. The accomplices in the hellish deed which had been perpetrated had all fled at my approach; at least I supposed so, for they were not to be seen.

"Now, blast your corn-shucking soul," said the victor (a youth about eighteen years old) as he rose from the ground, "come cutt'n your shines 'bout me agin, next time I come to the Courthouse, will you! Get your owl-eye in agin if you can!"

At this moment he saw me for the first time. He looked excessively embarrassed, and was moving off, when I called to him, in a tone imboldened by the sacredness of my office and the iniquity of his crime, "Come back, you brute! and assist me in relieving your fellow mortal, whom you have ruined for ever!"

My rudeness subdued his embarrassment in an instant; and, with a taunting curl of the nose, he replied, "You needn't kick before you're spurr'd. There a'nt nobody there, nor ha'nt been nother. I was jist seein' how I could 'a' *fout*." So saying, he bounded to his plough, which stood in the corner of the fence about fifty yards beyond the battle ground.

And, would you believe it, gentle reader! his report was true. All that I had heard and seen was nothing more nor less than a Lincoln rehearsal; in which the youth who had just left me had played all the parts of all the characters in a Courthouse fight.

I went to the ground from which he had risen, and there were the prints of his two thumbs, plunged up to the balls in the mellow earth, about the distance of a man's eyes apart; and the ground around was broken up as if two stags had been engaged upon it.

HALL

THE DANCE

Some years ago I was called by business to one of the frontier counties, then but recently settled. It became necessary for me, while there, to enlist the services of Thomas Gibson, Esq., one of the magistrates of the county, who resided about a mile and a half from my lodgings; and to this circumstance was I indebted for my introduction to him. I had made the intended disposition of my business, and was on the eve of my departure for the city of my residence, when I was induced to remain a day longer by an invitation from the squire to attend a dance at his house on the following day. Having learned from my landlord that I would probably "be expected at the frolic" about the hour of 10 in the forenoon, and being desirous of seeing all that passed upon the occasion, I went over about an hour before the time.

The squire's dwelling consisted of but one room, which answered the threefold purpose of dining-room, bedroom, and kitchen. The house was constructed of logs, and the floor was of *puncheons;* a term which, in Georgia, means split logs, with their faces a little smoothed with the axe or hatchet. To gratify his daughters, Polly and Silvy, the old gentleman and his lady had consented to *camp out* for a day, and to surrender the habitation to the girls and their young friends.

When I reached there I found all things in readiness for the promised amusement. . . .

I saw several fine, bouncing, ruddy-cheeked girls descending a hill about the eighth of a mile off. They, too, were attired in manufactures of their own hands. The refinements of the present day in female dress had not even reached our republican *cities* at this time; and, of course, the *country girls* were wholly ignorant of them. They carried no more cloth upon their arms or straw upon their heads than was necessary to cover them. They used no artificial means of spreading their frock tails to an interesting extent from their ankles. They had no boards laced to their breasts, nor any corsets laced to their sides; consequently, they looked, for all the world, like human beings, and could be distinctly recognised as such at the distance of two hundred paces. Their movements were as free and active as nature would permit them to be. Let me not be understood as interposing the least objection to any lady in this land of liberty dressing just as she pleases. If she choose to lay her neck and shoulders bare, what right have I to look at them? much less to find fault with them. If she choose to put three yards of muslin in a frock sleeve, what right have I to ask why a little strip of it was not put in the body? If she like the pattern of a hoisted umbrella for a frock, and the shape of a cheese-cask for her body, what is all that to me? But to return.

The girls were met by Polly and Silvy Gibson at some distance from the house, who welcomed them—"with a kiss, of course"—oh, no; but with something much less equivocal: a hearty shake of the hand and smiling countenances, which had some meaning.

[*Note.*—The custom of kissing, as practised in these days by the *amiables,* is borrowed from the French, and by them from Judas.]

The young ladies had generally collected before any of the young men appeared. It was not long, however, before a large number of both sexes were assembled, and they adjourned to the *ballroom.*

But for the snapping of a fiddle-string, the young people would have been engaged in the amusement of the day in less than three minutes from the time they entered the house. Here were no formal introductions to be given, no drawing for places or partners, no parade of managers, no ceremonies. It was perfectly understood that all were invited *to dance,* and that none were invited who were unworthy to be danced with; consequently, no gentleman hesitated to ask any lady present to dance with him, and no lady refused to dance with a gentleman merely because she had not been made acquainted with him.

In a short time the string was repaired, and off went the party to a good old republican six reel. I had been thrown among *fashionables* so long that I had almost forgotten my native dance. But it revived rapidly as they wheeled through its mazes, and with it returned many long-forgotten, pleasing recollections. Not only did the reel return to me, but the very persons who used to figure in it with me, in the heyday of youth.

Here was my old sweetheart, Polly Jackson, identically personified in Polly Gibson; and here was Jim Johnson's, in Silvy; and Bill Martin's, in Nancy Ware. Polly Gibson had my old flame's very steps as well as her looks. "Ah!" said I, "squire, this puts me in mind of old times. I have not seen a six reel for five-and-twenty years. It recalls to my mind many a happy hour, and many a jovial friend who used to enliven it with me. Your Polly looks so much like my old sweetheart, Polly Jackson, that, were I young again, I certainly should fall in love with her."

"That was the name of her mother," said the squire.

"Where did you marry her?" inquired I.

"In Wilkes," said he; "she was the daughter of old Nathan Jackson, of that county."

"It isn't possible!" returned I. "Then it is the very girl of whom I am speaking. Where is she?"

"She's out," said the squire, "preparing dinner for the young people; but she'll be in towards the close of the day. But come along, and I'll make you acquainted with her at once, if you'll promise not to run away with her, for I tell you what it is, she's the likeliest *gal* in all these parts yet."

"Well," said I, "I'll promise not to run away with her, but you must not let her know who I am. I wish to make myself known to her; and, for fear of the worst, you shall witness the introduction. But don't get jealous, squire, if she seems a little too glad to see me; for, I assure you, we had a strong notion of each other when we were young."

"No danger," replied the squire; "she hadn't seen *me* then, or she never could have loved such a hard favoured man as you are."

In the mean time the dance went on, and I employed myself in selecting from the party the best examples of the dancers of my day and Mrs. Gibson's for her entertainment. In this I had not the least difficulty; for the dancers before me and those of my day were in all respects identical. . . .

The dance grew merrier as it progressed; the young people became more easy in each other's company, and often enlivened the scene with most humorous remarks. Occasionally some sharp cuts passed between the boys, such as would have produced half a dozen duels at a city ball; but here they were taken as they were meant, in good humour. Jim Johnson being a little tardy in meeting his partner at a turn of the reel, "I *ax* pardon, Miss Chloe," said he, "Jake Slack went to make a cross-hop just now, and tied his legs in a hard knot, and I stop'd to help him untie them." A little after, Jake hung his toe in a crack of the floor, and nearly fell; "Ding my buttons," said he, "if I didn't know I should stumble over Jim Johnson's foot at last; Jim, draw your foot up to your own end of the reel." (Jim was at the other end of the reel, and had, in truth, a prodigious foot.)

Towards the middle of the day, many of the neighbouring farmers dropped in, and joined the squire and myself in talking of old times. At length dinner was announced. It consisted of plain *fare*, but there was a profusion of it. Rough planks, supported by stakes driven in the ground, served for a table; at which the old and young of both sexes seated themselves at the same time. I soon recognised Mrs. Gibson from all the matrons present. Thirty years had wrought great changes in her appearance, but they had left some of her features entirely unimpaired. Her eye beamed with all its youthful fire; and, to my astonishment, her mouth was still beautified with a full set of teeth, unblemished by time. The rose on her cheek had rather freshened than faded and her smile was the very same that first subdued my heart; but her fine form was wholly lost, and, with it, all the grace of her movements. Pleasing but melancholy reflections occupied my mind as I gazed on her dispensing her cheerful hospitalities. I thought of the sad history of many of her companions and mine, who used to carry light hearts through the merry dance. I compared my after life with the cloudless days of my attachment to Polly. Then I was light hearted, gay, contented, and happy. I aspired to nothing but a good name, a good wife, and an easy competence. The first and last were mine already; and Polly had given me too many little tokens of her favour to leave a doubt now that the second was at my command. But I was foolishly told that my talents were of too high an order to be employed in the drudgeries of a farm, and I more foolishly believed it. I forsook the pleasures which I had tried and proved, and went in pursuit of those imaginary joys which seemed to encircle the seat of Fame. From that moment to the present, my life had been little else than one unbroken scene of disaster, disappointment, vexation, and toil. And now, when I was too old to enjoy the pleasures which I had discarded, I found that my aim was absolutely hopeless; and that my pursuits had only served to unfit me for the humbler walks of life, and to exclude me from the higher. The gloom of these reflections was, however, lightened in a measure by the promises of the coming hour, when I was to live over again with Mrs. Gibson some of the happiest moments of my life.

After a hasty repast the young people returned to their amusement, followed by myself, with several of the elders of the company. An hour had scarcely elapsed before Mrs. Gibson entered, accompanied by a goodly number of matrons of her own age. This accession to the company produced its usual effects. It raised the tone of conversation a full octave, and gave it a triple time movement; added new life to the wit and limbs of the young folks, and set the old men to cracking jokes.

At length the time arrived for me to surprise and delight Mrs. Gibson. The young people insisted upon the old folks taking a reel; and this was just what I had been waiting for; for, after many plans for making the discovery, I had finally concluded upon that which I thought would make *her* joy general among the company: and that was, to announce myself, just before leading her to the dance, in a voice audible to most of the assembly. I therefore readily assented to the proposition of the young folks, as did two others of my age, and we made to the ladies for our partners. I, of course, offered my hand to Mrs. Gibson.

"Come," said I, "Mrs. Gibson, let us see if we can't out-dance these young people."

"Dear me, sir," said she, "I haven't danced a step these twenty years."

"Neither have I; but I've resolved to try once more, if you will join me, just for old time's sake."

"I really cannot think of dancing," said she.

"Well," continued I (raising my voice to a pretty high pitch, on purpose to be heard, while my countenance kindled with exultation at the astonishment and delight which I was about to produce), "you surely will dance with an old friend and sweetheart, who used to dance with you when a girl!"

At this disclosure her features assumed a vast variety of expressions; but none of them responded precisely to my expectation: indeed, some of them were of such an equivocal and alarming character, that I deemed it advisable not to prolong her suspense. I therefore proceeded:

"Have you forgot your old sweetheart, Abram Baldwin?"

"What!" said she, looking more astonished and confused than ever. "Abram Baldwin! Abram Baldwin! I don't think I ever heard the name before."

"Do you remember Jim Johnson?" said I.

"Oh, yes," said she, "mighty well," her countenance brightening with a smile.

"And Bill Martin?"

"Yes, perfectly well; why, *who* are you?"

Here we were interrupted by one of the gentlemen, who had led his partner to the floor, with, "Come, stranger, we're getting mighty tired o' standing. It won't do for old people that's going to dance to take up much time in standing; they'll lose all their *spryness*. Don't stand begging Polly Gibson, she never dances; but take my Sal there, next to her; she'll run a reel with you, to old Nick's house and back *agin*."

No alternative was left me, and therefore I offered my hand to Mrs. Sally—I didn't know who.

"Well," thought I, as I moved to my place, "the squire is pretty secure from jealousy; but Polly will soon remember me when she sees my steps in the reel. I will dance precisely as I used to in my youth, if it tire me to death." There was one step that was almost exclusively my own, for few of the dancers of my day could perform it at all, and none with the grace and ease that I did. "She'll remember Abram Baldwin," thought I, "as soon as she sees the *double cross-hop*." It was performed by rising and crossing the legs twice or thrice before lighting, and I used to carry it to the third cross with considerable ease. It was a step solely adapted to setting or balancing, as all will perceive; but I thought the occasion would justify a little perversion of it, and therefore resolved to lead off with it, that Polly might be at once relieved from suspense. Just, however, as I reached my place, Mrs. Gibson's youngest son, a boy about eight years old, ran in and cried out, "Mammy, old Boler's jump'd upon the planks, and dragg'd off a great hunk o' meat as big as your head, and broke a dish and two plates all to darn smashes!" Away went Mrs. Gibson, and off went the music. Still I hoped that matters would be adjusted in time for Polly to return and see the double cross-hop; and I felt the mortification which my delay in getting a partner had occasioned somewhat solaced by the reflection that it had thrown me at the foot of the reel.

The first and second couples had nearly completed their performances, and Polly had not returned. I began to grow uneasy, and to interpose as many delays as I could without attracting notice.

The six reel is closed by the foot couple balancing at the head of the set, then in the middle, then at the foot, again in the middle, meeting at the head, and leading down.

My partner and I had commenced balancing at the head, and Polly had not returned. I balanced until my partner forced me on. I now deemed it advisable to give myself up wholly to the double cross-hop; so that, if Polly should return in time to see any step, it should be this, though I was already nearly exhausted. Accordingly, I made the attempt to introduce it in the turns of the reel; but the first experiment convinced me of three things at once: 1st. That I could not have used the step in this way in my best days; 2d. That my strength would not more than support it in its proper place for the remainder of the reel; and, 3d. If I tried it again in this way, I should knock my brains out against the puncheons; for my partner, who seemed determined to confirm her husband's report of her, evinced no disposition to wait upon experiments; but, fetching me a jerk while I was up and my legs crossed, had wellnigh sent me head foremost to Old Nick's house, sure enough.

We met in the middle, my back to the door, and from the silence that prevailed in the yard, I flattered myself that Polly might be even now catching the first glimpse of the favourite step, when I heard her voice at some distance from the house: "Get you gone! G-e-e-e-t you gone! G-e-e-e-e-e-t you gone!" Matters out doors were now clearly explained. There had been a struggle to get the meat from Boler; Boler had triumphed, and retreated to the woods with his booty, and Mrs. Gibson was heaping indignities upon him in the last resort.

The three *"Get-you-gones"* met me precisely at the three closing balances; and the last brought my moral energies to a perfect level with my physical.

Mrs. Gibson returned, however, in a few minutes after, in a good humour; for she possessed a lovely disposition, which even marriage could not spoil. As soon as I could collect breath enough for regular conversation (for, to speak in my native dialect, I was *"mortal tired"*), I took a seat by her, resolved not to quit the house without making myself known to her, if possible.

"How much," said I, "your Polly looks and dances like you used to, at her age."

"I've told my old man so a hundred times," said she. "Why, who upon earth are you!"

"Did you ever see two persons dance more alike than Jim Johnson and Sammy Tant?"

"Never. Why, who can you be!"

"You remember Becky Lewis?"

"Yes!"

"Well, look at Chloe Dawson, and you'll see her over again."

"Well, law me! Now I know I must have seen you somewhere; but, to save my life, I can't tell where. Where did your father live?"

"He died when I was small."

"And where did you use to see me?"

"At your father's, and old Mr. Dawson's, and at Mrs. Barnes's, and at Squire Noble's, and many other places."

"Well, goodness me! it's mighty strange I can't call you to mind."

I now began to get petulant, and thought it best to leave her.

The dance wound up with the old merry jig, and the company dispersed.

The next day I set out for my residence. I had been at home rather more than two months, when I received the following letter from Squire Gibson:

"DEAR SIR: I send you the money collected on the notes you left with me. Since you left here, Polly has been thinking about old times, and she says, to save her life, she can't recollect you."

BALDWIN

10. The Spirit of the Times

The national literary organ for much of Southwestern humor was William T. Porter's sporting and theatrical periodical, *The Spirit of the Times*. Begun in 1831, it was one of the most popular American journals in the two decades before the Civil War. With a long list of prominent contributors, particularly Whig and Democratic politicians from the South and West, it did much to develop interest in the humor and nuances of American vernacular idiom. No source from the period touches so evocatively on the ways in which Americans amused themselves, and on how gentlemen of sporting inclinations looked at the way in which Americans amused themselves.

The race between Fashion and Boston was one of the great match races of the era; the Currier and Ives print (Illustration F12) shows the next great one three years later when Peytona, the Southern challenger, narrowly beat Fashion which news was immediately sent to Manhattan and Philadelphia via carrier pigeon). The Peleg White letters are typical of the dialect humor that was the magazine's specialty. Longstreet's "framing device" has in this case disappeared, and one senses no serious tension between the writer and the dialect character he creates. A long step is taken toward Huck Finn.

THE BEST RACE EVER RUN IN AMERICA!

Huzza for the Bonnets o' Blue!! Huzza for the Northern Champion!!
THE SOUTH BEATEN BY THE NORTH

IN

$7:32\frac{1}{2}—7:45.$

The great sectional Match for $20,000 a side, Four mile heats, between THE NORTH and THE SOUTH, came off on Tuesday last, the 10th inst. Since

William T. Porter, editor, *The Spirit of the Times; A Chronicle of the Turf, Agriculture, Field Sports, Literature, and the Stage*, 1839–1842.

the memorable contest between Eclipse and Henry, on the 27th of May, 1823, no race has excited so much interest and enthusiasm. It attracted hundreds of individuals from the remotest sections of the Union, and for months has been the theme of remark and speculation, not only in the Sporting Circles of this country but in England, where the success of the Northern Champion was predicted! It was a most thrilling and exciting race!—one which throws in the shade the most celebrated of those wonderful achievements which have conferred so much distinction upon the High Mettled Racers of America!

At an early hour on Tuesday morning our streets were filled with carriages of all descriptions, wending their way to the Ferries, while thousands upon thousands crossed over to the cars of the Long Island Rail Road Company. But after eleven o'clock the Company found it impossible to convey to the course the immense crowd which filled and surrounded the cars, though they continued to sell tickets after they were fully sensible of the fact! Indeed, from the first, the arrangements of the Company were an imposition! They charged the most extravagant price for the transportation of passengers, and their preparations were in no way equal to the occasion; above all, they continued to sell tickets after *they knew* that several thousand more persons had purchased them than they could transport. A train, bearing over two thousand passengers, did not reach the course until after the 1st heat, and hundreds who had purchased tickets, despairing of reaching the course in the cars, started on foot, and reached it before them. At half past eleven o'clock there were not less than five thousand persons waiting a conveyance by the cars at the Brooklyn terminus, all of whom had purchased tickets! Under these circumstances, it will not be very surprising to any one to hear that upon the return of the cars after the race, the indignant passengers rolled several of them off the track over the hill, and smashed others, while "a perfect mash" was made of the ticket office! The race was a golden harvest to the hack, cab, and omnibus proprietors. The anxiety to reach the course was so great that ten dollars were offered for a standing-up place in a charcoal cart! . . .

Upon reaching the course, such a tableau was presented as we never saw before. The field inside of the course was thronged with carriages and equestrians, while the fences, booths, and trees, were densely covered, so much so that several accidents occurred from their breaking down. It is stated that there were no less than Eight Thousand persons in the stands, and yet there were nearly as many more who could obtain but a partial view of the race, while many could not see it at all! The number of spectators in attendance is variously estimated at from FIFTY to SEVENTY THOUSAND!! Among them the U. S. Senate and House of Representatives, the British Army and Navy, as well as our own, the Bench and the Bar, and the Beauty and Fashion of New York were all represented. The Ladies' Stand was appropriately graced by the presence of a large number of the most brilliant of our city belles, who, with hardly an exception, gave the suffrage of "their most sweet voices" to the beautiful daughter of Bonnets o' Blue! The enclosed "privileged space" in front of the stands, reserved for the Members of the Jockey Club and strangers who were charged $10 for admission, without distinction!) was thronged with Turfmen, Breeders, and Amateurs! At one o'clock, however, owing to the want of an efficient police, and their inability to see the race, more than a thousand persons climbed over the pickets, from the field, into the enclosed space, while a mob on the outside tore down a length of fence, and stove through a door in the stand, and swarmed into the cleared space. For a time it seemed impossible for the match to take place at all! A crowd of loafers made a rush up the stairs leading to the Club Stand, but they were summarily ejected. At length YANKEE SULLIVAN, JEROLOMAN, RYNAS, and several other distinguished members of The Fancy, undertook to clear the course, which they did in an incredibly short time, by organizing a party of their friends, who formed in line, with clasped hands, quite across the space, and marched from one end to the other, thereby driving outside of the gate every person without a badge. Of course there were among this mob several ugly customers, but Yankee Sullivan had only to "let fly with his right," or Jeroloman give any one of them "a teaser on his smeller," to fix his business! On the whole, the mob conducted themselves very well under the circumstances; the great majority were in perfectly good humor, and had the proprietors taken the precaution to *paint* the tops of the pickets with a thick coat of *tar,* and engage a strong body of police, no such disgraceful scene would have occurred.

THE RACE

First Heat.—Boston on the inside went away with the lead at a rattling pace, the mare laying up within two lengths of him down the straight run on the backstretch; the half mile was run in 55 seconds. The same position was maintained to the end of the mile, (run in 1:53) but soon after Fashion made play and the pace improved. Both made strong running down the back stretch, over the hill (opposite the half mile post) and down the slight descent which succeeds, and though this seemed favorable ground for Boston, the mare gained on him, at this place, in this mile, and placed herself well up. Boston threw her off on the turn, and led through clear, running this mile in 1:50½. The pace seemed too good to last, and Boston's friends, as he led cleverly down the back stretch, were "snatching and eager" to take anything offered. Again Boston led through, this mile (the 3d) being run in 1:54, Fashion, keeping him up to the top of his rate. The contest was beautiful and exciting beyond description; there was no clambering, no faltering, no dwelling on the part of either; each ran with a long rating stroke, and at a pace that kills. Soon after commencing the 4th mile Joe Laird shook his whip over her head and gave Fashion an eye opener or two with the spur, and not 100 yards from the ground where Boston took the track from Charles Carter, *she collared and passed him in half a dozen strokes* at a flight of speed we never saw equalled, except in the desperate brush at the stand between Grey Medoc and Altorf, in their dead heat! When Fashion responded to the call upon her and took the track in such splendid style the cheers sent up from the "rude throats" of thousands might have been heard for miles! Fashion made her challenge after getting through the drawgate and took the lead opposite the quarter mile post. Boston, however, like a trump, as he is, did not give back an inch, and though it was manifest the Northern Phenomenon had the foot of him, he gave her no respite. He lapped her down the back stretch for 300 yards, when Gil. Patrick very sensibly took a strong bracing pull on him and bottled him up for a desperate brush up the hill, where Eclipse passed Henry. Here Gil. again let him out, but unfortunately he pulled him inside so near the fence that Boston struck his hip against a post, and hitting a sharp knot or a nail cut through the skin on his quarter for seven or eight inches! He struck hard enough to jar himself very much, and we observed him to falter; but he soon recovered, and though at this moment Fashion led him nearly three lengths, he gradually closed the gap round the turn to within a few feet. At this moment the excited multitude broke through all restraint in their anxiety to witness the termination of the heat, and the course was nearly blocked up! On coming out through a narrow gauntlet of thousands of spectators excited to the highest pitch, both horses very naturally faltered at the tremendous shouts which made the welkin ring! Up the quarter stretch Gil. made another desperate effort to win the race out of the fire. He applied his thong freely, while Joe Laird drew his whip on the mare more than once, and tapped her claret at the same time. Inside of the gate it was "a hollow thing," though Boston nearly closed the gap at the distance stand. Gil. fairly caught Joe by surprise, but the latter, shaking his whip over her head, gave Fashion the spur, and she instantly recovered her stride coming through about a length ahead with apparently something in hand to spare, closing the heat in 7:32½—the fastest, by all odds, ever run in America! . . .

Both horses cooled out well. Boston always blows tremendously, even after a gallop, but he seemed little distressed. Neither was Fashion; her action is superb, and as she came through on the 4th mile, it was remarked that she was playing her ears as if taking her exercise. She recovered sooner than Boston, and though her friends now offered large odds on her, Boston's were no less confident; the seventh mile they thought would "fetch her." We should not have been surprised to have seen both swell over the loins, nor to have found them greatly distressed. We examined them carefully after the heat, and state with great pleasure, that though they "blowed strong," they recovered in a few minutes, and came to the post again comparatively fresh. After the heat was over, the crowd rushed into the enclosed space *en masse;* an endeavor was made to clear a portion of the track of the multitude who had now taken possession of it, and after great exertions, a lane was formed, through which the horses came up for the

Second Heat: Fashion led off with a moderate stroke, and carried on the running down the back stretch with a lead of about three lengths. After making the ascent of the hill Boston challenged, closed the gap, and lapped her. A tremendous shout arose on all hands at this rally, but as it subsided on the part of Boston's friends, it was again more tumultuously caught up by the friends of the mare, as she outfooted him before reaching the head of the quarter stretch. She came through (in 1:59) three or four lengths ahead, and kept up her rate down the entire straight stretch on the rear of the Course. After getting over the hill, Boston, as before, made a rush, and succeeded in collaring the mare, while she, as before, again threw him off, and led through by two or three lengths in 1:57. Gil. relieved his horse for the next 600 yards, but instead of waiting for Fashion to ascend the hill at the half mile post alone, he called on Boston just before reaching it, and the two went over it nearly together; no sooner had they commenced the descending ground, then gathering all his energies for a final and desperate effort, Boston made a dash, and this time he succeeded in taking the track! The scene which ensued we have no words to describe. Such cheering, such betting, and so many long faces, was never seen nor heard before. After being compelled to give up the track, Joe Laird, with the utmost prudence and good sense, took his mare in hand, and gave her time to recover her wind. This run *took the shine out of* Boston! Instead of pulling him steadily, and refreshing him with a slight respite, Gil. Patrick kept him at his work after he took the track, and run this mile (the 3d) in 1:51½! The pace was tremendous! Nothing short of limbs of steel and sinews of catgut could stand up under such a press! On the first turn after passing the stand, Fashion, now fresh again, made a dash, and as Boston had not another run left in him, she cut him down in her stride opposite the quarter mile post, and *the thing was out!* The race, so far as Boston was concerned, was past praying for! If anything can parallel Fashion's turn of speed it is her invincible game. She now gradually dropped him, and without another effort on his part to retrieve the fortunes of the day, she came home a gallant and easy winner in 7:45! Boston pulled up inside of the distance stand, and walked over the score! As she came under the Judges' cord extended across the course, Boston was exactly sixty yards behind, though he could have placed himself in a better position had Gil. called upon him. As Joe Laird rode Fashion back to the stand, the shouts were so deafening, that had not the President of the Club and another gentleman held on to her bridle, she would have not only "enlarged the circle of her acquaintance" very speedily, but "made a mash" of some dozen of "the rank and file" then and there assembled. She looked as if another heat would not "set her back any." . . .

MISCELLANY

Original Theatrical Anecdote.—A correspondent writes us to the following effect:—Not long since the play of Othello was enacted in New Orleans. Among the audience placed in the pit were three up river boatmen, who had descended the Mississippi in a broad horn, or some such craft, and having sold out pretty well, thought they would treat themselves to a sight of the play-house, before starting for home. They were tall, stout, strapping fellows, who really looked as if they could whip their weight in wild cats. Their attention seemed to be deeply engrossed with the play as it proceeded. At length when it came to that part in which the Moor, in the interview with Desdemona, says "The Handkerchief!"—"The handkerchief!!"—"The handkerchief!!!" Our boatman did not understand all this, and when the Moor had reached the third exclamation, and was again pausing, one of them cried out "Oh, d—m it, my friend, why *don't you blow your nose with your fingers, and let the play go on?"*

J. M. FIELD's version of *"The Artful Dodger"* has set them *"all dying"* in Philadelphia. This piece, which has had an immense run in London, is still *preserved in MSS.* by the original performer of the part. It would really be a pity, by an *international copy-right law*—to stop the ingenuity of us Dodgers.

The following is a portion of Field's song in the piece.

THE DODGERS

They're dodging in the palace, for
   The "artful" they've an itching;
They're dodging in the parlor, and
   They're dodging in the kitchen:
The parson is a dodger,
   Often dodges round his text;
And his hearers, dodging through *this* world,
   Through him would dodge the *next!*
     And we're all dodging, &c.

The Editor's a dodger,
   Whether Democrat or Whig;
He makes the other side sing small,
   Himself but talking big;
And candidates are dodgers, "what
   They'll do"—and "what they've done;"
Their dodge, to serve their country best—
   Best serving *number one!*
     And we're all dodging, &c.

Victoria is a dodger, when
   She goes to France to lodge;
Louis Philippe, as the "Artful," too,
   Will soon return the dodge!
Across the other channel, Dan,
   Says let 'em dodge and wheel;
I'm the boy, and, by the holy, they
   Shall never dodge "Repeal!"
     And we're all dodging, &c.

There's Dickens! he's a dodger when
   He seeks to prove his art in
Shewing up the Yankee doodles in
   His *funny* story, "Martin;"
And the Yankees, just as artful, say,
   Each number as they quit,
There's plenty of the "Chuzzle," but
   They cannot see the "*wit!*"
     And we're all dodging, &c.

The annexed "good 'un" is from the Boston "Morning Post," one of the very best daily journals in the Union, edited by our esteemed friend Charles Gordon Greene, Esq. You won't "see anything *green*" in the following paragraph:—

In a town some fifty miles from Boston, the members of a religious society were in the practice of holding conference meetings in the church, at which they made a kind of audible confession, technically called recounting one's "experience." A very pious member of the church, Mr. D——, was in the habit of inviting his neighbor Mr. L——, who was not a member, to attend these meetings, at one of which Mr. D—— got up and stated to the congregation that he was a great sinner—that he sinned daily, and with his eyes open—that he wilfully and knowingly sinned—that goodness dwelt not in him—that he was absolutely and totally depraved—that nothing but the boundless mercy and infinite goodness of God could save him from eternal damnation. After this confession of Mr. D——, Mr. L——, who had by accident been placed upon the "anxious seat," was called to recount his "experience." He arose, and with most imperturbable gravity, stated that he had very little to say of himself, but the brethren would remember that he had lived for five-and-twenty years the nearest neighbor of Mr. D.—that he knew him well—more intimately so than any other man—and it gave him great pleasure, because he could do it with entire sincerity, *to confirm the truth of all brother D. had confessed of himself.* When Mr. L. sat down under the visible and audible smile of the whole congregation, the parson not excepted, Mr. D. went up to him and said, "You are a rascal and a liar, and I'll lick you when you get out of church."

Saunders' *Metallic Tablet and Razor Strop.*—These Strops have probably done as much for the observance of the third commandment as half the preaching on the subject of profane swearing, for so kindly do they induce amiability in that class of bipeds doomed to use a razor, that he must be a sinner indeed who does not feel grateful to the inventor for putting in his hands an instrument wherewith he defies the torment of wiry-edged razors, and the miseries of a scraped and half shaved face. We have just been presented with one of these strops, and have hardly put it by since we surprised a pair of ruthless, rascally razors into a state of entire obedience with a few touches over its metallic surface.

We Give in.—Greene, of the Boston Post, may have that old razor. We give it up freely after reading the following:—

Dr. Hitchcock pulls teeth so easily that a man the other day begged him to "finish the row," after he had removed a decayed one—he said he *enjoyed* it.

We had scarcely finished reading the above when we noticed the following in the Boston Transcript. Those Boston wags are ahead yet. We pass:—

Good Fishing.—It is said that trout are so plenty in Granville, in this state, that when one man is fishing for them, another is obliged to stand by the hook, with a club, to prevent more than one from biting at a time!

Conscientiousness.—"I shall prevent the use of ardent spirits," as the innkeeper said when he watered the liquors.

And here in the Granite State the girls never pretend to *waste* candles in such business. "Debby," said a certain old lady, "Debby, don't let me catch you burnin' candles out a-sparking; tallow is *scurse* and perhaps you mayn't get the schoolmaster *after all!*" Debby dutifully obeyed her ma'am.

N. H. Argus.

Nothing exceeds the modesty of the Hawkeye girls. They won't be courted by daylight, nor in the evening unless the candles are extinguished.

Chicago Democrat.

"PELEG WHITE" AMONG THE CORN DODGERS OUT WEST.

DODGINSVILLE, (a leetle spell west of sundown,)

May the fust, 1840.

Mister Spirit,—Major Downing rit a letter a leetle spell ago from the Log Cabing tu North Bend, when he was a stayin with the Gineral, a helpin him keep the hogs out of his cornfields, and tell'd all the folks down East that the Ohio had riz, and maybe it would be rizer. The Major warnt fur out of the way there, but it ain't so now, for the Ohio has got down agin, amost out of sight, and maybe it will be got *downer*. The Ohio is the all-firedest unsartin consarn in all natur. You may fill it clean up tu the brim, and a leetle more tu, and afore a feller can run a gray hoss around a tall cornfield three times, and he may lick the critter tu the tip eend of his speed tu, it will git down agin. Great mistake in natur in not makin the bottom on't tight enough to hold water during a pressure.

But maybe you would like tu know who in natur I am, and what kind o broughten up I have got. Wal, unskin your head, knock under, and take a glass of *hard cider* with me, and I will tell you all about it. I was born of my mammy, sired by my daddy (so folks say), and got my broughten up pretty much as I could ketch it, which is pretty fair considerin the times. I have been takin a short tower round the country, just pretty much on account of my *hulsum* [wholesome], and tu git a leetle more insight intu the works of natur and art. I have bin stoppin here a short spell, just to see how the land lies, and the way the folks dew have tu work tu keep the grass from growin in the streets is pesky perplexious.

The land is so mucky and rich here, that the meanest kind of fence-posts bear moss-roses, and I guess it is about one of the most moralistist places this side of old Weathersfield, Conn. Yesterday a feller let his hosses run away, with the wagin hitched tu 'um, and the way they did streak it down the street would have troubled a streak of greased lightning amazingly. As soon as they got the feller who owned the horses they had a committee appinted (for you must know everything is done here amost by a committee of great folks), and they fined him $5, and reprimanded him pretty hard tu. They did it, they said, 'cause they had an idea that it had an immoral tendency, as a great many wimmen hearin the noise, run tu their doors tu look out, with *nothin* on their feet but their *stockins!* But the way natur does look pretty on the mountaings, and in the gardings, round about here, is tryin tu a feller, if he has got a speck of poetry in his feelins. The air is so full of parfume of roses, vialets, and hunny-suckles, that if you go out in the mornin suddingly, and take a good strong snuff on't, it will almost knock you down about as quick as a clap of lightnin', and oh! lordy! such lots of pretty gals as there are here, and so hulsum-lookin tu— it eanamost gives a feller the spazams tu look on 'em.

This is the country arter all—burn a hole in my old hat, but the people are a pretty sharp set. You may stick a feller so full of college larnin in the East that he is amost ready to go ravin-distracted mad a knowin so much, and then send him out here, and I can pick out a boy, scarcely fifteen till next gineral muster time, who can larn him more about cutting eye-teeth than he ever hearn of before in all his born days. Why, there is one feller out here who brags that he never went to skule but four days in his life (and them was rainy days, tu), that has got so much larnin that he don't know what tu du with it. T'other day I seen him agoin round town with it in a cart, sellin it out for twenty-five cents a corn-basket full, and heaped up measure at that. You can git just as much on't of him as you want for *tu-and-six,* children half price, and poor folks sixpence. Seein this feller made me think on what old Uncle Jo Negus used to say to me when I was a boy, just agoin intu the world tu seek my fortun. Says he tu me, says he—"Peleg, mind you one thing, and when you git grown up tu be a man, if you don't find it so then you may call uncle Jo a pocky old fool." Says he—"Peleg, I have seen a great deal of the world in my day, and studied human nature pretty hard, and I have got a notion intu my head that it takes nigh about all God Almighty's creation to make a world; and in fact," says he, stoppin a spell, appearantly tu git his idees together, "I don't know but I would fling in Indianny and Illanoy tu boot, and they do say," says he, "that the ager is so powerful thick out there that they can cut it with a knife, and in the best ager season amost all the children are born, and no thanks tu the doctors neither. One good ager shake is better than ten doctors." "Now," says I, "Uncle Jo, you don't believe that, du you?" "It's a fact," says he. "What a savin of expense it must be," says I. "Yes," says he; "when there is a large family." "Now," says I, "Uncle Jo, that story is amost equal to Pete Whetstone's *Bum* fly story," and Deacon Hitchcock said that that was an almighty tuff one for a Christian to swaller. With tender feelins, your friend,

PELEG WHITE

DODGINSVILLE, HARD CIDER Co., nigh the "Western Resarve,"

July 1st, 1840.

Mister Spirit,—I tell'd you a short spell ago, that jist as sewn as I could git my idees up, I would write you again. Wal, here it comes, for better or for *wus,* as minister said to Uncle Josh. Hills, when he married him to Aunt Sally Fox, at the age of sixty-five. In these most mortal tuf times, it is pesky hard for a feller to git any new idees, axceptin' he gits 'em on credit, and that's gittin' pretty much run out every where—specially in big cities. The only place I know on, where a chap can git ara speck of credit on time, and live 'bove board, in these all-squeezin', pinchin' times, is in the woods, 'mong the mountings and Injins, a shootin' catamounts, painters, chipinucks, and sich like wild varmints. I often think on't, what happy fellers Ingins must be, a livin' in the woods, and a roamin' jist where natur takes a notion;—no note to pay at sixty days sight, and three days grace, *without defalcation.* All days, days of grace with Injins—no shavin' shops—no three per cent. a month—no sheriffs tu bother 'em—no temperance—no 'malgamation societies—no long poles, with a leetle silk *pus* on the eend on't stuck at 'em every time amost they go tu meetin', but plenty good squaw, fresh bear meat, and cold spring water—maybe, *some* whiskey. O'ny tu think on't! how the grand folks that live in big cities, set around in hot weather, a puffin' and a blowin', amost melted away with the overpowerin' heat, a swearin' like possest—the cussed muskeeters a suckin' their very *inards* out on 'em, and sich a parchin' thirst!—amost as bad as the yaller fever. O'ny tu think on't, how the Ingins, arter a hard day's hunt, a breathin' the *hulsum* air on the mountings, come to a clear cold spring, the water jist amost as clear as chrystal, and lay right down on their bellies, and jist suck up through their teeth, as much as they want on't, and no fears bein' pizened by alcohol, and log-wood bein mixed in't,—then a good big piece of bear's meat roasted, maybe *some* salt, a smoke of the pipe, a fresh bed of leaves, a sleepin' sound, and no feers of bed bugs nither. Then tu think on't, how they are waked up in the mornin' by the warblin' notes of natur's songsters, not by a cussed *short stapled* crittur a ringin' a bell around their ears—and then, arter breakfast, they can go on their own way rejoicin'—no boot-black tu pay, nor landlord a runnin' arter 'em, a hollerin' out, "Mister an't you forgot your chalk?" "Oh my? but what du you think?" but don't I wish I was a Ingin savage! But I arn't though.

And here I am tu the Dodginsville tavern, the winder to my room histed up so that I can look right out on tu LAW BELLY RIVER, not the river of STICKS, but the Ohio filled amost with old logs, a floating on tu Etarnity— or some *other* place down South. Sometimes I wish I was a log, a floatin' down the Ohio, coolly and comfortably punchin' in the sides of a steam boat now and then, or tu be split up and made intu merlasses hogsheads, or licker barrels, or tu be filled with *hard cider*, and drinked around tu all the log-cabing meetins. It would be amost lappin' nice though, that's a fact—and then the idee of bein' well filled, bunged tight, and hooped so strong as tu be actilly beyend the fear of *bustin' biler*. It would be nigh on as much as human natur could stand—that's a fact. Wal, as I was a sayin', here I am to the Dodginsville tavern, a spendin' my time pritty much a studyin' human natur. A great study is human natur—I used to have an idee, I had got pretty well larnt in it, but I begin to estimate I han't got inter the picturs *skasely* yit. It's a great book, is human natur—it has got a great many *pritty pieces* rit in it, and if a feller don't keep a studyin' them pritty much all the hull spell, he will git clean behind the times—a poor benighted crittur—that's a fact. "Keep your left eye skinned tight, and your eye-teeth *filed sharp*," is my motto, now-a-days. . . .

There is nothin' amost in this world, that polishes a feller off so much, and gives him so good an idea of mankind, and womankind in general, as travellin' around the world. Larnin' in books, with picters in 'em, is all very well, and ought to be incouraged, but a feller won't know much arter all about human natur, if he don't go around and see folks, and git acquainted with 'em, and hear 'em *"blow off."* Some great writer (I forgit his name now, but I kinder think it is BILLY MARSH, the poet) has said that there are more things in Haaven and Airth than is dreamed on in the *purtiest kind of books*. Wal, that's just my notion, and if people aint satisfied on that pint, jist let 'em come out here and stay a short spell, and drink spruce beer, made out of the *hulsumist* kinds of *arbs*, for three cents a glass, smoke *Victoria* cigars at *one-and-six* a hundred, go to bed at half past eight in the evenin', and if they don't git the *city rile* out on 'em, in a short spell, then it's my *treat*. Then if they wants tu see the raal, honest patriots—the lovers of the Constitution and the Laws, and the *bone* and *sinew* of the country, let them go to a log cabing barbacue and they'll see 'em. Folks don't turn out here tu go tu 'em, jist *bekase* they can git a belly-full of hard cider, and roast beef, and mutton, *for nothin'.* No, No! they *scorn* the idea. They turn out jist *bekase* they *love their country so,* and want to pay honor to the great, the good, the honest, and the brave men, who *fit* and periled their lives in battle, tu save the risin' generations from the etarnal bondage of the Ingins and British. Then, arter dinner, tu see the patriotism *gush out* from the multitude, and hear the *stump speakin',* and the cannons a roarin', and the *piercin'* sound of the shrill fife, and the martial notes of the sonorous drum, and see the stars and stripes a flyin', and the hard cider a *runnin',* and look upon the grayheaded, war-worn old sogers, who fit with the Gineral, and see 'em fight their battles over agin with the *cussed Ingins,* and hear 'em tell how they licked that *tarnal British Rebel* Burgine out—it will twitch the tears out of any feller, if he han't got a heart as hard as a stun. It seems so nateral like—amost like bein' in war. I *swow,* you can eanemost hear the infarnal savages a yellin'. Hard cider and roast beef does make a feller's patriotism and courage *stick out so.* It's amost amazin' that's a fact. I'll be darned if I don't kalkilate it's a leetle more inspirin' than a *real battle field* with the *inamy in sight.*

11. Dream and Reality

Illustrations

1. "Sarah Sully, the Artist's wife," by Thomas Sully, 1848.

2. "An Impartial Judge," 1836.

3. *"Domestic Happiness,"*
   1847.

4. *"The Novel Reader,"* *1853.*

5. *"Dismissal of a School on an October Afternoon," by Henry Inman, 1845.*

6. *"The Village School in an Uproar,"* 1830.

7. *"The Thriving City of Eden (as it appeared on paper and in fact)," 1844.*

8. *"Bargaining for a Horse," by William Sydney Mount, 1835.*

9. *"Pittsburgh Horse Market," by David G. Blythe, c. 1858.*

10. *"The Peaceable Kingdom," by Edward Hicks, c. 1835.*

11. *"A Militia Muster," c. 1829.*

12. Broadsides

The broadside was essentially a half-folk, half-commercial adaptation of the ballad tradition for a literate public. The form of publication easiest to produce and cheapest to buy, it offers a rich source of folk wisdom and humor often applied to current happenings. Though broadsides as literary form increasingly gave ground in the nineteenth century to the newspaper and the cheap magazine, the tradition retained enough vitality to produce such earthy folk humor as "The Courting Song"* and such unflinching descriptions of human suffering as the ballad of "Mariah Hocrij." Because tragedies, personal and public, often instigated these songs, they offer one of the best clues as to how relatively simple people handled and attempted to explain the presence of evil and terror in what was accepted as the most progressive society in a progressing and ordered universe.

DREADFUL RIOT ON NEGRO HILL **

Dear SISSER,

I hab sad tiding to enform you, O a few night since I taught my lass day surely come, a great number de white Truckerman got angry wid count I spose so many bad girl who lib here and treten to molish all de brack peeples housen! I don't know dat I can gib you more sblime description of de dredful sort of work, den in de langrage of Massa Pope and Milton.

> 'Twas ten o'clock or dareabout
> When Pomp and I got snug in bed,
> And just I blow de candle out,
> A noise uncommon struck my head.

* The first and last of these songs are in Library of Congress collections. The others are from the Houghton Library of Harvard University.
** In the late 1820's Boston experienced some riots against houses of prostitution, some of which spilled over into attacks on the surrounding black community. The "letter" is dated "180027."

My husband say, "O don't be fright,
   'Tis noting but some roguish boys,
Who come pon Neger Hill to fight
   And sturbe de peeples wid dare noise:

Well den I try to reste me,
   But minuit fore I close my eye,
O such a creech!—Gau blesse me,
   Some scream for help, some murder cry.

It pere dare was a tousand men,
   Look like so many goose in flock;
Each wid a cudgel in he hand,
   And dressen most in whiten frock.

O Pomp, said I what shall we do,
   Spose deff dis night should be our fate,
Spose day should kill both I and you,
   Ah what become of little Kate!

Or only tink dear Pomp said I,
   If day shood kill you wid a stone,
Now den your Phillesee wood cry
   To see you kick and hear you groan.

Pomp den get up and seize he gun.
   And say 'tis brack folk voice I hear,
He charge he piece and bout to run,
   I beg him not to interfere.

Juss as I spoke a shower of stone,
   Come rattle bang again our door,
One truck poor Pomp upon de shin
   And bring him senseless to de floor!

Anoder truck poor Katy head,
   Which was he not fleec'd well wid wool,
Wood kill'd de little angel dead,
   Or made de child a natral fool!!

I tell 'um Pomp he poor old man,
   Not by keep girl he gain he food,
For while I wash, do all I can,
   Pomp earn'd a trifle sawing wood.

"Hold your brack jaw! one said to me;
    "Or soon I break your Callabash!
Anoder said ah soon you see,
    Wid club you Cocanut we smash!

Wang bang again de stone day flew,
    Crack went de crockry on de shef,
Great Goff said *I* what shall we do;
    While Pomp cry—Phillis save yourself!

I then seize Kate up garret fly,
    And into smoke house softly creep,
And still as Musquash dare we lie,
    Till darkness fled and day-light peep.

Pomp! Pomp! cry I, pray how are you,
    "O Phillis!—juss alive, dat all
Stone come so thick, so swiftly flew;
    I was oblige up chimbly crawl.

Poor creature, he come creep to me,
    Hobbling pon he wounded foot;
I neber such an image see,
    Cover'd from head to feet wid soot.

O such a condition my house in
    I cood set down whole day and cry,
And Pomp too wid his broken shin,
    Prehaps poor creature yet may die.

De damage done no tongue can tell,
    But *I* will try to let you know,
Long on de subject I cant dwell,
    It make me feel all over so!

My parlour fill'd wid dirt and stone,
    My Bureau smash and Table split,
My Bedstead broke, de Curtain torn,
    And quite destroy my Dining Set,

My Carpet rip from end to end,
    And crack my clock and split de case,
My Silver Spoon all bruize and bend,
    My Sopha Cushee much deface.

My hogany Desk wid polish shine,
  My Toilet, Screen and Battledore,
My Coffee Urn and pipe of Wine,
  Lie heap of rubbish on de floor.

O for a tousen tongues to tell,
  And hearts to bear de woeful sight,
And eyes to weep for dose who fell
  Wed kick and blow dat awful night,

Some broken shin some bleeding head,
  Some sprained arm some bruizen thigh,
And brack man lying almost dead,
  Most ebery where wood meet your eye,

But yesterday poor Pompey he
  Could say One Hundred Pound my lot,
But Sisser if you will believe me,
  One broken shin now all he got.

Here from de country late we move.
  Juss wed more ease ourself maintain,˙
But chance we get for cash or love,
  Pomp swear he move right back again.

Dear Sisser, I am yours fectionately,

PHILLIS.

N.B. By de great detruction of my Furniture you will perceive my house
was pretty genteel furnish—common Furniture will do in de country, but
in Bosson or Providence if a body wish to be rekon any thing day muss
conform to de fashon ob de place.

BOSTCRIPT.

Mail wait for me to let you know.
  Pomp get no better wid he shin;
De Doctors now advise him go.
  Wid much delay to Balltown Spring,
Doubtless day tink day so much pain
  Proceed from fracture of de brain.

A BALM FOR THE AFFLICTED

Written on the death of ASA DEARBORN, Esq. of Portsmouth, N.H. who died
in Boston Hospital, June 8, 1829, aged 58. He had a tumour under his arm,

and it was thought best by the physicians to take it out, in order to prolong his life. The operation of extracting the tumour lasted more than one hour. The severity of the operation, and the loss of so many blood vessels, destroyed all the circulation on that side of the body, and mortification took place and death ensued.

COMPOSED BY ELDER JOSEPH BOODY, OF NEW-DURHAM, JUNE 16, 1829, AND SUBMITTED TO THE MOURNING WIDOW.

1 IS ASA dead? he was my friend,
Is DEARBORN's journey at an end?
The eighth of June he took his leave,
And left his friends to mourn and grieve.

2 In eighteen hundred twenty-nine,
Our friend did leave the shores of time;
In Boston Hospital he fled,
To mingle with the silent dead.

3 A tumour rose upon his side,
Which spread its course both deep and wide;
Aged fifty-eight or thereabout,
His days did end, his sands run out.

4 The surgeons cut the tumour out,
Which shortened life, we have no doubt;
Though 'twas intended for the best,
But oh! how great was his distress.

5 Almost two weeks he languished there,
His pains were more than he could bear;
All circulation ceased to flow,
All mortified from top to toe.

6 They for his wife and children sent,
From Portsmouth they to Boston went;
His wife and son did there arrive,
In time to see him just alive.

7 But oh! how shocking was the sight,
All racked with pain both day and night;
His mind impaired, his body weak,
With only strength enough to speak.

8 At six o'clock on the next day,
His soul did take its flight away;
To find in heaven a long reward,
Among the followers of the Lord.

OLD MAID'S LAST PRAYER

Come all you pretty maidens some older some younger,
Who all have got sweethearts but I must stay longer,
Some sixteen some eighteen are happily married,
Alas! how unequally such things are carried
    A limner a penman a tinker a tailor,
    A fidler, a pedlar, a ploughman a sailer,
    Come gentle, come simple come foolish or witty
    Don't let me die a maid take me out of pity.

I have a sister Sally who's younger than I am,
Has so many sweethearts she's forc'd to deny them,
I never was guilty of denying many
The Lord knows my heart I'd be very glad for any,
    A limner, a penman, etc.

I have a sister Susan though ugly ill shapen,
Before she was sixteen years old she was taken,
Before she was eighteen a son and a daughter,
And I'm six and thirty and never had an offer.
    A limner, a penman, etc.

It has often been said by my mother and father,
That going to one wedding makes way for another,
If that be the case I will go without bidding,
And let the world judge if I don't want a wedding,
    A limner, a penman, etc.

I never will scold and I'll never be jealous,
My husband shall have money to go to the alehous.
While he is there spending I'll be at home saving,
And leave it to you all, if I an't worth having.
    A limner, a penman, etc.

COURTING SONG

Adam at first was formed of dust
    As Scripture doth record:
And did receive a wife called Eve;
    From his creator, Lord.

From Adam's side, a crooked bride
    The Lord was pleased to form.
Ordained that they in bed might lay,
    To keep each other warm.

To court, indeed they had no need,
   She was his wife at first,
And she was made to be his aid,
   Whose origin was dust.

This new made pair full happy were,
   And happy might remained,
If his help mate had never ate,
   The fruit that was restrain'd.

Though Adam's wife destroyed his life,
   In a manner that was awful,
Yet marriage now we allow,
   To be both just and lawful.

But women must be courted first,
   Because it is the fashion
And so at times commit great crimes,
   Caus'd by a lustful passion.

And now a days there are two ways,
   Which of the two is right,
To lie between sheets sweet and clean,
   Or sit up all the night.

But some suppose bundling in clothes,
   Doth heaven sorely vex,
Then let me know which way to go,
   To court the female sex:

Whether they must be hugg'd and kiss'd,
   When sitting by the fire;
Or, whether they in bed may lay,
   Which doth the Lord require?

But some pretend to recommend
   The sitting up all night:
Courting in chairs as doth appear,
   To them to be most right.

Nature's request, is grant me rest,
   Our bodies seek repose,
Night is the time and 'tis no crime,
   To bundle in their clothes,

Since in bed a man and maid,
   May bundle and be chaste:
It does no good to burn out wood,
   It is a needless waste;

Let coats and gowns be laid aside,
    And breeches take their flight,
An honest man and woman can
    Lay quiet all the night.

In Genesis no knowledge is
    Of this thing to be got
Whether young men did bundle then,
    Or whether they did not.

The sacred book says wives they took,
    It don't say how they courted,
Whether that they in bed did lay,
    Or by the fire sported.

. . .

Since bundling is not quite the thing,
    That judgment will procure:
Go on young men and bundle then,
    And keep your bodies pure.

ABR'M PRESCOTT'S CONFESSION,

OF THE MURDER OF MRS. SALLY COCHRAN, OF PEMBROKE, N.H.—JUNE 23, 1833. *
BY A PRIVATE INDIVIDUAL AT THE BAR.

Ye people all, assembled here,
    To see me suffer death—
Draw nigh the guilty wretch and hear
    Words of my dying breath.

Insanity I do not plead—
    'Tis useless now and vain;
Therefore I pray you all take heed,
    I shall not long remain!

Soon will this life the forfeit pay,
    Of villany and crime;
Soon will my soul be launched away,
    To eternity of time!

* The motivation for the murder was much less clear than the broadside
pretends. The defense made a strong case for acquittal on the grounds of
temporary insanity. Prescott had earlier attacked both Mr. and Mrs. Cochran
with an ax while they slept, but the couple, believing the attack unintended,
continued to employ him. Good "help" was hard to find in America.

My God and Judge will soon appear!
    Oh! on that dreadful day,
What friend of mine will then be near
    To wash my sins away?

The hand of God is on me laid,
    For mischief I have done;
Nature's great debt, will soon be paid,
    My earthly race soon run!

Curs'd be the hour that gave me birth,
    Curs'd be the life I led;
Why did I kill that happy wife?
    Why did I bruise her head?

Curs'd be the stake, with which I did
    Inflict the deadly blow;
Curs'd be the spot on which I hid
    Her body as you know!

Oh! lust, accursed lust! 'twas this
    For which I did the deed;
Forfeiting heaven, and life, and bliss,
    Forfeiting all I need.

The trees and flowers, and all were bright,
    'Twas strawberry-time, and she,
Thinking no harm, in broad day-light
    Went to the fields with me.

The beautious one, I basely slew,
    Was lovely to behold,
Was kind and good to all she knew,
    Precious as shining gold!

She had a mother been to me,
    In health and sickness kind;
O what a wretch was I, to be
    To all her goodness blind!

Hell was within my breast, and rage
    Fill'd my soul with guilt—
I must my foul desire assuage;
    Thus was her life's blood spilt!

We pick'd some berries red and rare,
    Red as her blushing face—
Then with a stake I kill'd her there,
    All in that lonely place!

I fear'd her husband's wrath, for he
    I once had tried to kill;
I fear'd his rage would murder me,
    I fear his person still.

'Twas done—a ruin'd man was I,
    Hated by great and small—
Soon on the gallows, I must die,
    A spectacle for all!!

Then view me here, ye bright and gay,
    Behold my dreadful end;
Forsake your sins, while now you may,
    Your wicked ways now mend.

ADAM AND EVE

Sung by Mr. Finn, at the Tremont theatre.[*]

People build houses high as a steeple—
There are more play-houses than people!
In my young days, when I was little,
People built meeting-houses without any steeple,
    Singing, Heigho, I grieve, I grieve, for the good old days of
        Adam and Eve.

Oh dear, oh dear, how I dream now,
Every thing it goes by steam now;
In ancient times, when I was little,
The only steam came from the kettle,
    Singing, Heigho, etc.

Gentlemen wear stays and laces,
Horses' girths around their waces;
Times are not now as times have been,
Father *laced* I with a cowskin,
    Singing, Heigho, etc.

[*] Henry J. Finn was a popular actor, manager, playwright and humorist, who was killed in the burning of the steamer Lexington.

The dandies now look slim and pale,
Once they look'd hearty, fresh and hale;
Their voices sound like a squeaking fiddle,
And they're small as a wasp around the middle!
    Singing, Heigho, etc.

Now, ladies, what I'm going to say is true,
But hope it's no offence to you;
Your grandmas wore round their necks pretty laces,
Wore their own hair and made their own dresses,
With a little short sleeve, tuck'd up with a button,
Now you wear dashing sacks, call'd a leg of mutton,
    Singing, Heigho, etc.

Now my lads, for a slap at you—
What I'm going to say, is equally true;
Your grandfathers got up to see larks rising,
But now these things you are despising,
For now to you I truly say,
You see larks by night, and not by day,
    Singing, Heigho, etc.

In my young days we all dress'd plain,
Bu' now the boys have grown quite vain;
Once they wore jackets, like a sailor,
They now strut in fine coats, and cheat the tailor,
    Singing, Heigho, etc.

A BALLAD ON THE
BURNING OF THE STEAMER
LEXINGTON,

WHEN ONE HUNDRED AND FIFTY SOULS PERISHED, AND ONLY FIVE RESCUED FROM
THE DEVOURING ELEMENT, IN LONG ISLAND SOUND, ON HER PASSAGE TO STON-
INGTON, CONNECTICUT, ON THE NIGHT OF THE 13TH OF JANUARY, 1840.

1

On Monday last, at three o'clock,
    With streamers floating gay,
A Steamer called the LEXINGTON
    From New-York sailed away.

2

One hundred souls, or more that time,
    She carried with her along;
Whose cruel fate, it was decreed,
    Should never see another morn.

3

The gentlemen, who went on board
   Were full of life and glee;
Expecting soon their relatives
   And numerous friends to see.

4

When opposite to Eaton's neck,
   A cry of fire was heard;
On which they all rushed on the deck,
   So sore they were afraid!

5

The fire soon got so far ahead
   It rose in volumes high;
The flames soon spread along its sides,
   While dreadful was the cry.

6

And as the flames in volumes rolled,
   To hear them shriek and moan
Would cause the stoutest heart to break
   Of marble or of stone!

7

The life boat soon was lowered down,
   The steamer under weigh,
When twenty souls were all upset,
   And buried in the sea!

8

Two other boats under her bow
   Were sunk along its side;
They all looked on, with horror struck,
   And wrung their hands and cried.

9

Hilliard, a mariner on board,
   A captain bold and brave,
Quick got out his fragile boat
   And rode the stormy wave!

10

To save themselves from the dreadful fire,
   They plunged into the wave;
And all the souls who were on board
   Soon found a watery grave!

11

Of a hundred souls, or more,
   Who left the port that day,
But five were saved to tell the tale
   Of their sad destiny.

12

The cruel men were all to blame,
   The owners of the boat:
To stow their cotton on the deck
   With such a precious freight.

13

Their consciences will lash them sore,
   And haunt them many a day;
When they think on the hundred souls
   Gone into eternity!

14

So here I close my mournful lay,
   While children yet unborn
Shall to their sons tell the sad tale
   And fate of the Lexington.

THE ALPHABETICAL SONG,*

REVISED AND ADAPTED TO THE PRESENT TIMES

A stands for Adams, whose Administration
   Was like a dead weight on the neck of the nation.
B stands for Banks, and also for Biddle,
   Their tune they must alter or hang up their fiddle.
C stands for Clay, for the potter unfit,
   He ne'er can be moulded to honor a whit.
D stands for Dollars, half Dollars and Dimes,
   Then speedily give us good hard money times.
E stands for Eagle, our country's proud bird,
   He soars where the thunder of battle is heard.
F stands for the Federal faction, who fain
   Would be lords o'er the poor and skin them for gain.
G stands for the Game which the bank swindlers play,
   But the people have called for a reckoning day,
H stands for Hemp for a halter to hang
   Webb and Wise and the rest of the duelling gang.

* The following three songs were manufactured for the election of 1840.

I stands for the Impudent lies that are told
   By the aristocratic party, those liars of old.
J stands for Jackson, who never would flinch
   Nor yield to the foes of his country an inch.
K stands for Knavery of every kind;
   Examine the banks and enough on't you'll find.
L stands for Liberty, which we revere,
   A blessing to all honest democrats dear.
M stands for Morton, the people's firm friend,
   Who ne'er would to proud aristocracy bend.
N stands for National glory and fame,
   Which Washington won for America's name.
O stands for Old times, when equality reigned,
   Ere the whigs had the altar of freedom profaned.
P stands for Priestcraft, whose object is power,
   And loaves and fishes enough to devour.
Q stands for Question—and so I will ask
   What makes Henry Clay wear a demagogue's mask?
R stands for Ruin brought close to our doors,
   By State legislation and "corporate powers."
S stands for Sub-Treasury—so down with pet banks,
   The public has suffered enough by their pranks.
T stands for Turncoat; just as the wind veers,
   Intent on his interest, the time-server steers.
U stands for Union;—long may it remain,
   And our enemies' plots prove forever in vain.
V stands for Van Buren whom the whigs cannot scare,
   Too true to his trust to deviate a hair.
W stands for Webster, Webb, Wickliffe and Wise,
   Full of plausible slang like the father of lies.
X stands a mere cross—and truth will declare
   What sad and sore crosses the whigs have to bear.
Y stands for Yeoman, our strength and support,
   Who'll maintain to the last our republican fort.
Z stands for false Zealots, and much they abound—
   Only see how they're tossing their firebrands round.
And so to conclude I will bring in poor & [and,]
   And call him Omega and come to stand.

THE HERO PLOWMAN

Tune, *"Yankee Doodle."*

The hero plowman of North Bend,
   According to my notion,
Who did our cabins long defend,
   Is worthy of promotion.

Then for the plowman we'll array,
　　Our gallant Buckeye forces—
Van Buren's collar men K K °
　　They soon will fly their courses.

Van cannot bribe us with his Price,
　　Nor will we be Swartwouted;
We'll stick to Tip like any vise,
　　Until the foe is routed.
　　　　　Then for, etc.

Come one come all, the spoilsmen clan,
　　Who jump at Matty's orders;
We'll clear his kitchen to a man,
　　And boost them from our borders.
　　　　　Then for, etc.

The false magician long has play'd
　　His feats of hocus pocus;
Has congregated and array'd,
　　His rabid Loco Focos.
　　　　　But for, etc.

The treas'ry-Kraut is wholly spoil'd,
　　It never was half salted,
But spoilsmen gulp it down unboil'd,
　　But just a little scalded.
　　　　　Then for, etc.

Our Buckeye hero, true and tried,
　　Is rightly nam'd old granny;
To deliver (is his pride)
　　The house of little Vanny.
　　　　　Then for, etc.

But granny never works by halves,
　　He's eke a famous doctor,
He'll ease the nation of her knaves,
　　As he did Gen'ral Proctor.
　　　　　Then for, etc.

The spoilsmen will be forc'd to slope;
　　To take unto their scrapers;
Old Tip will grant them, soon I hope,
　　Authentic walking papers.
　　　　　So for, etc.

° K K means can't come it.

And then the famous Kinderhook,
   Sir Martin will reside in;
He'll find some cranny nook or crook,
   His infamy to hide in.
       Then for, etc.

Now here's a health to Harrison:
   His fame keeps circling wider;
Ohio's boast Virginia's son—
   We'll toast him on hard cider.
       Then for, etc.

THE LOG CABIN AND HARD CIDER CANDIDATE

Tune, *"Auld Lang Syne."*

Should good old cider be despised,
   And ne'er regarded more?
Should plain log cabins be despised,
   Our fathers built of yore?
For the true old style, my boys!
   For the true old style?
Let's take a mug of cider, now,
   For the true old style.

We've tried experiments enough
   Of fashions new and vain,
And now we long to settle down
   To good old times again.
For the good old ways, my boys!
   For the good old ways,
Let's take a mug of cider, now,
   For the good old ways.

We've tried your purse-proud lords, who love
   In palaces to shine;
But we'll have a plowman President
   Of the Cincinnatus line.
For old North Bend, my boys!
   For old North Bend,
We'll take a mug of cider, yet,
   For old North Bend.

We've tried the "greatest and the best,"
   And found him bad enough;
And he who "in the footsteps treads"
   Is yet more sorry stuff.

For the brave old Thames, my boys!
  For old North Bend,
We'll take a mug of cider, yet,
  For the brave old Thames.

VERSES ON MARIAH HOCRIJ,

OF EATON, N.Y. WHO WAS SCALDED TO DEATH, JUNE, 1843

VERSES ON MARIAH HORCRIJ,

MARIAH was a pleasant and dutiful child;
Her manners were charming, her temper was mild:
The pride of her father, her mother's bright joy;
Her image and virtue death cannot destroy.
She early attain'd to woman-hood's bloom;
Being scarcely fifteen, when call'd to the tomb:
Her charms and her beauty, and all the sweet train
Of tender affections are sever'd in twain

Her parents no more behold their sweet child;
Her brothers and sister, by death are beguil'd
Of one who was lovely and tender and Kind;
In Whom a sweet sister they always could find.
Mong th' young men and maidens that dwelt in the place
She shone with unusual beauty and grace:
Though artless and plain, without science or *Wealth*,
She attracted by her own intrinsical *Worth*.

She was easy and free, yet modest reserve
Secur'd their respect, their affection and love;
But she has now bid them a lasting adieu,
And her lovely charms no more they will view.
As her folks were at Work in the dairy, one day,
A scalding the curd, for the cheese, in the *Whey*,
They let down the *Kettle* by a *Windless* or crank,
Below the first floor, into a Caldron or tank

The caldron was boiling, with Water, half full;
They used it, sometimes, for their hogs and the fowl,
To boil up their food and to fatten them well,
Twas adjoining the place where those animals dwell.
The kettle being rais'd, she was steadying the same,
When she slip'd, and into the caldron she came.
Her father let go of the *Windless* and *Crain*,
To save his dear child from the scalding and pain

Being in haste, he was careless, did not make them fast,
And the kettle went down on this dear creature's breast
Where it held her so fast, that two minutes, or more,
Elaps'd, before he his child could restore.
In that liquid flame, What tortor she felt;
Her cries would have made, e'en an adamant melt.
Submerged in the boiling hot Water, she lay,
Held down by the *Kettle* of hot scalding *Whey*

Her face and her hands, they only escap'd
This hot bath of fire, that she had to take;
And she was so scalded that her flesh it gave way,
In taking her out of the place where she lay.
As they took off her clothes, the skin and the flesh
Came off in large masses, *we* here do confess:
Her blood turned inward, and so freely did flow;
Out of the cavities made, it forced its way through.

Her feet and her ankles were bare to the bone!
But *Words* cant describe this heart rending scene.
A higher'd man and her father were all that were there
Her mother was confin'd, and could not appear:
They scalded their hands, as her form they did lift,
And the flesh where they grasp'd her did also come off
On her shoulders, and elsewhere, this *was* the case
For she was quite heavy and her clothes not tightlaced
Yet she liv'd for some hours, though greatly distress'd
And her God and her friends alternately address'd.
She said she felt peace, thro' the blood of the Lamb,
And for her redemption, could trust in his name.

THE ROYAL CHRISTENING

Bring forth the babe in pomp and lace,
While thousands starve and curse the light;
But what of that? on Royal face,
Shame knows no blush, however slight.

Bring forth the babe—a nation's moans,
Will Ring sweet music in its ear,
For well we know a nation's groans,
To Royal ears were always dear.

Bring forth the babe—down, courtiers, down;
And bow your lackey knees in dust,
Before a child's beslobbered gown;
Our children cannot find a crust.

When Christ was born, no servile throng,
Around the Saviour's manger met;
No flatterer's Raised their fulsome song—
But what was Christ to Alfred's pet?

God, who has heard the widow's moan;
God who has heard the Orphan's cry—
Thou, *too,* dost sit upon a throne,
But none round thee of *famine* die.

Things like this babe of Royal birth,
Who boast their "princely Right divine,"
Are but thy parodies on earth:
Theirs is oppression—mercy thine.

Bring forth the babe: from foreign lands,
Fresh Kingly vampires flock to greet,
This new one in its nurse's hands—
(For Royal mothers give no teat;)

Bring forth the toy of princely whim,
And let your prayers mount night and day;
For ought we not to *pray for him?*
Who'll *Prey on us* enough some day?

Oh! who would grudge to squander gold,
On such a glorious babe as this?
What tho' *our* babes are starved and cold,
They have no claim to earthly bliss.

Ours are no *mongrel, German breed,*
But English born and English bred;
Then let them live and die in need,
While the plump Coburg thing is fed.

Christen the babe, Archbishop proud—
Strange servant thou of lowly Christ!
Thousands are to *your* purse allowed,
For *him* the smallest loaf sufficed.

Though holy water's scanty now,
My lord you may dismiss your fears;
Take to baptise the infant's brow,
A starving people's bitter tears.

LINES WRITTEN ON THE
MURDER OF DR. PARKMAN BY PROF. WEBSTER,

IN THE CITY OF BOSTON, ON THE 23D OF NOVEMBER, 1849. *

What fine inventions, schemes and arts,
Can now be viewed in different parts;
Our telegraphs and steam engines,
Which pass along through different lines,
And run their courses with such speed,
They're truly wonderful indeed.
We surely own a lovely nation,
That's worthy of our admiration.
Our schools of learning they are great,
No nation does with us compete.
Our institutions they are free,
In this blest land of liberty;
Our printing and our printing presses
All other nations far surpasses;
Our publications are so cheap,
In every free enlightened state;
Our churches they do thickly stand,
In every corner of the land;
Each may enjoy his own opinion,
Throughout the extent of our Union.
Religious men, with one accord,
May weekly meet to serve the Lord,
And earnestly his blessing seek,
With his direction through the week.
Our noble ships can stand the breeze,
We send them far across the seas.
In California's richest mines,
The star of independence shines.
Our enemies we put to flight,
They driven are out of our sight.
Our rights we nobly have defended,
And now we trust our wars are ended.
Our laws are wholesome, just and good,
Our government hath firmly stood;
We stand upon a sure foundation,
Our choicest men do rule the nation.
Yet we have reason to lament,
That crime is like a judgment sent,
To mar our comforts and our joys,
And show them oft like idle toys.

* George Parkman's murder by one of his Harvard colleagues was a *cause
célèbre* in the period. Sixteen years earlier Parkman had given medical testimony as to Abraham Prescott's probable insanity.

How strange it is that learned men,
With crime their characters should stain;
Yet very many such are found,
To tread the surface of the ground.
How many times hath man's condition
Been ruined sadly by ambition.
We've seen the rich, the learn'd, the brave,
Come to a sad untimely grave.
Though sciences are still increasing,
And new discoveries never ceasing,
The light of knowledge on doth shine,
Yet still we hear of guilt and crime.
This awful news which now we hear,
Doth fill our hearts with dread and fear.
A gentleman, high and respected,
A murderer hath been detected!!
He was professor in a college,
Possessed of scientific knowledge—
A learned man, with noble parts,
Well skilled in many useful arts;
A teacher of the highest order,
That now is found within our border.
His victim was a Dr. P——,
A man of strict veracity.
Possessed of wealth, he ever stood
Prepared to do the needful good.
Professor Webster was his debter,
Which proved to be a dreadful matter;
For when he justly sought his own,
By that foul fiend he was struck down;
And melancholy to relate,
This awful monster sealed his fate.

The city was quite overthrown,
When he a missing was made known.
They searched for him, both far and near,
With deep anxiety and fear.
A general search there was directed,
When in the college was detected,
In Webster's laboratory screened,
Some fragments of our worthy friend!
Part of his body was found burned,
A part into a privy turned;
A portion was concealed in tan,
Of this great philanthropic man.
Professor Webster has been tried,
A jury has been satisfied,

By proofs which were to them submitted,
That he the murder had committed.
Now gentle reader, pause and think,
How low poor wicked man may sink;
Think on the awful guilt of crime,
Oh, think upon it—think in time.

WAR ODES *

Desperate for the saltpetre necessary for gunpowder, the Confederacy sent out agents to locate and collect deposits of it. The agent for Selma, Alabama advertised in the local paper:

"The ladies of Selma are respectfully requested to preserve the chamber lye collected about their premises for the purpose of making nitre. A barrel will be sent around daily to collect it."

John Harrelson, Agent, Nitre and Mining Bureau

AN APPEAL TO JOHN HARRELSON

John Harrelson, John Harrelson, You are a wretched creature,
You've added to this bloody war a new and awful feature.
You'd have us think while every man is bound to be a fighter,
The ladies, bless the pretty dears, should save their p—— for nitre.

John Harrelson, John Harrelson, where did you get this notion,
To send your barrel round the town to gather up this lotion?
We thought the girls had work enough in making shirts and kissing,
But you have put the pretty dears to patriotic p——g.

John Harrelson, John Harrelson, do pray invent a neater
And somewhat less immodest mode of making your saltpetre;
For 'tis an awful idea, John, gunpowdery and cranky,
That when a lady lifts her skirt, she's killing off a Yankee.

YANKEE VERSION

John Harrelson, John Harrelson, we've read in song and story
How woman's tears through all the years have moistened fields of glory,
But never was it told before, how, mid such scenes of slaughter,
Your Southern beauties dried their tears and went to making water.

No wonder that your boys are brave, who couldn't be a fighter,
If every time he shot a gun he used his sweetheart's nitre?
And, vice-versa, what could make a Yankee soldier sadder,
Than dodging bullets fired by a pretty woman's bladder.

* These poems were discovered by Professor E. B. Smith in the Francis Blair papers in the Library of Congress.

13. Fashion

ANNA CORA MOWATT

"Fashion" was the social equivalent of the Jacksonians' "monster bank": an enemy so encrusted with vice and stupidity that one could argue that its defeat would usher in the golden age even though the most bothersome aspects of the social system were left untouched. Mrs. Mowatt's solution to business corruption is certainly sentimental; presumably all is cured when fashionable wife and daughter are shipped from New York City to a rural retreat to learn country virtues from the good uncle who has stayed pure of heart and principle (and incidentally *really* rich) back on the farm. But it's hardly more sentimental than the Jacksonians' curing industrial ills by slaying the national bank, or Horace Greeley's countering them by Utopian Associationism.

Mrs. Mowatt eloped at fifteen with a prosperous New York merchant to the temporary dismay of her wealthy and prominent family. Her husband's impoverishment and illness gave her an excuse for making a career of writing and the theater, which she had always loved. She gave public readings in 1841, in 1845 *Fashion* began its successful run at the Park Theatre in New York, and a few months later Mrs. Mowatt made her acting debut. There followed a theatrical career that made her a favorite actress, as well as a successful playwright, in both the United States and England. Upon her husband's death in 1851, she retired from the stage, remarried, and enjoyed a successful literary career, highlighted by her charming *Autobiography of an Actress* (1854). *Fashion* was the most popular of early American social comedies, and offers a fairly clever resume of the stock stereotypes and sentiments intended to satirize American fashionable life.

Anna Cora Mowatt, *Fashion; or, Life in New York* (London, 1850), 1–62. Many of the plot complications are omitted here: the Count's attempt to seduce Gertrude; Gertrude's discovery that the Count is in reality a pastry cook who was once Millinette's lover; and Gertrude's plot to expose the imposer which goes awry, causing everyone, briefly, to suspect her virtue. Five acts were considered necessary proof of an author's literary seriousness.

ACT I

SCENE I. *A splendid Drawing Room in the House of* MRS. TIFFANY. *Open folding doors discovering a Conservatory. On either side glass windows down to the ground. Doors on right and left. Mirror, couches, ottomans, a table with albums, &c., beside it an arm-chair.* MILLINETTE *dusting furniture, &c.* ZEKE *in a dashing livery, scarlet coat, &c.*

ZEKE. Dere's a coat to take de eyes ob all Broadway! Ah! Missy, it am de fixins dat make de natural *born* gemman. A libery for ever! Dere's a pair ob insuppressibles to 'stonish de colored population.

MILLINETTE. Oh, *oui*, Monsieur Zeke [*Very politely.*] I not *comprend* one word he say![*Aside.*]

ZEKE. I tell 'ee what, Missy, I'm 'stordinary glad to find dis a bery spectabul like situation! Now as you've made de acquaintance ob dis here family, and dere you've had a supernumerary advantage ob me—seeing dat I only receibed my appointment dis morning. What I wants to know is your publicated opinion, privately expressed, ob de domestic circle.

MILLINETTE. You mean vat *espèce*, vat kind of *personnes* are Monsieur and Madame Tiffany? Ah! Monsieur is not de same ting as Madame,— not at all.

ZEKE. Well, I s'pose he ain't altogether.

MILLINETTE. Monsieur is man of business,—Madame is lady of fashion. Monsieur make de money,—Madame spend it. Monsieur nobody at all, —Madame everybody altogether. Ah! Monsieur Zeke, de money is all dat is *necessaire* in dis country to make one lady of fashion. Oh! it is quite anoder ting in *la belle France!*

ZEKE. A bery lucifer explanation. Well, now we've disposed ob de heads ob de family, who come next?

MILLINETTE. First, dere is Mademoiselle Seraphina Tiffany. Mademoiselle is not at all one proper *personne*. Mademoiselle Seraphina is one coquette. Dat is not de mode in *la belle France;* de ladies, dere, never learn *la coquetrie* until dey do get one husband.

ZEKE. I tell'ee what, Missy, I disreprobate dat proceeding altogeder!

MILLINETTE. Vait! I have not tell you all *la famille* yet. Dere is Ma'mselle Prudence—Madame's sister, one very *bizarre personne*. Den dere is Ma'mselle Gertrude, but she not anybody at all; she only teach Mademoiselle Seraphina *la musique*.

ZEKE. Well, now, Missy, what's your own special defunctions?

MILLINETTE. I not understand, Monsieur Zeke.

ZEKE. Den I'll amplify. What's de nature ob your exclusive services?

MILLINETTE. *Ah, oui! je comprend.* I am Madame's *femme de chambre* —her lady's maid, Monsieur Zeke. I teach Madame *les modes de Paris,* and Madame set de fashion for all New York. You see, Monsieur Zeke, dat it is me, *moi-même,* dat do lead de fashion for all de American *beau monde!*

ZEKE. Yah! yah! yah! I hab de idea by de heel. Well, now, p'raps you can 'lustrify my officials?

MILLINETTE. Vat you will have to do? Oh! much tings, much tings. You vait on de table,—you tend de door,—you clean de boots,—you run de errands,—you drive de carriage,—you rub de horses,—you take care of de flowers,—you carry de water,—you help cook de dinner,—you wash de dishes,—and den you always remember tó do everything I tell you to!

ZEKE. Wheugh, am dat *all?*

MILLINETTE. All I can tink of now. Today is Madame's day of reception, and all her grand friends do make her one *petite* visit. You mind run fast ven de bell do ring.

ZEKE. Run? If it wasn't for dese superfluminous trimmings, I tell 'ee what, Missy, I'd run—

MRS. TIFFANY [*outside*]. Millinette!

MILLINETTE. Here comes Madame! You better go, Monsieur Zeke.

ZEKE. Look ahea, Massa Zeke, doesn't dis open rich! [*Aside.*]

[*Exit* ZEKE.]

[*Enter* MRS. TIFFANY *dressed in the most extravagant height of fashion.*]

MRS. TIFFANY. Is everything in order, Millinette? Ah! very elegant, very elegant indeed! There is a *jenny-says-quoi* look about this furniture,— an air of fashion and gentility perfectly bewitching. Is there not, Millinette?

MILLINETTE. Oh, *oui,* Madame!

MRS. TIFFANY. But where is Miss Seraphina? It is twelve o'clock; our visitors will be pouring in, and she has not made her appearance. But I hear that nothing is more fashionable than to keep people waiting.— None but vulgar persons pay any attention to punctuality. Is it not so, Millinette?

MILLINETTE. Quite *comme il faut.*—Great *personnes* always do make little *personnes* wait, Madame.

MRS. TIFFANY. This mode of receiving visitors only upon one specified day of the week is a most convenient custom! It saves the trouble of keeping the house continually in order and of being always dressed. I flatter myself that *I* was the first to introduce it amongst the New York *ee-light.* You are quite sure that it is strictly a Parisian mode, Millinette?

MILLINETTE. Oh, *oui,* Madame; entirely *mode de Paris.*

MRS. TIFFANY. This girl is worth her weight in gold. [*Aside.*] Millinette, how do you say *arm-chair* in French?

MILLINETTE. *Fauteuil,* Madame.

MRS. TIFFANY. *Fo-tool!* That has a foreign—an out-of-the-wayish sound that is perfectly charming—and so genteel! There is something about our American words decidedly vulgar. *Fowtool!* how refined. *Fowtool! Arm-chair!* what a difference!

MILLINETTE. Madame have one *charmante* pronunciation. *Fowtool!* [*Mimicking aside.*] *Charmante,* Madame!

MRS. TIFFANY. Do you think so, Millinette? Well, I believe I have. But a woman of refinement and of fashion can always accommodate herself to everything foreign! And a week's study of that invaluable work— "*French without a Master,*" has made me quite at home in the court language of Europe! But where is the new valet? I'm rather sorry that he is black, but to obtain a white American for a domestic is almost impossible; and they call this a free country! What did you say was the name of this new servant, Millinette?

MILLINETTE. He do say his name is Monsieur Zeke.

MRS. TIFFANY. Ezekiel, I suppose. Zeke! Dear me, such a vulgar name will compromise the dignity of the whole family. Can you not suggest something more aristocratic, Millinette? Something *French!*

MILLINETTE. Oh, *oui,* Madame; *Adolph* is one very fine name.

MRS. TIFFANY. A-dolph! Charming! Ring the bell, Millinette! [MILLI-NETTE *rings the bell.*] I will change his name immediately, besides giving him a few directions.

[*Enter* ZEKE. MRS. TIFFANY *addresses him with great dignity.*]

Your name, I hear, is *Ezekiel.*—I consider it too plebeian an appellation to be uttered in my presence. In future you are called A-dolph. Don't reply,—never interrupt me when I am speaking. A-dolph, as my guests arrive, I desire that you will inquire the name of every person, and then announce it in a loud, clear tone. *That* is the fashion in Paris.

[MILLINETTE *retires up the stage.*]

ZEKE. Consider de office discharged, Missus.

[*Speaking very loudly.*]

MRS. TIFFANY.   Silence! Your business is to obey and not to talk.

ZEKE.   I'm dumb, Missus!

MRS. TIFFANY [*pointing up stage*].   A-dolph, place that *fow-tool* behind me.

ZEKE [*looking about him*].   I habn't got dat far in de dictionary yet. No matter, a genus gets his learning by nature. [*Takes up the table and places it behind* MRS. TIFFANY, *then expresses in dumb show great satisfaction.* MRS. TIFFANY, *as she goes to sit, discovers the mistake.*]

MRS. TIFFANY.   You dolt! Where have you lived not to know that *fow-tool* is the French for *arm-chair?* What ignorance! Leave the room this instant.

[MRS. TIFFANY *draws forward an arm-chair and sits.* MILLINETTE *comes forward suppressing her merriment at* ZEKE's *mistake and removes the table.*]

ZEKE.   Dem's de defects ob not having a libery education.   [*Exit.*]

[PRUDENCE *peeps in.*]

PRUDENCE.   I wonder if any of the fine folks have come yet. Not a soul,— I knew they hadn't. There's Betsy all alone. [*Walks in.*] Sister Betsy!

MRS. TIFFANY.   Prudence! how many times have I desired you to call me *Elizabeth? Betsy* is the height of vulgarity.

PRUDENCE.   Oh! I forgot. Dear me, how spruce we do look here, to be sure,—everything in first rate style now, Betsy.

[MRS. TIFFANY *looks at her angrily.*]

Elizabeth, I mean. Who would have thought, when you and I were sitting behind that little mahogany-colored counter, in Canal Street, making up flashy hats and caps—

MRS. TIFFANY.   Prudence, what *do* you mean? Millinette, leave the room.

MILLINETTE.   *Oui,* Madame.

[MILLINETTE *pretends to arrange the books upon a side table, but lingers to listen.*]

PRUDENCE.   But I always predicted it,—I always told you so, Betsy,—I always said you were destined to rise above your station!

MRS. TIFFANY.   Prudence! Prudence! have I not told you that—

PRUDENCE.   No, Betsy, it was *I* that told *you,* when we used to buy our silks and ribbons of Mr. Antony Tiffany—"*talking Tony,*" you know we used to call him, and when you always put on the finest bonnet in our shop to go to his,—and when you staid so long smiling and chattering with him, I always told you that *something* would grow out of it—and didn't it?

MRS. TIFFANY.   Millinette, send Seraphina here instantly. Leave the room.

MILLINETTE.   *Oui*, Madame. So dis *Americaine* lady of fashion vas one *milliner?* Oh, vat a fine country for *les marchandes des modes!* I shall send for all my relation by de next packet! [*Aside.*] [*Exit* MILLINETTE.]

MRS. TIFFANY.   Prudence! never let me hear you mention this subject again. Forget what we *have* been, it is enough to remember that we *are* of the *upper ten thousand!*

[PRUDENCE *goes up and sits down.*]

[*Enter* SERAPHINA, *very extravagantly dressed.*]

MRS. TIFFANY.   How bewitchingly you look, my dear! Does Millinette say that that head dress is strictly Parisian?

SERAPHINA.   Oh yes, Mamma, all the rage! They call it a *lady's tarpaulin,* and it is the exact pattern of one worn by the Princess Clementina at the last court ball.

MRS. TIFFANY.   Now, Seraphina, my dear, don't be too particular in your attentions to gentlemen not eligible. There is Count Jolimaitre, decidedly the most fashionable foreigner in town,—and so refined,—so much accustomed to associate with the first nobility in his own country that he can hardly tolerate the vulgarity of Americans in general. You may devote yourself to him. Mrs. Proudacre is dying to become acquainted with him. By the by, if she or her daughters should happen to drop in, be sure you don't introduce them to the Count. It is not the fashion in Paris to introduce—Millinette told me so.

[*Enter* ZEKE.]

ZEKE [*in a very loud voice*].   Mister T. Tennyson Twinkle!

MRS. TIFFANY.   Show him up.   [*Exit* ZEKE.]

PRUDENCE.   I must be running away! [*Going.*]

MRS. TIFFANY.   Mr. T. Tennyson Twinkle—a very literary young man and a sweet poet! It is all the rage to patronize poets! Quick, Seraphina, hand me that magazine.—Mr. Twinkle writes for it.

[SERAPHINA *hands the magazine,* MRS. TIFFANY *seats herself in an armchair and opens the book.*]

PRUDENCE [*returning*].   There's Betsy trying to make out that reading without her spectacles. [*Takes a pair of spectacles out of her pocket and hands them to* MRS. TIFFANY.] There, Betsy, I knew you were going to ask for them. Ah! they're a blessing when one is growing old!

MRS. TIFFANY.   What do you mean, Prudence? a woman of fashion *never* grows old! Age is always out of fashion.

PRUDENCE.   Oh, dear! what a delightful thing it is to be fashionable.

[*Exit* PRUDENCE.]

[MRS. TIFFANY *resumes her seat.*]
[*Enter* TWINKLE. *He salutes* SERAPHINA.]

TWINKLE.   Fair Seraphina! the sun itself grows dim,
　　　　　Unless you aid his light and shine on him!

SERAPHINA.   Ah! Mr. Twinkle, there is no such thing as answering you.

TWINKLE [*looks around and perceives* MRS. TIFFANY]. The "New Monthly Vernal Galaxy." Reading my verses, by all that's charming! Sensible woman! I won't interrupt her. [*Aside.*]

MRS. TIFFANY [*rising and coming forward*]. Ah! Mr. Twinkle, is that you? I was perfectly *abimé* at the perusal of your very *distingué* verses.

TWINKLE.   I am overwhelmed, Madam. Permit me. [*Taking the magazine.*] Yes, they do read tolerably. And you must take into consideration, ladies, the rapidity with which they were written. Four minutes and a half by the stop watch! The true test of a poet is the *velocity* with which he composes. Really they do look very prettily, and they read tolerably —*quite* tolerably—*very* tolerably,—especially the first verse. [*Reads.*] "To Seraphina T——."

SERAPHINA.   Oh! Mr. Twinkle!

TWINKLE [*reads*]. "Around my heart"—

MRS. TIFFANY.   How touching! Really, Mr. Twinkle, quite tender!

TWINKLE [*recommencing*]. "Around my heart"—

MRS. TIFFANY.   Oh, I must tell you. Mr. Twinkle! I heard the other day that poets were the aristocrats of literature. That's one reason I like them, for I do dote on all aristocracy!

TWINKLE.   Oh, Madame, how flattering! Now pray lend me your ears! [*Reads.*] "Around my heart thou weavest"—

SERAPHINA.   That is such a *sweet* commencement, Mr. Twinkle!

TWINKLE [*aside*]. I wish she wouldn't interrupt me!
[*Reads.*] "Around my heart thou weavest a spell"—

MRS. TIFFANY.   Beautiful! But excuse me one moment, while I say a word to Seraphina! Don't be too affable, my dear! Poets are very ornamental appendages to the drawing room, but they are always as poor as their own verses. They don't make eligible husbands! [*Aside to* SERAPHINA.]

TWINKLE.   Confound their interruptions! [*Aside.*] My dear Madam, unless you pay the utmost attention you cannot catch the ideas. Are you ready? Well, now you shall hear it to the end! [*Reads.*]

"Around my heart thou weavest a spell
"Whose"—

[*Enter* ZEKE.]

ZEKE. Mister Augustus Fogg! A bery misty lookin young gemman!
[*Aside.*]

MRS. TIFFANY. Show him up, Adolph!

[*Exit* ZEKE.]

TWINKLE. This is too much!

SERAPHINA. Exquisite verses, Mr. Twinkle,—exquisite!

TWINKLE. Ah, lovely Seraphina! your smile of approval transports me to the summit of Olympus.

SERAPHINA. Then I must frown, for I would not send you so far away.

TWINKLE. Enchantress! It's all over with her. [*Aside.*]

[*Retire up and converse.*]

MRS. TIFFANY. Mr. Fogg belongs to one of our oldest families,—to be sure he is the most difficult person in the world to entertain, for he never takes the trouble to talk, and never notices anything or anybody,—but then I hear that nothing is considered so vulgar as to betray any emotion, or to attempt to render oneself agreeable!

[*Enter* MR. FOGG, *fashionably attired but in very dark clothes.*]

FOGG [*bowing stiffly*]. Mrs. Tiffany, your most obedient. Miss Seraphina, yours. How d'ye do, Twinkle?

MRS. TIFFANY. Mr. Fogg, how do you do? Fine weather,—delightful, isn't it?

FOGG. I am indifferent to weather, Madam.

MRS. TIFFANY. Been to the opera, Mr. Fogg? I hear that the *bow monde* make their *debutt* there every evening.

FOGG. I consider operas a bore, Madam.

SERAPHINA [*advancing*]. You must hear Mr. Twinkle's verses, Mr. Fogg!

FOGG. I am indifferent to verses, Miss Seraphina.

SERAPHINA. But Mr. Twinkle's verses are addressed to me!

TWINKLE. Now pay attention, Fogg! [*Reads.*]

"Around my heart thou weavest a spell
"Whose magic I"—

[*Enter* ZEKE.]

ZEKE. Mister—No, he say he ain't no Mister—

TWINKLE. "Around my heart thou weavest a spell,
    "Whose magic I can never tell!"

MRS. TIFFANY. Speak in a loud, clear tone, A-dolph!

TWINKLE. This is terrible!

ZEKE. Mister Count Jolly-made-her!

MRS. TIFFANY. Count Jolimaitre! Good gracious! Zeke, Zeke—A-dolph I mean.—Dear me, what a mistake! [*Aside.*] Set that chair out of the way,—put that table back. Seraphina, my dear, are you all in order? Dear me! dear me! Your dress is so tumbled![*Arranges her dress.*] What are you grinning at? [*To* ZEKE.] Beg the Count to *honor* us by walking up!   [*Exit* ZEKE.]

Seraphina, my dear [*aside to her*], remember now what I told you about the Count. He is a man of the highest,—good gracious! I am so flurried; and nothing is so ungenteel as agitation! what will the Count think! Mr. Twinkle, pray stand out of the way! Seraphina, my dear, place yourself on my right! Mr. Fogg, the conservatory—beautiful flowers,—pray amuse yourself in the conservatory.

FOGG. I am indifferent to flowers, Madam.

MRS. TIFFANY. Dear me! the man stands right in the way,—just where the Count must make his *entray!* [*Aside.*] Mr. Fogg,—pray—

[*Enter* COUNT JOLIMAITRE, *very dashingly
dressed, wears a moustache.*]

MRS. TIFFANY. Oh, Count, this unexpected honor—

SERAPHINA. Count, this inexpressible pleasure—

COUNT. Beg you won't mention it, Madam! Miss Seraphina, your most devoted!

[*Crosses.*]

MRS. TIFFANY. What condescension! [*Aside.*] Count, may I take the liberty to introduce—Good gracious! I forgot. [*Aside.*] Count, I was about to remark that we never introduce in America. All our fashions are foreign, Count.

[TWINKLE, *who has stepped forward to be introduced, shows great
indignation.*]

COUNT. Excuse me, Madam, our fashions have grown antediluvian before you Americans discover their existence. You are lamentably behind the age—lamentably! 'Pon my honor, a foreigner of refinement finds great difficulty in existing in this provincial atmosphere.

MRS. TIFFANY. How dreadful, Count! I am very much concerned. If there is anything which I can do, Count—

SERAPHINA. Or I, Count, to render your situation less deplorable—

COUNT. Ah! I find but one redeeming charm in America—the superlative loveliness of the feminine portion of creation,—and the wealth of their obliging papas. [*Aside.*]

MRS. TIFFANY.   How flattering! Ah! Count, I am afraid you will turn the head of my simple girl here. She is a perfect child of nature, Count.

COUNT.   Very possibly, for though you American women are quite charming, yet, demme, there's a deal of native rust to rub off!

MRS. TIFFANY.   *Rust?* Good gracious, Count! where do you find any rust? [*Looking about the room.*]

COUNT.   How very unsophisticated!

MRS. TIFFANY.   Count, I am so much ashamed,—pray excuse me! Although a lady of large fortune, and one, Count, who can boast of the highest connections, I blush to confess that I have never travelled,— while you, Count, I presume are at home in all the courts of Europe.

COUNT.   *Courts?* Eh? Oh, yes, Madam, very true. I believe I am pretty well known in some of the courts of Europe—*police courts.* [*Aside, crossing.*] In a word, Madam, I had seen enough of civilized life— wanted to refresh myself by a sight of barbarous countries and customs —had my choice between the Sandwich Islands and New York—chose New York!

MRS. TIFFANY.   How complimentary to our country! And, Count, I have no doubt you speak every conceivable language? You talk English like a native.

COUNT.   Eh, what? Like a native? Oh, ah, demme, yes, I am something of an Englishman. Passed one year and eight months with the Duke of Wellington, six months with Lord Brougham, two and a half with Count d'Orsay—knew them all more intimately than their best friends—no heroes to me—hadn't a secret from me, I assure you,—*especially of the toilet.* [*Aside.*]

MRS. TIFFANY.   Think of that, my dear! Lord Wellington and Duke Broom! [*Aside to* SERAPHINA.]

SERAPHINA.   And only think of Count d'Orsay, Mamma! [*Aside to* MRS. TIFFANY.] I am so wild to see Count d'Orsay!

COUNT.   Oh! a mere man milliner. Very little refinement out of Paris! Why, at the very last dinner given at Lord—Lord Knows-who, would you believe it, Madam, there was an individual present who wore a *black* cravat and took *soup twice!*

MRS. TIFFANY.   How shocking! the sight of him would have spoilt my appetite! Think what a great man he must be, my dear, to despise lords and counts in that way. [*Aside to* SERAPHINA.] I must leave them together. [*Aside.*] Mr. Twinkle, your arm. I have some really very *foreign exotics* to show you.

TWINKLE. I fly at your command. I wish all her exotics were blooming in their native soil! [*Aside, and glancing at the* COUNT.]

MRS. TIFFANY. Mr. Fogg, will you accompany us? My conservatory is well worthy a visit. It cost an immense sum of money.

FOGG. I am indifferent to conservatories, Madam; flowers are such a bore!

MRS. TIFFANY. I shall take no refusal. Conservatories are all the rage,—I could not exist without mine! Let me show you,—let me show you.

[*Places her arm through* MR. FOGG'S, *without his consent. Exeunt* MRS. TIFFANY, FOGG, *and* TWINKLE *into the conservatory, where they are seen walking about.*]

SERAPHINA. America, then, has no charms for you, Count?

COUNT. Excuse me,—some exceptions. I find you, for instance, particularly charming! Can't say I admire your country. Ah! if you had ever breathed the exhilarating air of Paris, ate creams at Tortoni's, dined at the Café Royale, or if you had lived in London—felt at home at St. James's, and every afternoon driven a couple of Lords and a Duchess through Hyde Park, you would find America—where you have no kings, queens, lords, nor ladies—insupportable!

SERAPHINA. Not while there was a Count in it?

[*Enter* ZEKE, *very indignant.*]

ZEKE. Where's de Missus?

[*Enter* MRS. TIFFANY, FOGG, *and* TWINKLE, *from the conservatory.*]

MRS. TIFFANY. Whom do you come to announce, A-dolph?

ZEKE. He said he wouldn't trust me—no, not eben wid so much as his name; so I wouldn't trust him up stairs, den he ups wid *his stick* and I *cuts mine.*

MRS. TIFFANY. Some of Mr. Tiffany's vulgar acquaintances. I shall die with shame. [*Aside.*] A-dolph, inform him that I am *not at home.*

[*Exit* ZEKE.]

My nerves are so shattered, I am ready to sink. Mr. Twinkle, that *fow tool,* if you please!

TWINKLE. What? What do you wish, Madam?

MRS. TIFFANY. The ignorance of these Americans! [*Aside.*] Count, may I trouble you? That *fow tool,* if you please!

COUNT. She's not talking English, nor French, but I suppose it's American. [*Aside.*]

TRUEMAN [*outside*]. Not at home!

ZEKE. No, Sar—Missus say she's not at home.

TRUEMAN. Out of the way, you grinning nigger!

[*Enter* ADAM TRUEMAN, *dressed as a farmer, a stout cane in his hand, his boots covered with dust.* ZEKE *jumps out of his way as he enters.*]

[*Exit* ZEKE.]

TRUEMAN.   Where's this woman that's not *at home* in her own house? May I be shot! if I wonder at it! I shouldn't think she'd ever feel *at home* in such a show-box as this!

[*Looking round.*]

MRS. TIFFANY.   What a plebeian looking old farmer! I wonder who he is? [*Aside.*] Sir—[*Advancing very agitatedly.*] what do you mean, Sir, by this *ow*dacious conduct? How dare you intrude yourself into my parlor? Do you know who I am, Sir? [*With great dignity.*] You are in the presence of Mrs. Tiffany, Sir!

TRUEMAN.   Antony's wife, eh? Well now, I might have guessed that—ha! ha! ha! for I see you make it a point to carry half your husband's shop upon your back! No matter; that's being a good helpmate—for he carried the whole of it once in a pack on his own shoulders—now you bear a share!

MRS. TIFFANY.   How dare you, you impertinent, *ow*dacious, ignorant old man! It's all an invention. You're talking of somebody else. What will the Count think! [*Aside.*]

TRUEMAN.   Why, I thought folks had better manners in the city! This is a civil welcome for your husband's old friend, and after my coming all the way from Catteraugus to see you and yours! First a grinning nigger tricked out in scarlet regimentals—

MRS. TIFFANY.   Let me tell you, Sir, that liveries are all the fashion!

TRUEMAN.   The fashion, are they? To make men wear the *badge of servitude* in a free land,—that's the fashion, is it? Hurrah, for republican simplicity! I will venture to say, now, that you have your coat of arms too!

MRS. TIFFANY.   Certainly, Sir; you can see it on the panels of my *voyture.*

TRUEMAN.   Oh! no need of that. I know what your escutcheon must be! A bandbox *rampant* with a bonnet *couchant*, and a pedlar's pack *passant!* Ha, ha, ha! that shows both houses united!

MRS. TIFFANY.   Sir! you are most profoundly ignorant,—what do you mean by this insolence, Sir? How shall I get rid of him? [*Aside.*]

TRUEMAN [*looking at* SERAPHINA]. I hope that is not Gertrude! [*Aside.*]

MRS. TIFFANY.   Sir, I'd have you know that—Seraphina, my child, walk with the gentlemen into the conservatory.

[*Exeunt* SERAPHINA, TWINKLE, FOGG *into conservatory.*]

Count Jolimaitre, pray make due allowances for the errors of this rustic! I do assure you, Count—[*Whispers to him.*]

TRUEMAN.   Count! She calls that critter with a shoe brush over his mouth, Count! To look at him, I should have thought he was a tailor's walking advertisement! [*Aside.*]

COUNT [*addressing* TRUEMAN *whom he has been inspecting through his eye-glass*].   Where did you say you belonged, my friend? Dug out of the ruins of Pompeii, eh?

TRUEMAN.   I belong to a land in which I rejoice to find that you are a foreigner.

COUNT.   What a barbarian! He doesn't see the honor I'm doing his country! Pray, Madam, is it one of the aboriginal inhabitants of the soil? To what tribe of Indians does he belong—the Pawnee or Choctaw? Does he carry a tomahawk?

TRUEMAN.   Something quite as useful,—do you see that?

[*Shaking his stick.* COUNT *runs behind* MRS. TIFFANY.]

MRS. TIFFANY.   Oh, dear! I shall faint! Millinette! [*Approaching.*] Millinette!

[*Enter* MILLINETTE, *without advancing into the room.*]

MILLINETTE.   *Oui,* Madame.

MRS. TIFFANY.   A glass of water! [*Exit* MILLINETTE.] Sir, [*Crossing to* TRUEMAN.] I am shocked at your plebeian conduct! This is a gentleman of the highest standing, Sir! He is a *Count,* Sir!

[*Enter* MILLINETTE, *bearing a salver with a glass of water. In advancing towards* MRS. TIFFANY, *she passes in front of the* COUNT, *starts and screams. The* COUNT, *after a start of surprise, regains his composure, plays with his eye-glass, and looks perfectly unconcerned.*]

MRS. TIFFANY.   What is the matter? What *is* the matter?

MILLINETTE.   Noting, noting,—only—[*Looks at* COUNT *and turns away her eyes again.*] only—noting at all!

TRUEMAN.   Don't be afraid, girl! Why, did you never see a live Count before? He's tame,—I dare say your mistress there leads him about by the ears.

MRS. TIFFANY.   This is too much! Millinette, send for Mr. Tiffany instantly!

[*Crosses to* MILLINETTE, *who is going.*]

MILLINETTE.   He just come in, Madame!

TRUEMAN. My old friend! Where is he? Take me to him,—I long to have one more hearty shake of the hand!

MRS. TIFFANY [*crosses to him*]. Count, honor me by joining my daughter in the conservatory, I will return immediately.

[COUNT *bows and walks towards conservatory.* MRS. TIFFANY *following part of the way and then returning to* TRUEMAN.]

TRUEMAN. What a Jezebel! These women always play the very devil with a man, and yet I don't believe such a damaged bale of goods as *that* [*Looking at* MRS. TIFFANY.] has smothered the heart of little Antony!

MRS. TIFFANY. This way, Sir, sal vous plait.

[*Exit with great dignity.*]

TRUEMAN. *Sal vous plait.* Ha, ha, ha! We'll see what Fashion has done for him. [*Exit.*]

END OF ACT I

ACT II

SCENE I. *Inner apartment of* MR. TIFFANY'S *Counting House.* MR. TIFFANY, *seated at a desk looking over papers.* MR. SNOBSON, *on a high stool at another desk, with a pen behind his ear.*

SNOBSON [*rising, advances to the front of the stage, regards* TIFFANY *and shrugs his shoulders*]. How the old boy frets and fumes over those papers, to be sure! He's working himself into a perfect fever—ex-actly, —therefore *bleeding's* the prescription! So here goes! [*Aside.*] Mr. Tiffany, a word with you, if you please, Sir?

TIFFANY [*sitting still*]. Speak on, Mr. Snobson, I attend.

SNOBSON. What I have to say, Sir, is a matter of the first importance to the credit of the concern—the *credit* of the concern, Mr. Tiffany!

TIFFANY. Proceed, Mr. Snobson.

SNOBSON. Sir, you've a handsome house—fine carriage—nigger in livery —feed on the fat of the land—everything first rate—

TIFFANY. Well, Sir?

SNOBSON. My salary, Mr. Tiffany!

TIFFANY. It has been raised three times within the last year.

SNOBSON. Still it is insufficient for the necessities of an honest man,— mark me, an *honest* man, Mr. Tiffany.

TIFFANY [*crossing*].   What a weapon he has made of that word! [*Aside.*] Enough—another hundred shall be added. Does that content you?

SNOBSON.   There is one other subject which I have before mentioned, Mr. Tiffany,—your daughter,—what's the reason you can't let the folks at home know at once that I'm to be *the man?*

TIFFANY.   Villain! And must the only seal upon this scoundrel's lips be placed there by the hand of my daughter? [*Aside.*] Well, Sir, it shall be as you desire.

SNOBSON.   And Mrs. Tiffany shall be informed of your resolution?

TIFFANY.   Yes.

SNOBSON.   Enough said! That's the ticket! The CREDIT *of the concern's safe,* Sir!

[*Returns to his seat.*]

TIFFANY.   How low have I bowed to this insolent rascal! To rise himself he mounts upon my shoulders, and unless I can shake him off he must crush me! [*Aside.*]

[*Enter* TRUEMAN.]

TRUEMAN.   Here I am, Antony, man! I told you I'd pay you a visit in your money-making quarters. [*Looks around.*] But it looks as dismal here as a cell in the States' prison!

TIFFANY [*forcing a laugh*]. Ha, ha, ha! States' prison! You are so facetious! Ha, ha, ha!

TRUEMAN.   Well, for the life of me I can't see anything so amusing in that! I should think the States' prison plaguy uncomfortable lodgings. And you laugh, man, as though you fancied yourself there already.

TIFFANY.   Ha, ha, ha!

TRUEMAN [*imitating him*]. Ha, ha, ha! What on earth do you mean by that ill-sounding laugh, that has nothing of a laugh about it! This *fashion*-worship has made heathens and hypocrites of you all! *Deception* is your household God! A man laughs as if he were crying, and cries as if he were laughing in his sleeve. Everything is something else from what it seems to be. I have lived in your house only three days, and I've heard more lies than were ever invented during a Presidential election! First your fine lady of a wife sends me word that she's not at home— I walk up stairs, and she takes good care that *I* shall not be *at home*— wants to turn me out of doors. Then *you* come in—take your old friend by the hand—whisper, the deuce knows what, in your wife's ear, and the tables are turned in a tangent! Madam curtsies—says she's enchanted to see me—and orders her grinning nigger to show me a room.

TIFFANY.   We were exceedingly happy to welcome you as our guest!

TRUEMAN.   Happy? *You* happy? Ah! Antony! Antony! that hatchet face of yours, and those criss-cross furrows tell quite another story! It's many a long day since you were *happy* at anything! You look as if you'd melted down your flesh into dollars, and mortgaged your soul in the bargain! Your warm heart has grown cold over your ledger—your light spirits heavy with calculation! You have traded away your youth—your hopes—your tastes for wealth! and now you *have* the wealth you coveted, what does it profit you? Pleasure it cannot buy; for you have lost your *capacity* for enjoyment—Ease it will not bring; for the love of gain is never satisfied! It has made your counting-house a penitentiary, and your home a fashionable *museum* where there is no niche for you! You have spent so much time *ciphering* in the one, that you find yourself at last a very *cipher* in the other! See me, man! seventy-two last August!—strong as a hickory and every whit as sound!

TIFFANY.   I take the greatest pleasure in remarking your superiority, Sir.

TRUEMAN.   Bah! no man takes pleasure in remarking the superiority of another! Why the deuce, can't you speak the truth, man? But it's not the *fashion,* I suppose! I have not seen one frank, open face since—no, no, I can't say that either, though lying *is* catching! There's that girl, Gertrude, who is trying to teach your daughter music—but Gertrude was bred in the country!

TIFFANY.   A good girl; my wife and daughter find her very useful.

TRUEMAN.   Useful? Well, I must say you have queer notions of *use!*— But come, cheer up, man! I'd rather see one of your old smiles, than know you'd realized another thousand! I hear you are making money on the true, American, high pressure system—better go slow and sure— the more steam, the greater danger of the boiler's bursting! All sound, I hope? Nothing rotten at the core?

TIFFANY.   Oh, sound—quite sound!

TRUEMAN.   Well, that's pleasant—though I must say you don't look very pleasant about it!

TIFFANY.   My good friend, although I am solvent, I may say, perfectly solvent—yet you—the fact is, you can be of some assistance to me!

TRUEMAN.   That's the *fact,* is it? I'm glad we've hit upon one *fact* at last! Well—

[SNOBSON, *who during this conversation has been employed in writing, but stops occasionally to listen, now gives vent to a dry, chuckling laugh.*]

TRUEMAN.   Hey? What's that? Another of those deuced ill-sounding, city laughs! [*Sees* SNOBSON.] Who's that perched up on the stool of repentance—eh, Antony?

SNOBSON.   The old boy has missed his text there—*that's* the stool of repentance!

[*Aside and looking at* TIFFANY's *seat.*]

TIFFANY.   One of my clerks—my confidential clerk!

TRUEMAN.   Confidential? Why, he looks for all the world like a spy—the most inquisitorial, hang-dog face—ugh! the sight of it makes my blood run cold! Come, [*Crosses.*] let us talk over matters where this critter can't give us the benefit of his opinion! Antony, the next time you choose a confidential clerk, take one that carries his credentials in his face—those in his pocket are not worth much without!

[*Exeunt* TRUEMAN *and* TIFFANY.]

SNOBSON [*jumping from his stool and advancing*].   The old prig has got the tin, or Tiff would never be so civil! All right—Tiff will work every shiner into the concern—all the better for me! Now I'll go and make love to Seraphina. The old woman needn't try to knock me down with any of her French lingo! Six months from today if I ain't driving my two footmen tandem, down Broadway—and as fashionable as Mrs. Tiffany herself, then I ain't the trump I thought I was! that's all. [*Looks at his watch.*] Bless me! eleven o'clock and I haven't had my julep yet! Snobson, I'm ashamed of you!

[*Exit.*]

SCENE 2.   *The interior of a beautiful conservatory; walk through the centre; stands of flower pots in bloom; a couple of rustic seats.* GERTRUDE, *attired in white, with a white rose in her hair; watering the flowers.* COLONEL HOWARD, *regarding her.*

HOWARD.   I am afraid you lead a sad life here, Miss Gertrude?

GERTRUDE [*turning round gaily*].   What! amongst the flowers?

[*Continues her occupation.*]

HOWARD.   No, amongst the thistles, with which Mrs. Tiffany surrounds you; the tempests, which her temper raises!

GERTRUDE.   They never harm me. Flowers and herbs are excellent tutors. I learn prudence from the reed, and bend until the storm has swept over me!

HOWARD.   Admirable philosophy! But still this frigid atmosphere of fashion must be uncongenial to you? Accustomed to the pleasant companionship of your kind friends in Geneva, surely you must regret this cold exchange?

GERTRUDE.   Do you think so? Can you suppose that I could possibly prefer a ramble in the woods to a promenade in Broadway? A wreath of scented wild flowers to a bouquet of these sickly exotics? The odor of new-mown hay to the heated air of this crowded conservatory? Or can you imagine that I could enjoy the quiet conversation of my Geneva friends, more than the edifying chit-chat of a fashionable drawing room? But I see you think me totally destitute of taste?

HOWARD. You have a merry spirit to jest thus at your grievances!

GERTRUDE. I have my *mania*,—as some wise person declares that all mankind have,—and mine is a love of independence! In Geneva, my wants were supplied by two kind old maiden ladies, upon whom I know not that I have any claim. I had abilities, and desired to use them. I came here at my own request; for here I am no longer *dependent! Voilà tout,* as Mrs. Tiffany would say.

HOWARD. Believe me, I appreciate the confidence you repose in me!

GERTRUDE. Confidence! Truly, Colonel Howard, the *confidence* is entirely on your part, in supposing that I confide that which I have no reason to conceal! I think I informed you that Mrs. Tiffany only received visitors on her reception day—she is therefore not prepared to see you. Zeke—Oh! I beg his pardon—Adolph, made some mistake in admitting you.

HOWARD. Nay, Gertrude, it was not Mrs. Tiffany, nor Miss Tiffany, whom I came to see; it—it was—

GERTRUDE. The conservatory perhaps? I will leave you to examine the flowers at leisure!

[*Crosses.*]

HOWARD. Gertrude—listen to me. If I only dared to give utterance to what is hovering upon my lips! [*Aside.*] Gertrude!

GERTRUDE. Colonel Howard!

HOWARD. Gertrude, I must—must—

GERTRUDE. Yes, indeed you *must,* must leave me! I think I hear somebody coming—Mrs. Tiffany would not be well pleased to find you here— pray, pray leave me—that door will lead you into the street.

[*Hurries him out through door; takes up her watering pot, and commences watering flowers, tying up branches, &c.*]

What a strange being is man! Why should he hesitate to say—nay, why should I prevent his saying, what I would most delight to hear? Truly man *is* strange—but woman is quite as incomprehensible!

[*Exit. Enter Trueman followed by Prudence.*]

PRUDENCE. What a nice old man he is, to be sure! I wish he would say something! [*Aside.*]

[*Crosses, walks after him, turning when he turns—after a pause.*]

Don't mind *me*, Mr. Trueman!

TRUEMAN. Mind you? Oh, no, don't be afraid—I wasn't minding you. Nobody seems to mind you much!

[*Continues walking and examining the flowers*—PRUDENCE *follows.*]

PRUDENCE. Very pretty flowers, ain't they? Gertrude takes care of them.

TRUEMAN. Gertrude? So I hear—I suppose you can tell me now who this Gertrude—

PRUDENCE. Who she's in love with? I *knew* you were going to say that! I'll tell you all about it! Gertrude, she's in love with—Mr. Twinkle! and he's in love with her. And Seraphina she's in love with Count Jolly —what-d'ye-call-it: but Count Jolly don't take to her at all—but Colonel Howard—he's the man—he's desperate about her!

TRUEMAN. Why, you feminine newspaper! Howard in love with that quintessence of affectation! Howard—the only frank, straightforward fellow that I've met since—I'll tell him my mind on the subject! And Gertrude hunting for happiness in a rhyming dictionary! The girl's a greater fool than I took her for!

PRUDENCE. So she is—you see I know all about them!

TRUEMAN. I see you do! You've a wonderful knowledge—wonderful—of *other people's concerns!* It may do here, but take my word for it, in the county of Catteraugus you'd get the name of a great *busy-body*. But perhaps you know that, too?

PRUDENCE. Oh! I always know what's coming. I feel it beforehand all over me. I knew something was going to happen the day you came here —and what's more I can always tell a married man from a single—I felt right off that you were a bachelor!

TRUEMAN. Felt right off I was a bachelor, did you? you were sure of it— sure?—quite sure? [PRUDENCE *assents delightedly.*] Then you felt wrong!—a bachelor and a widower are not the same thing!

PRUDENCE. Oh! but it all comes to the same thing—a widower's as good as a bachelor any day! And besides I knew that you were a farmer *right off.*

TRUEMAN. On the spot, eh? I suppose you saw cabbages and green peas growing out of my hat?

PRUDENCE. No, I didn't—but I knew all about you. And I knew— [*Looking down and fidgeting with her apron.*] I knew you were for getting married soon! For last night I dream't I saw your funeral going along the streets, and the mourners all dressed in white. And a funeral is a sure sign of a wedding, you know! [*Nudging him with her elbow.*]

TRUEMAN [*imitating her voice*]. Well, I can't say that I *know* any such thing! you know! [*Nudging her back.*]

PRUDENCE. Oh! it does, and there's no getting over it! For my part, I like farmers—and I know all about setting hens and turkeys, and feeding chickens, and laying eggs, and all that sort of thing!

TRUEMAN. May I be shot! if mistress newspaper is not putting in an advertisement for herself! This is your city mode of courting, I suppose, ha, ha, ha! [*Aside.*]

PRUDENCE. I've been west, a little; but I never was in the county of Catteraugus, myself.

TRUEMAN. Oh! you were not? And you have taken a particular fancy to go there, eh?

PRUDENCE. Perhaps I shouldn't object—

TRUEMAN. Oh!—ah!—so I suppose. Now pay attention to what I am going to say, for it is a matter of great importance to yourself.

PRUDENCE. Now it's coming—I know what he's going to say! [*Aside.*]

TRUEMAN. The next time you want to tie a man for life to your apron-strings, pick out one that don't come from the county of Catteraugus—for green horns are scarce in those parts, and modest women plenty!

[*Exit.*]

PRUDENCE. Now who'd have thought he was going to say that! But I won't give him up yet—I won't give him up. [*Exit.*]

END OF ACT II

ACT III

SCENE I. MRS. TIFFANY'S *Parlor.*

[*Enter* MRS. TIFFANY, *followed by* MR. TIFFANY.]

TIFFANY. Your extravagance will ruin me, Mrs. Tiffany!

MRS. TIFFANY. And your stinginess will ruin me, Mr. Tiffany! It is totally and *toot a fate* impossible to convince you of the necessity of *keeping up appearances.* There is a certain display which every woman of fashion is forced to make!

TIFFANY. And pray who made *you* a woman of fashion?

MRS. TIFFANY. What a vulgar question! All women of fashion, Mr. Tiffany—

TIFFANY. In this land are *self-constituted*, like you, Madam—and *fashion* is the cloak for more sins than charity ever covered! It was for *fashion's* sake that you insisted upon my purchasing this expensive house—it was for *fashion's* sake that you ran me in debt at every exorbitant upholsterer's and extravagant furniture warehouse in the city—it was for *fashion's* sake that you built that ruinous conservatory—hired more servants than they have persons to wait upon—and dressed your footman like a harlequin!

MRS. TIFFANY.   Mr. Tiffany, you are thoroughly plebeian, and insufferably *American,* in your grovelling ideas! And, pray, what was the occasion of these very *mal-ap-pro-pos* remarks? Merely because I requested a paltry fifty dollars to purchase a new style of headdress—a *bijou* of an article just introduced in France.

TIFFANY.   Time was, Mrs. Tiffany, when you manufactured your own French headdresses—took off their first gloss at the public balls, and then sold them to your shortest-sighted customers. And all you knew about France, or French either, was what you spelt out at the bottom of your fashion plates—but now you have grown so fashionable, forsooth, that you have forgotten how to speak your mother tongue!

MRS. TIFFANY.   Mr. Tiffany, Mr. Tiffany! Nothing is more positively vulgarian—more *unaristocratic* than any allusion to the past!

TIFFANY.   Why, I thought, my dear, that *aristocrats* lived principally upon the past—and traded in the market of fashion with the bones of their ancestors for capital?

MRS. TIFFANY.   Mr. Tiffany, such vulgar remarks are only suitable to the counting house, in my drawing room you should—

TIFFANY.   Vary my sentiments with my locality, as you change your *manners* with your *dress!*

MRS. TIFFANY.   Mr. Tiffany, I desire that you will purchase Count d'Orsay's "Science of Etiquette," and learn how to conduct yourself—especially before you appear at the grand ball, which I shall give on Friday!

TIFFANY.   Confound your balls, Madam; they make *footballs* of my money, while you dance away all that I am worth! A pretty time to give a ball when you know that I am on the very brink of bankruptcy!

MRS. TIFFANY.   So much the greater reason that nobody should suspect your circumstances, or you would lose your credit at once. Just at this crisis a ball is absolutely *necessary* to save your reputation! There is Mrs. Adolphus Dashaway—she gave the most splendid fête of the season—and I hear on very good authority that her husband has not paid his baker's bill in three months. Then there was Mrs. Honeywood—

TIFFANY.   Gave a ball the night before her husband shot himself—perhaps you wish to drive me to follow his example?

MRS. TIFFANY.   Good gracious! Mr. Tiffany, how you talk! I beg you won't mention anything of the kind. I consider black the most unbecoming color. I'm sure I've done all that I could to gratify you. There is that vulgar old torment, Trueman, who gives one the lie fifty times a day—haven't I been very civil to him?

TIFFANY.   Civil to his *wealth*, Mrs. Tiffany! I told you that he was a rich, old farmer—the early friend of my father—my own benefactor—and that I had reason to think he might assist me in my present embarrassments. Your civility was *bought*—and like most of your *own* purchases has yet to be *paid* for. [*Crosses.*]

MRS. TIFFANY.   And will be, no doubt! The condescension of a woman of fashion should command any price. Mr. Trueman is insupportably indecorous—he has insulted Count Jolimaitre in the most outrageous manner. If the Count was not so deeply interested—so *abimé* with Seraphina, I am sure he would never honor us by his visits again!

TIFFANY.   So much the better—he shall never marry my daughter!—I am resolved on that. Why, Madam, I am told there is in Paris a regular matrimonial stock company, who fit out indigent dandies for this market. How do I know but this fellow is one of its creatures, and that he has come here to increase its dividends by marrying a fortune?

MRS. TIFFANY.   Nonsense, Mr. Tiffany. The Count, the most fashionable young man in all New York—the intimate friend of all the dukes and lords in Europe—not marry my daughter? Not permit Seraphina to become a Countess? Mr. Tiffany, you are out of your senses!

TIFFANY.   That would not be very wonderful, considering how many years I have been united to you, my dear. Modern physicians pronounce lunacy infectious!

MRS. TIFFANY.   Mr. Tiffany, he is a man of fashion—

TIFFANY.   Fashion makes fools, but cannot *feed* them. By the bye, I have a request,—since you are bent upon ruining me by this ball, and there is no help for it,—I desire that you will send an invitation to my confidential clerk, Mr. Snobson.

MRS. TIFFANY.   Mr. Snobson! Was there ever such an *you-nick* demand! Mr. Snobson would cut a pretty figure amongst my fashionable friends! I shall do no such thing, Mr. Tiffany.

TIFFANY.   Then, Madam, the ball shall not take place. Have I not told you that I am in the power of this man? That there are circumstances which it is happy for you that you do not know—which you cannot comprehend,—but which render it essential that you should be civil to Mr. Snobson? Not you merely, but Seraphina also? He is a more appropriate match for her than your foreign favorite.

MRS. TIFFANY. A match for Seraphina, indeed! [*Crosses.*] Mr. Tiffany, you are determined to make a *fow pas.*

ACT IV

SCENE I. *Ball Room splendidly illuminated. A curtain hung at the further end.* MR. *and* MRS. TIFFANY, SERAPHINA, GERTRUDE, FOGG, TWINKLE, COUNT, SNOBSON, COLONEL HOWARD, *a number of guests—some seated, some standing. As the curtain rises, a cotillion is danced;* GERTRUDE *dancing with* HOWARD, SERAPHINA *with* COUNT.

[*Enter* TRUEMAN, *yawning and rubbing his eyes.*]

TRUEMAN.   What a nap I've had, to be sure! [*Looks at his watch.*] Eleven o'clock, as I'm alive! Just the time when country folks are comfortably *turned in,* and here your grand *turn-out* has hardly begun yet!

[*To* TIFFANY, *who approaches.*]

GERTRUDE [*advancing*]. I was just coming to look for you, Mr. Trueman. I began to fancy that you were paying a visit to dreamland.

TRUEMAN.   So I was, child—so I was—and I saw a face—like yours—but brighter!—even brighter. [*To* TIFFANY.] There's a smile for you, man! It makes one feel that the world has something worth living for in it yet! Do you remember a smile like that, Antony? Ah! I see you don't —but I do—I do! [*Much moved.*]

HOWARD [*advancing*].   Good evening, Mr. Trueman. [*Offers his hand.*]

TRUEMAN.   That's right, man; give me your whole hand! When a man offers me the tips of his fingers, I know at once there's nothing in him worth seeking beyond his fingers ends.

[TRUEMAN *and* HOWARD, GERTRUDE *and* TIFFANY *converse.*]

MRS. TIFFANY [*advancing*].   I'm in such a fidget lest that vulgar old fellow should disgrace us by some of his plebeian remarks! What it is to give a ball, when one is forced to invite vulgar people! Dear me, Mr. Trueman, you are very late—quite in the fashion, I declare!

TRUEMAN.   Fashion! And pray what is *fashion,* madam? An agreement between certain persons to live without using their souls! to substitute etiquette for virtue—decorum for purity—manners for morals! to affect a shame for the works of their Creator! and expend all their rapture upon the works of their tailors and dressmakers!

MRS. TIFFANY.   You have the most *ow-tray* ideas, Mr. Trueman—quite rustic, and deplorably *American!* But pray walk this way . . .

TRUEMAN [encountering FOGG, who is hurrying alone to the supper room].
Mr. Fogg, never mind the supper, man! Ha, ha, ha! Of course you are
indifferent to suppers!

FOGG.   Indifferent! suppers—oh, ah—no, Sir—suppers? no—no—I'm not
indifferent to suppers! [Hurries away towards table.]

TRUEMAN.   Ha, ha, ha! Here's a new discovery I've made in the fashionable world! Fashion don't permit the critters to have heads or hearts,
but it allows them stomachs! [To TIFFANY, who advances.] So it's not
fashionable to feel, but it's fashionable to feed, eh, Antony? ha, ha, ha!

[TRUEMAN and TIFFANY retire towards supper room.]

ACT V

SCENE I. Mrs. Tiffany's Drawing Room—same Scene as Act First. GER-
TRUDE seated at a table. She lets TRUEMAN read a letter explaining her
actions.

TRUEMAN.   Thunder and lightning! I see it all! Come and kiss me, girl!
[GERTRUDE evinces surprise.] No, no—I forgot—it won't do to come to
that yet! She's a rare girl! I'm out of my senses with joy! I don't know
what to do with myself! Tol, de rol, de rol, de ra! [Capers and sings.]

GERTRUDE.   What a remarkable old man! [Aside.] Then you do me
justice, Mr. Trueman?

TRUEMAN.   I say I don't! Justice! You're above all dependence upon justice! Hurrah! I've found one true woman at last! True? [Pauses thought-
fully.] Humph! I didn't think of that flaw! Plotting and manœuvering—
not much truth in that? An honest girl should be above stratagems!

GERTRUDE.   But my motive, Sir, was good.

TRUEMAN.   That's not enough—your actions must be good as well as
your motives! Why could you not tell the silly girl that the man was an
impostor?

GERTRUDE.   I did inform her of my suspicions—she ridiculed them; the
plan I chose was an imprudent one, but I could not devise—

TRUEMAN.   I hate devising! Give me a woman with the firmness to be
frank! But no matter—I had no right to look for an angel out of Paradise; and I am as happy—as happy as a Lord! that is, ten times happier
than any Lord ever was! Tol, de rol, de rol! Oh! you—you—I'll thrash
every fellow that says a word against you!

GERTRUDE.   You will have plenty of employment then, Sir, for I do not
know of one just now who would speak in my favor!

TRUEMAN.   Not *one*, eh? Why, where's your dear Mr. Twinkle? I know all about it—can't say that I admire your choice of a husband! But there's no accounting for a girl's taste.

GERTRUDE.   Mr. Twinkle! Indeed you are quite mistaken!

TRUEMAN.   No—really? Then you're not taken with him, eh?

GERTRUDE.   Not even with his rhymes.

TRUEMAN.   Hang that old mother meddle-much! What a fool she has made of me. And so you're quite free, and I may choose a husband for you myself? Heart-whole, eh?

GERTRUDE.   I—I—I trust there is nothing *unsound* about my heart.

TRUEMAN.   There it is again. Don't prevaricate, girl! I tell you an *evasion* is *a lie in contemplation,* and I hate lying! Out with the truth! Is your heart *free* or not?

GERTRUDE.   Nay, Sir, since you *demand* an answer, permit *me* to demand by what right you ask the question?

[*Enter* HOWARD.]

Colonel Howard here!

TRUEMAN.   I'm out again! What's the Colonel to her? [*Retires up.*]

HOWARD [*crosses to her*].   I have come, Gertrude, to bid you farewell. Tomorrow I resign my commission and leave this city, perhaps for ever. You, Gertrude, it is you who have exiled me! After last evening—

TRUEMAN [*coming forward to* HOWARD].   What the plague have you got to say about last evening?

HOWARD.   Mr. Trueman!

TRUEMAN.   What have you got to say about last evening? and what have you to say to that little girl at all? It's Tiffany's precious daughter you're in love with.

HOWARD.   Miss Tiffany? Never! I never had the slightest pretension—

TRUEMAN.   That lying old woman! But I'm glad of it! Oh! Ah! Um! [*Looking significantly at* GERTRUDE *and then at* HOWARD.] I see how it is. So you don't choose to marry Seraphina, eh? Well, now, whom do you choose to marry? [*Glancing at* GERTRUDE.]

HOWARD.   I shall not marry at all!

TRUEMAN.   You won't? [*Looking at them both again.*] Why, you don't mean to say that you don't like—

[*Points with his thumb to* GERTRUDE.]

GERTRUDE.   Mr. Trueman, I may have been wrong to boast of my good nature, but do not presume too far upon it.

HOWARD.   You like frankness, Mr. Trueman, therefore I will speak plainly.

I have long cherished a dream from which I was last night rudely awakened.

TRUEMAN. And that's what you call speaking plainly? Well, I differ with you! But I can guess what you mean. Last night you suspected Gertrude there of—[*Angrily.*] of what no man shall ever suspect her again while I'm above ground! You did her injustice,—it was a mistake! There, now that matter's settled. Go, and ask her to forgive you,—she's woman enough to do it! Go, go!

HOWARD. Mr. Trueman, you have forgotten to whom you dictate.

TRUEMAN. Then you won't do it? you won't ask her pardon?

HOWARD. Most undoubtedly I will not—not at any man's bidding. I must first know—

TRUEMAN. You won't do it? Then if I don't give you a lesson in politeness—

HOWARD. It will be because you find me your *tutor* in the same science. I am not a man to brook an insult, Mr. Trueman! but we'll not quarrel in presence of the lady.

TRUEMAN. Won't we? I don't know that—   [*Crosses.*]

GERTRUDE. Pray, Mr. Trueman—Colonel Howard, pray desist, Mr. Trueman, for my sake! [*Taking hold of his arm to hold him back.*] Colonel Howard, if you will read this letter it will explain everything.

[*Hands letter to* HOWARD, *who reads.*]

TRUEMAN. He don't deserve an explanation! Didn't I tell him that it was a mistake? Refuse to beg your pardon! I'll teach him, I'll teach him!

HOWARD [*after reading*]. Gertrude, how have I wronged you!

TRUEMAN. Oh, you'll beg her pardon now?   [*Between them.*]

HOWARD. Hers, Sir, and yours! Gertrude, I fear—

TRUEMAN. You needn't,—she'll forgive you. You don't know these women as well as I do,—they're always ready to pardon; it's their nature, and they can't help it. Come along, I left Antony and his wife in the dining room; we'll go and find them. I've a story of my own to tell! As for you, Colonel, you may follow. Come along, come along!

[*Leads out* GERTRUDE, *followed by* HOWARD.]

[*Enter* MR. *and* MRS. TIFFANY, MR. TIFFANY *with a bundle of bills in his hand.*]

MRS. TIFFANY. I beg you won't mention the subject again, Mr. Tiffany. Nothing is more plebeian than a discussion upon economy—nothing more *ungenteel* than looking over and fretting over one's bills!

TIFFANY. Then I suppose, my dear, it is quite as ungenteel to *pay* one's bills?

MRS. TIFFANY.   Certainly! I hear the *ee-light* never condescend to do anything of the kind. The honor of their invaluable patronage is sufficient for the persons they employ!

TIFFANY.   *Patronage* then is a newly invented food upon which the working classes fatten? What convenient appetites poor people must have! Now listen to what I am going to say. As soon as my daughter marries Mr. Snobson—

[*Enter* PRUDENCE, *a three-cornered note in her hand.*]

PRUDENCE.   Oh, dear! oh, dear! what shall we do! Such a misfortune! Such a disaster! Oh, dear! oh, dear!

MRS. TIFFANY.   Prudence, you are the most tiresome creature! What *is* the matter?

PRUDENCE [*pacing up and down the stage*].   Such a disgrace to the whole family! But I always expected it. Oh, dear! oh, dear!

TIFFANY.   Gone! where?

PRUDENCE.   Off!—eloped—eloped with the Count! Dear me, dear me! I always told you she would!

TIFFANY.   Then I am ruined!   [*Stands with his face buried in his hands.*]

MRS. TIFFANY.   Oh, what a ridiculous girl! And she might have had such a splendid wedding! What could have possessed her?

TIFFANY.   The devil himself possessed her, for she has ruined me past all redemption! Gone, Prudence, did you say gone? Are you *sure* they are gone?

PRUDENCE.   Didn't I tell you so! Just look at this note—one might know by the very fold of it—

TIFFANY [*snatching the note*].   Let me see it! [*Opens the note and reads.*] "My dear Ma,—When you receive this I shall be a *countess!* Isn't it a sweet title? The Count and I were forced to be married privately, for reasons which I will explain in my next. You must pacify Pa, and put him in a good humor before I come back, though now I'm to be a countess I suppose I shouldn't care!" Undutiful huzzy! "We are going to make a little excursion and will be back in a week.

 "Your dutiful daughter—Seraphina."
A man's curse is sure to spring up at his own hearth,—here is mine! The sole curb upon that villain gone, I am wholly in his power! Oh! the first downward step from honor—he who takes it cannot pause in his mad descent and is sure to be hurried on to ruin!

MRS. TIFFANY.   Why, Mr. Tiffany, how you do take on! And I dare say to elope was the most fashionable way after all!

[*Enter* TRUEMAN, *leading* GERTRUDE, *and followed by* HOWARD.]

TRUEMAN.   Where are all the folks? Here, Antony, you are the man I
want. We've been hunting for you all over the house. Why—what's the
matter? There's a face for a thriving city merchant! Ah! Antony, you
never wore such a hang-dog look as that when you trotted about the
country with your pack upon your back! Your shoulders are no broader
now—but they've a heavier load to carry—that's plain!

MRS. TIFFANY.   Mr. Trueman, such allusions are highly improper! What
would my daughter, *the Countess*, say!

GERTRUDE.   The Countess? Oh! Madam!

MRS. TIFFANY.   Yes, the Countess! My daughter Seraphina, the Countess
dee Jolimaitre! What have you to say to that? No wonder you are surprised after your *recherché, abimé* conduct! I have told you already,
Miss Gertrude, that you were not a proper person to enjoy the inestim-
able advantages of my patronage. You are dismissed—do you understand? Discharged!

TRUEMAN.   Have you done? Very well, it's my turn now. Antony, perhaps
what I have to say don't concern you as much as some others—but I
want you to listen to me. You remember, Antony, [*His tone becomes
serious.*] a blue-eyed, smiling girl—

TIFFANY.   Your daughter, Sir? I remember her well.

TRUEMAN.   None ever saw her to forget her! Give me your hand, man.
There—that will do! Now let me go on. I never coveted wealth—yet
twenty years ago I found myself the richest farmer in Catteraugus.
This cursed money made my girl an object of speculation. Every idle
fellow that wanted to feather his nest was sure to come courting Ruth.
There was one—my heart misgave me the instant I laid eyes upon him
—for he was a city chap, and not over fond of the truth. But Ruth—ah!
she was too pure herself to look for guile! His fine words and his fair
looks—the old story—she was taken with him—I said, "no"—but the girl
liked her own way better than her old father's—girls always do! and
one morning—the rascal robbed me—not of my money, he would have
been welcome to that—but of the only treasure I cherished—my
daughter!

TIFFANY.   But you forgave her!

TRUEMAN.   I did! I knew she would never forgive herself—that was
punishment enough! The scoundrel thought he was marrying my gold
with my daughter—he was mistaken! I took care that they should never
want; but that was all. She loved him—what will not woman love?
The villain broke her heart—mine was tougher, or it wouldn't have

stood what it did. A year after they were married, he forsook her! She came back to her old home—her old father! It couldn't last long—she pined—and pined—and—then—she died! Don't think me an old fool —though I am one—for grieving won't bring her back. [*Bursts into tears.*]

TIFFANY. It was a heavy loss!

TRUEMAN. So heavy, that I should not have cared how soon I followed her, but for the child she left! As I pressed that child in my arms, I swore that my unlucky wealth should never curse it, as it had cursed its mother! It was all I had to love—but I sent it away—and the neighbors thought it was dead. The girl was brought up tenderly but humbly by my wife's relatives in Geneva. I had her taught true independence— she had hands—capacities—and should use them! Money should never buy her a husband! for I resolved not to claim her until she had made her choice, and found the man who was willing to take her for herself alone. She turned out a rare girl! and it's time her old grandfather claimed her. Here he is to do it! And there stands Ruth's child! Old Adam's heiress! Gertrude, Gertrude!—my child!

PRUDENCE [*after a pause*]. Do tell; I want to know! But I knew it! I always said Gertrude would turn out somebody, after all!

MRS. TIFFANY. Dear me! Gertrude an heiress! My dear Gertrude, I always thought you a very charming girl—quite YOU-NICK—an heiress! I must give her a ball! I'll introduce her into society myself—of course an heiress must make a sensation!   [*Aside.*]

HOWARD. I am too bewildered even to wish her joy. Ah! there will be plenty to do that now—but the gulf between us is wider than ever.
                                                                      [*Aside.*]

TRUEMAN. Step forward, young man, and let us know what you are muttering about. I said I would never claim her until she had found the man who loved her for herself. I *have* claimed her—yet I never break my word—I think I *have* found that man! and here he is. [*Strikes* HOWARD *on the shoulder.*] Gertrude's yours! There—never say a word, man—don't bore me with your thanks—you can cancel all obligations by making that child happy! There—take her!—Well, girl, and what do you say?

GERTRUDE. That I rejoice too much at having found a parent for my first act to be one of disobedience!   [*Gives her hand to* HOWARD.]

TRUEMAN. How very dutiful! and how disinterested!

[TIFFANY *retires up—and paces the stage, exhibiting great agitation.*]

PRUDENCE [*to* TRUEMAN]. All the *single folks* are getting married!

TRUEMAN. No, they are not. You and I are single folks, and we're not likely to get married.

MRS. TIFFANY. My dear Mr. Trueman—my sweet Gertrude, when my daughter, the Countess, returns, she will be delighted to hear of this *deenooment!* I assure you that the Countess will be quite charmed!

GERTRUDE. The Countess? Pray, Madam, where *is* Seraphina?

MRS. TIFFANY. The Countess *dee* Jolimaitre, my dear, is at this moment on her way to—to Washington! Where after visiting all the fashionable curiosities of the day—including the President—she will return to grace her native city!

GERTRUDE. I hope you are only jesting, Madam? Seraphina is not married?

MRS. TIFFANY. Excuse me, my dear, my daughter had this morning the honor of being united to the Count *dee* Jolimaitre!

GERTRUDE. Madam! He is an impostor!

MRS. TIFFANY. Good gracious! Gertrude, how can you talk in that disrespectful way of a man of rank? An heiress, my dear, should have better manners! The Count—

[*Enter* MILLINETTE, *crying.*]

MILLINETTE. Oh! Madame! I will tell everyting—oh! dat *monstre!* He break my heart!

MRS. TIFFANY. Millinette, what is the matter?

MILLINETTE. Oh! he promise to marry me—I love him much—and now Zeke say he run away vid Mademoiselle Seraphina!

MRS. TIFFANY. What insolence! The girl is mad! Count Jolimaitre marry my *femmy de chamber!*

MILLINETTE. Oh! Madam, he is not one Count, not at all! Dat is only de title he go by in dis country. De foreigners always take de large title ven dey do come here. His name *à Paris* vas Gustave Tread-mill. But he not one Frenchman at all, but he do live one long time *à Paris*. First he live vid Monsieur Vermicelle—dere he vas de head cook! Den he live vid Monsieur Tire-nez, de barber! After dat he live vid Monsieur le Comte Frippon-fin—and dere he vas le Comte's valet! Dere, now I tell everyting I feel one great deal better!

MRS. TIFFANY. Oh! good gracious! I shall faint! Not a Count! What will everybody say? It's no such thing! I say he *is* a Count! One can see the foreign *jenny says quoi* in his face! Don't you think I can tell a Count when I see one? I say he *is* a Count!

[*Enter* SNOBSON, *his hat on—his hands thrust in his pocket—evidently a little intoxicated.*]

SNOBSON. I won't stand it! I say I won't!

TIFFANY [*rushing up to him*]. Mr. Snobson, for heaven's sake—[*Aside.*]

SNOBSON. Keep off! I'm a hard customer to get the better of! You'll see if I don't come out strong!

TRUEMAN [*quietly knocking off* SNOBSON's *hat with his stick*]. Where are your manners, man?

SNOBSON. My business ain't with you, Catteraugus; you've waked up the wrong passenger!—Now the way I'll put it into Tiff will be a caution. I'll make him wince! That extra mint julep has put the true pluck in me. Now for it! [*Aside.*] Mr. Tiffany, Sir—you needn't think to come over me, Sir—you'll have to get up a little earlier in the morning before you do *that*, Sir! I'd like to know, Sir, how you came to assist your daughter in running away with that foreign loafer? It was a downright swindle, Sir. After the conversation I and you had on that subject she wasn't your property, Sir.

TRUEMAN. What, Antony, is that the way your city clerk bullies his boss?

SNOBSON. You're drunk, Catteraugus—don't expose yourself—you're drunk! Taken a little too much toddy, my old boy! Be quiet! I'll look after you, and they won't find it out. If you want to be busy, you may take care of my *hat*—I feel so deuced weak in the chest, I don't think I *could* pick it up myself.—Now to put the screws to Tiff. [*Aside.*] Mr. Tiffany, Sir—you have broken your word, as no virtuous individual— no honorable member—of—the—com—mu—ni—ty—

TIFFANY. Have some pity, Mr. Snobson, I beseech you! I had nothing to do with my daughter's elopement! I will agree to anything you desire —your salary shall be doubled—trebled—[*Aside to him.*]

SNOBSON [*aloud*]. No, you don't. No bribery and corruption.

TIFFANY. I implore you to be silent. You shall become partner of the concern, if you please—only do not speak. You are not yourself at this moment. [*Aside to him.*]

SNOBSON. Ain't I though? I feel *twice* myself. I feel like two Snobsons rolled into one, and I'm chock full of the spunk of a dozen! Now, Mr. Tiffany, Sir—

TIFFANY. I shall go distracted! Mr. Snobson, if you have one spark of manly feeling—   [*Aside to him.*]

TRUEMAN. Antony, why do you stand disputing with that drunken jackass? Where's your nigger? Let him kick the critter out, and be of use for once in his life.

SNOBSON.   Better be quiet, Catteraugus. This ain't your hash, so keep your spoon out of the dish. Don't expose yourself, old boy.

TRUEMAN.   Turn him out, Antony!

SNOBSON.   He daren't do it! Ain't I up to him? Ain't he in my power? Can't I knock him into a cocked hat with a word? And now he's got my steam up—I *will* do it!

TIFFANY [*beseechingly*].   Mr. Snobson—my friend—

SNOBSON.   It's no go—steam's up—and I don't stand at anything!

TRUEMAN.   You won't *stand* here long unless you mend your manners— you're not the first man I've *upset* because he didn't know his place.

SNOBSON.   I know where Tiff's place is, and that's in the *States' Prison!* It's bespoke already. He would have it! He wouldn't take pattern of me, and behave like a gentleman! He's a *forger*, Sir! [TIFFANY *throws himself into a chair in an attitude of despair; the others stand transfixed with astonishment.*] He's been forging Dick Anderson's endorsements of his notes these ten months. He's got a couple in the bank that will send him to the wall any how—if he can't make a raise. I took them there myself! Now you know what he's worth. I said I'd expose him, and I have done it!

MRS. TIFFANY.   Get out of the house! You ugly, little, drunken brute, get out! It's not true. Mr. Trueman, put him out; you have got a stick—put him out!

[*Enter* SERAPHINA, *in her bonnet and shawl—a parasol in her hand.*]

SERAPHINA.   I hope Zeke hasn't delivered my note.
     [*Stops in surprise at seeing the persons assembled.*]

MRS. TIFFANY.   Oh, here is the Countess!   [*Advances to embrace her.*]

TIFFANY [*starting from his seat, and seizing* SERAPHINA *violently by the arm*].   Are—you—married?

SERAPHINA.   Goodness, Pa, how you frighten me! No, I'm not married, *quite.*

TIFFANY.   Thank heaven.

MRS. TIFFANY [*drawing* SERAPHINA *aside*].   What's the matter? Why did you come back?

SERAPHINA.   The clergyman wasn't at home—I came back for my jewels —the Count said nobility couldn't get on without them.

TIFFANY.   I may be saved yet! Seraphina, my child, you will not see me disgraced—ruined! I have been a kind father to you—at least I have tried to be one—although your mother's extravagance made a *madman* of me! The Count is an impostor—you seemed to like him—[*Pointing to* SNOBSON.] Heaven forgive me! [*Aside.*] Marry *him* and save *me*. You, Mr. Trueman, you will be my friend in this hour of extreme need—you will advance the sum which I require—I pledge myself to return it. My wife—my child—who will support them were I—the thought makes me frantic! You will aid me? You had a child yourself.

TRUEMAN.   But I did not *sell* her—it was her own doings. Shame on you, Antony! Put a price on your own flesh and blood! Shame on such foul traffic!

TIFFANY.   Save me—I conjure you—for my father's sake.

TRUEMAN.   For your *father's* SON's sake I will *not* aid you in becoming a greater villain than you are!

GERTRUDE.   Mr. Trueman—Father, I should say—save him—do not embitter our happiness by permitting this calamity to fall upon another—

TRUEMAN.   Enough—I did not need your voice, child. I am going to settle this matter my own way.

[*Goes up to* SNOBSON—*who has seated himself and fallen asleep—tilts him out of the chair.*]

SNOBSON [*waking up*].   Eh? Where's the fire? Oh! it's you, Catteraugus.

TRUEMAN.   If I comprehend aright, you have been for some time aware of your principal's forgeries?

[*As he says this, he beckons to* HOWARD, *who advances as witness.*]

SNOBSON.   You've hit the nail, Catteraugus! Old chap saw that I was up to him six months ago; left off throwing dust into my eyes—

TRUEMAN.   Oh, he did!

SNOBSON.   Made no bones of forging Anderson's name at my elbow.

TRUEMAN.   Forged at your elbow? You saw him do it?

SNOBSON.   I did.

TRUEMAN.   Repeatedly?

SNOBSON.   Re—pea—ted—ly.

TRUEMAN.   Then you, Rattlesnake, if he goes to the States' Prison, you'll take up your quarters there too. You are an accomplice, an *accessory!*

[TRUEMAN *walks away and seats himself,* HOWARD *rejoins* GERTRUDE. SNOBSON *stands for some time bewildered.*]

SNOBSON.   The deuce, so I am! I never thought of that! I must make myself scarce. I'll be off! Tif, I say, Tif! [*Going up to him and speaking confidentially.*] that drunken old rip has got us in his power. Let's give him the slip and be off. They want men of genius at the West,— we're sure to get on! You—you can set up for a writing master, and teach copying *signatures;* and I—I'll give lectures on *temperance!* You won't come, eh? Then I'm off without you. Good bye, Catteraugus! Which is the way to California? [*Steals off.*]

TRUEMAN.   There's one debt your city owes me. And now let us see what other nuisances we can abate. Antony, I'm not given to preaching, therefore I shall not say much about what you have done. Your face speaks for itself,—the crime has brought its punishment along with it.

TIFFANY.   Indeed it has, Sir! In *one year* I have lived a *century* of misery.

TRUEMAN.   I believe you, and upon one condition I will assist you—

TIFFANY.   My friend—my first, ever kind friend,—only name it!

TRUEMAN.   You must sell your house and all these gew gaws, and bundle your wife and daughter off to the country. There let them learn economy, true independence, and home virtues, instead of foreign follies. As for yourself, continue your business—but let moderation, in future, be your counsellor, and let *honesty* be your confidential clerk.

TIFFANY.   Mr. Trueman, you have made existence once more precious to me! My wife and daughter shall quit the city tomorrow, and—

PRUDENCE.   It's all coming right! It's all coming right! We'll go to the county of Catteraugus. [*Walking up to* TRUEMAN.]

TRUEMAN.   No, you won't,—I make that a stipulation, Antony; keep clear of Catteraugus. None of your fashionable examples there!

[JOLIMAITRE *appears in the Conservatory and peeps into the room unperceived.*]

COUNT.   What can detain Seraphina? We ought to be off!

MILLINETTE [*turns round, perceives him, runs and forces him into the room*]. Here he is! Ah, Gustave, *mon cher* Gustave! I have you now and we never part no more. Don't frown, Gustave, don't frown—

TRUEMAN.   Come forward, Mr. Count! and for the edification of fashionable society confess that you're an impostor.

COUNT.   An impostor? Why, you abominable old—

TRUEMAN.   Oh, your feminine friend has told us all about it, the cook—the valet—barber and all that sort of thing. Come, confess, and something may be done for you.

COUNT.   Well, then, I do confess I am no count; but really, ladies and gentlemen, I may recommend myself as the most capital cook.

MRS. TIFFANY.   Oh, Seraphina!

SERAPHINA.   Oh, Ma! [*They embrace and retire up.*]

TRUEMAN.   Promise me to call upon the whole circle of your fashionable acquaintances with your own advertisements and in your cook's attire, and I will set you up in business tomorrow. Better turn stomachs than turn heads!

MILLINETTE.   But you will marry me?

COUNT.   Give us your hand, Millinette! Sir, command me for the most delicate *paté*—the daintiest *croquette à la royale*—the most transcendent *omelette soufflée* that ever issued from a French pastry-cook's oven. I hope you will pardon my conduct, but I heard that in America, where you pay homage to titles while you profess to scorn them—where *Fashion* makes the basest coin current—where you have no kings, no princes, no *nobility*—

TRUEMAN.   Stop there! I object to your use of that word. When justice is found only among lawyers—health among physicians—and patriotism among politicians, *then* may you say that there is no *nobility* where there are no titles! But we *have* kings, princes, and nobles in abundance —of *Nature's stamp*, if not of *Fashion's*,—we have honest men, warm hearted and brave, and we have women—gentle, fair, and true, to whom no *title* could add *nobility*.

EPILOGUE

PRUDENCE.   I told you so! And now you hear and see. I told you *Fashion* would the fashion be!

TRUEMAN.   Then both its point and moral I distrust.

COUNT.   Sir, is that liberal?

HOWARD.   Or is it just?

TRUEMAN.   The guilty have escaped!

TIFFANY.   Is, therefore, sin
   Made charming? Ah! there's punishment within!
   Guilt ever carries his own scourge along.

GERTRUDE.   Virtue her own reward!

TRUEMAN.   You're right, I'm wrong.

MRS. TIFFANY.   How we have been deceived!

PRUDENCE.   I told you so.

SERAPHINA.   To lose at once a title and a beau!

COUNT.   A count no more, I'm no more of *account*.

TRUEMAN.   But to a nobler title you may mount,
   And be in time—who knows?—an honest man!

COUNT.   Eh, Millinette?

MILLINETTE.   Oh, *oui*,—I know you can!

GERTRUDE [*to audience*].   But, ere we close the scene, a word with you,—
   We charge you answer,—Is this picture true?

Some little mercy to our efforts show,
Then let the world your honest verdict know.
Here let it see portrayed its ruling passion,
And learn to prize at its just value—*Fashion*.

THE END

14. Americans at Play

Illustrations

1. *Boston Museum Playbill, 1851.*

2. *"Hiram Powers' Greek Slave," by R. Thew, 1843.*

3. *"The Power of Music," by William Sydney Mount, 1847.*

4. *"Christmas Party," c. 1840.*

5. *"Rip Van Winkle at Nicholas Vedder's Tavern," by John Quidor, 1839.*

6. *"The Drunkard's Progress," Currier and Ives, 1848.*

202

7. *"The Flax Scutching Bee,"* c. 1860.

8. *"Camp-Meeting," c. 1825.*

15. The Celestial Railroad

NATHANIEL HAWTHORNE

Hawthorne contributed to the *Democratic Review* much as he participated in Brook Farm or wrote for ladies' annuals or served in the Salem custom-house or turned out a campaign biography of his Bowdoin classmate, Franklin Pierce: with ostensible commitment that never really covered a bemused skepticism. Such was apparently his relation to American society: few literary figures took such willing part in the mundane business of society superficially, few intellectually so deeply separated themselves from it. Hawthorne's alleged "escape" to the Puritan past in his work was to give literary form to his cryptic message to a society that refused to admit that sin was an essential part of human life: both honesty and humanity required that man be able to admit and live with his and other people's capacity for evil. *Pilgrim's Progress* becomes the natural model for Hawthorne's most trenchant and witty picture of his society's loudly trumpeted technological and secular progress toward "the celestial city."

Not a great while ago, passing through the gate of dreams, I visited that region of the earth in which lies the famous City of Destruction. It interested me much to learn that by the public spirit of some of the inhabitants a railroad has recently been established between this populous and flourishing town and the Celestial City. Having a little time upon my hands, I resolved to gratify a liberal curiosity by making a trip thither. Accordingly, one fine morning after paying my bill at the hotel and directing the porter to stow my luggage behind a coach, I took my seat in the vehicle and set out for the station house. It was my good fortune to enjoy the company of a gentleman—one Mr. Smooth-it-away—who, though he had never actually visited the Celestial City, yet seemed as

Nathaniel Hawthorne, "The Celestial Railroad," in the Riverside edition of *The Complete Works* (Boston, 1882), II, 212–234.

well acquainted with its laws, customs, policy, and statistics as with those of the City of Destruction, of which he was a native townsman. Being moreover a director of the railroad corporation and one of its largest stockholders, he had it in his power to give me all desirable information respecting that praiseworthy enterprise.

Our coach rattled out of the city, and at a short distance from its outskirts passed over a bridge of elegant construction, but somewhat too slight, as I imagined, to sustain any considerable weight. On both sides lay an extensive quagmire, which could not have been more disagreeable, either to sight or smell, had all the kennels of the earth emptied their pollution there.

"This," remarked Mr. Smooth-it-away, "is the famous Slough of Despond —a disgrace to all the neighborhood; and the greater, that it might so easily be converted into firm ground."

"I have understood," said I, "that efforts have been made for that purpose from time immemorial. Bunyan mentions that above twenty thousand cartloads of wholesome instructions had been thrown in here without effect."

"Very probably! And what effect could be anticipated from such unsubstantial stuff?" cried Mr. Smooth-it-away. "You observe this convenient bridge. We obtained a sufficient foundation for it by throwing into the slough some editions of books of morality; volumes of French philosophy and German rationalism, tracts, sermons, and essays of modern clergymen; extracts from Plato, Confucius, and various Hindoo sages, together with a few ingenious commentaries upon texts of Scripture,—all of which, by some scientific process, have been converted into a mass like granite. The whole bog might be filled up with similar matter."

It really seemed to me, however, that the bridge vibrated and heaved up and down in a very formidable manner; and, spite of Mr. Smooth-it-away's testimony to the solidity of its foundation, I should be loath to cross it in a crowded omnibus, especially if each passenger were encumbered with as heavy luggage as that gentleman and myself. Nevertheless we got over without accident, and soon found ourselves at the station house. This very neat and spacious edifice is erected on the site of the little wicket gate, which formerly, as all old pilgrims will recollect, stood directly across the highway, and, by its inconvenient narrowness, was a great obstruction to the traveller of liberal mind and expansive stomach. . . .

A large number of passengers were already at the station house awaiting the departure of the cars. By the aspect and demeanor of these persons it was easy to judge that the feelings of the community had undergone a very favorable change in reference to the celestial pilgrimage. It would have done Bunyan's heart good to see it. Instead of a lonely and ragged man with a huge burden on his back, plodding along sorrowfully on foot while the whole city hooted after him, here were parties of the first gentry and most respectable people in the neighborhood setting forth towards the Celestial City as cheerfully as if the pilgrimage were merely a summer tour. Among the gentlemen were characters of deserved eminence— magistrates, politicians, and men of wealth, by whose example religion could not but be greatly recommended to their meaner brethren. In the ladies' apartment, too, I rejoiced to distinguish some of those flowers of fashionable society who are so well fitted to adorn the most elevated circles of the Celestial City. There was much pleasant conversation about the news of the day, topics of business, and politics, or the lighter matters of amusement; while religion, though indubitably the main thing at heart, was thrown tastefully into the background. Even an infidel would have heard little or nothing to shock his sensibility.

One great convenience of the new method of going on pilgrimage I must not forget to mention. Our enormous burdens, instead of being carried on our shoulders as had been the custom of old, were all snugly deposited in the baggage car, and, as I was assured, would be delivered to their respective owners at the journey's end. Another thing, likewise, the benevolent reader will be delighted to understand. It may be remembered that there was an ancient feud between Prince Beelzebub and the keeper of the wicket gate, and that the adherents of the former distinguished personage were accustomed to shoot deadly arrows at honest pilgrims while knocking at the door. This dispute, much to the credit as well of the illustrious potentate above mentioned as of the worthy and enlightened directors of the railroad, has been pacifically arranged on the principle of mutual compromise. The prince's subjects are now pretty numerously employed about the station house, some in taking care of the baggage, others in collecting fuel, feeding the engines, and such congenial occupations; and I can conscientiously affirm that persons more attentive to their business, more willing to accommodate, or more generally agreeable to the passengers, are not to be found on any railroad. Every good heart must surely exult at so satisfactory an arrangement of an immemorial difficulty.

"Where is Mr. Greatheart?" inquired I. "Beyond a doubt the directors have engaged that famous old champion to be chief conductor on the railroad?"

"Why, no," said Mr. Smooth-it-away, with a dry cough. "He was offered the situation of brakeman; but, to tell you the truth, our friend Greatheart has grown preposterously stiff and narrow in his old age. He has so often guided pilgrims over the road on foot that he considers it a sin to travel in any other fashion. Besides, the old fellow had entered so heartily into the ancient feud with Prince Beelzebub that he would have been perpetually at blows or ill language with some of the prince's subjects, and thus have embroiled us anew. So, on the whole, we were not sorry when honest Greatheart went off to the Celestial City in a huff and left us at liberty to choose a more suitable and accommodating man. Yonder comes the engineer of the train. You will probably recognize him at once."

The engine at this moment took its station in advance of the cars, looking, I must confess, much more like a sort of mechanical demon that would hurry us to the infernal regions than a laudable contrivance for smoothing our way to the Celestial City. On its top sat a personage almost enveloped in smoke and flame, which, not to startle the reader, appeared to gush from his own mouth and stomach as well as from the engine's brazen abdomen.

"Do my eyes deceive me?" cried I. "What on earth is this! A living creature? If so, he is own brother to the engine he rides upon!"

"Poh, poh, you are obtuse!" said Mr. Smooth-it-away, with a hearty laugh. "Don't you know Apollyon, Christian's old enemy, with whom he fought so fierce a battle in the Valley of Humiliation? He was the very fellow to manage the engine; and so we have reconciled him to the custom of going on pilgrimage, and engaged him as chief engineer."

"Bravo, bravo!" exclaimed I, with irrepressible enthusiasm; "this shows the liberality of the age; this proves, if any thing can, that all musty prejudices are in a fair way to be obliterated. And how will Christian rejoice to hear of this happy transformation of his old antagonist! I promise myself great pleasure in informing him of it when we reach the Celestial City."

The passengers being all comfortably seated, we now rattled away merrily, accomplishing a greater distance in ten minutes than Christian probably trudged over in a day. It was laughable, while we glanced along, as it were, at the tail of a thunderbolt, to observe two dusty foot travellers in the old pilgrim guise, with cockle shell and staff, their mystic rolls of parchment in their hands and their intolerable burdens on their backs. The preposterous obstinacy of these honest people in persisting to groan and stumble along the difficult pathway rather than take advantage of modern improvements, excited great mirth among our wiser brotherhood. We greeted the two pilgrims with many pleasant gibes and a roar of laughter; whereupon they gazed at us with such woful and absurdly compassionate visages that our merriment grew tenfold more obstreperous. Apollyon also entered heartily into the fun, and contrived to flirt the smoke and flame of the engine, or of his own breath, into their faces, and envelop them in an atmosphere of scalding steam. These little practical jokes amused us mightily, and doubtless afforded the pilgrims the gratification of considering themselves martyrs.

At some distance from the railroad Mr. Smooth-it-away pointed to a large, antique edifice, which, he observed, was a tavern of long standing, and had formerly been a noted stopping-place for pilgrims. In Bunyan's road book it is mentioned as the Interpreter's House.

"I have long had a curiosity to visit that old mansion," remarked I.

"It is not one of our stations, as you perceive," said my companion. "The keeper was violently opposed to the railroad; and well he might be, as the track left his house of entertainment on one side, and thus was pretty certain to deprive him of all his reputable customers. But the footpath still passes his door; and the old gentleman now and then receives a call from some simple traveller, and entertains him with fare as old fashioned as himself." . . .

The respectable Apollyon was now puttting on the steam at a prodigious rate, anxious, perhaps, to get rid of the unpleasant reminiscences connected with the spot where he had so disastrously encountered Christian. Consulting Mr. Bunyan's road book, I perceived that we must now be within a few miles of the Valley of the Shadow of Death, into which doleful region, at our present speed, we should plunge much sooner than seemed at all desirable. In truth, I expected nothing better than to find myself in the ditch on one side or the quag on the other; but on communicating my apprehensions to Mr. Smooth-it-away, he assured me that the difficulties of this passage, even in its worst condition, had been vastly exaggerated, and that, in its present state of improvement, I might consider myself as safe as on any railroad in Christendom.

Even while we were speaking, the train shot into the entrance of this dreaded Valley. Though I plead guilty to some foolish palpitations of the heart during our headlong rush over the causeway here constructed, yet it were unjust to withhold the highest encomiums on the boldness of its original conception and the ingenuity of those who executed it. It was gratifying, likewise, to observe how much care had been taken to dispel the everlasting gloom and supply the defect of cheerful sunshine, not a ray of which has ever penetrated among these awful shadows. For this purpose, the inflammable gas which exudes plentifully from the soil is collected by means of pipes, and thence communicated to a quadruple row of lamps along the whole extent of the passage. Thus a radiance has been created even out of the fiery and sulphurous curse that rests forever upon the valley—a radiance hurtful, however, to the eyes, and somewhat bewildering, as I discovered by the changes which it wrought in the visages of my companions. In this respect, as compared with natural daylight, there is the same difference as between truth and falsehood; but if the reader has ever traveled through the dark Valley, he will have learned to be thankful for any light that he could get—if not from the sky above, then from the blasted soil beneath. Such was the red brilliancy of these lamps that they appeared to build walls of fire on both sides of the track, between which we held our course at lightning speed, while a reverberating thunder filled the Valley with its echoes. Had the engine run off the track—a catastrophe, it is whispered, by no means unprece-dented—the bottomless pit, if there be any such place, would undoubtedly have received us. Just as some dismal fooleries of this nature had made my heart quake, there came a tremendous shriek, careering along the valley as if a thousand devils had burst their lungs to utter it, but which proved to be merely the whistle of the engine on arriving at a stopping place. . . .

At the end of the valley, as John Bunyan mentions, is a cavern, where, in his days, dwelt two cruel giants, Pope and Pagan, who had strown the ground about their residence with the bones of slaughtered pilgrims. These vile old troglodytes are no longer there; but into their deserted cave another terrible giant has thrust himself, and makes it his business to seize upon honest travellers and fatten them for his table with plentiful meals of smoke, mist, moonshine, raw potatoes, and sawdust. He is a German by birth, and is called Giant Transcendentalist; but as to his form, his features, his substance, and his nature generally, it is the chief peculiarity of this huge miscreant that neither he for himself, nor any body for him, has ever been able to describe them. As we rushed by the cavern's mouth we caught a hasty glimpse of him, looking somewhat like an ill-propor-tioned figure, but considerably more like a heap of fog and duskiness. He shouted after us, but in so strange a phraseology that we knew not what he meant, nor whether to be encouraged or affrighted.

It was late in the day when the train thundered into the ancient city of Vanity, where Vanity Fair is still at the height of prosperity, and exhibits an epitome of whatever is brilliant, gay, and fascinating beneath the sun. As I purposed to make a considerable stay here, it gratified me to learn that there is no longer the want of harmony between the town's people and pilgrims, which impelled the former to such lamentably mistaken measures as the persecution of Christian and the fiery martyrdom of Faithful. On the contrary, as the new railroad brings with it great trade and a constant influx of strangers, the lord of Vanity Fair is its chief patron, and the capitalists of the city are among the largest stockholders. Many passengers stop to take their pleasure or make their profit in the Fair, instead of going onward to the Celestial City. Indeed, such are the charms of the place that people often affirm it to be the true and only heaven; stoutly contending that there is no other, that those who seek further are mere dreamers, and that, if the fabled brightness of the Celestial City lay but a bare mile beyond the gates of Vanity, they would not be fools enough to go thither. Without subscribing to these perhaps exaggerated encomiums, I can truly say that my abode in the city was mainly agreeable, and my intercourse with the inhabitants productive of much amusement and instruction.

Being naturally of a serious turn, my attention was directed to the solid advantages derivable from a residence here, rather than to the effervescent pleasures which are the grand object with too many visitants. The Christian reader, if he have had no accounts of the city later than Bunyan's time, will be surprised to hear that almost every street has its church, and that the reverend clergy are nowhere held in higher respect than at Vanity Fair. And well do they deserve such honorable estimation; for the maxims of wisdom and virtue which fall from their lips come from as deep a spiritual source, and tend to as lofty a religious aim, as those of the sagest philosophers of old. In justification of this high praise I need only mention the names of the Rev. Mr. Shallow-deep, the Rev. Mr. Stumble-at-truth, that fine old clerical character the Rev. Mr. This-to-day, who expects shortly to resign his pulpit to the Rev. Mr. That-to-morrow; together with the Rev. Mr. Bewilderment, the Rev. Mr. Clog-the-spirit, and, last and greatest, the Rev. Dr. Wind-of-doctrine. The labors of these eminent divines are aided by those of innumerable lecturers, who diffuse such a various profundity, in all subjects of human or celestial science, that any man may acquire an omnigenous erudition without the trouble of even learning to read. Thus literature is etherealized by assuming for its medium the human voice; and knowledge, depositing all its heavier particles, except, doubtless, its gold, becomes exhaled into a sound, which forthwith steals into the ever-open ear of the community. These ingenious methods constitute a sort of machinery, by which thought and study are done to every person's hand without his putting himself to the slightest inconvenience in the matter. There is another species of machine for the wholesale manufacture of individual morality. This excellent result is effected by societies for all manner of virtuous purposes, with which a man has merely to connect himself, throwing, as it were, his quota of virtue into the common stock, and the president and directors will take care that the aggregate amount be well applied. All these, and other wonderful improvements in ethics, religion, and literature, being made plain to my comprehension by the ingenious Mr. Smooth-it-away, inspired me with a vast admiration of Vanity Fair. . . .

There was a sort of stock or script, called Conscience, which seemed to be in great demand, and would purchase almost any thing. Indeed, few rich commodities were to be obtained without paying a heavy sum in this particular stock, and a man's business was seldom very lucrative unless he knew precisely when and how to throw his hoard of conscience into the market. Yet, as this stock was the only thing of permanent value, whoever parted with it was sure to find himself a loser in the long run. Several of the speculations were of a questionable character. Occasionally a member of Congress recruited his pocket by the sale of his constituents; and I was assured that public officers have often sold their country at very moderate prices. Thousands sold their happiness for a whim. Gilded chains were in great demand, and purchased with almost any sacrifice. In truth, those who desired, according to the old adage, to sell any thing valuable for a song, might find customers all over the Fair; and there were innumerable messes of pottage, piping hot, for such as chose to buy them with their birthrights. A few articles, however, could not be found genuine at Vanity Fair. If a customer wished to renew his stock of youth the dealers offered him a set of false teeth and an auburn wig; if he demanded peace of mind, they recommended opium or a brandy bottle. . . .

Day after day, as I walked the streets of Vanity, my manners and deportment became more and more like those of the inhabitants. The place began to seem like home; the idea of pursuing my travels to the Celestial City was almost obliterated from my mind. I was reminded of it, however, by the sight of the same pair of simple pilgrims at whom we had laughed so heartily when Apollyon puffed smoke and steam into their faces at the commencement of our journey. There they stood, amid the densest bustle of Vanity; the dealers offering them their purple and fine linen and jewels, the men of wit and humor gibing at them, a pair of buxom ladies ogling them askance, while the benevolent Mr. Smooth-it-away whispered some of his wisdom at their elbows, and pointed to a newly-erected temple; but there were these worthy simpletons, making the scene look wild and monstrous, merely by their sturdy repudiation of all part in its business or pleasures.

One of them—his name was Stick-to-the-right—perceived in my face, I suppose, a species of sympathy and almost admiration, which, to my own great surprise, I could not help feeling for this pragmatic couple. It prompted him to address me.

"Sir," inquired he, with a sad, yet mild and kindly voice, "do you call yourself a pilgrim?"

"Yes," I replied, "my right to that appellation is indubitable. I am merely a sojourner here in Vanity Fair, being bound to the Celestial City by the new railroad."

"Alas, friend," rejoined Mr. Stick-to-the-right, "I do assure you, and beseech you to receive the truth of my words, that that whole concern is a bubble. You may travel on it all your lifetime, were you to live thousands of years, and yet never get beyond the limits of Vanity Fair. Yea, though you should deem yourself entering the gates of the blessed city, it will be nothing but a miserable delusion." . . .

This incident made a considerable impression on my mind, and contributed with other circumstances to indispose me to a permanent residence in the city of Vanity; although, of course, I was not simple enough to give up my original plan of gliding along easily and commodiously by railroad. Still, I grew anxious to be gone. There was one strange thing that troubled me. Amid the occupations or amusements of the Fair, nothing was more common than for a person—whether at feast, theatre, or church, or trafficking for wealth and honors, or whatever he might be doing, and however unseasonable the interruption—suddenly to vanish like a soap bubble, and be never more seen of his fellows; and so accustomed were the latter to such little accidents that they went on with their business as quietly as if nothing had happened. But it was otherwise with me.

Finally, after a pretty long residence at the fair, I resumed my journey towards the Celestial City, still with Mr. Smooth-it-away at my side. . . .

My recollections of the journey are now, for a little space, dim and confused, inasmuch as a singular drowsiness here overcame me, owing to the fact that we were passing over the enchanted ground, the air of which encourages a disposition to sleep. . . . The engine now announced the close vicinity of the final station house by one last and horrible scream, in which there seemed to be distinguishable every kind of wailing and woe, and bitter fierceness of wrath, all mixed up with the wild laughter of a devil or a madman. Throughout our journey, at every stopping-place,

Apollyon had exercised his ingenuity in screwing the most abominable sounds out of the whistle of the steam engine; but in this closing effort he outdid himself and created an infernal uproar, which, besides disturbing the peaceful inhabitants of Beulah, must have sent its discord even through the celestial gates.

While the horrid clamor was still ringing in our ears, we heard an exulting strain, as if a thousand instruments of music, with height, and depth, and sweetness in their tones, at once tender and triumphant, were struck in unison, to greet the approach of some illustrious hero, who had fought the good fight and won a glorious victory, and was come to lay aside his battered arms forever. Looking to ascertain what might be the occasion of this glad harmony, I perceived, on alighting from the cars, that a multitude of shining ones had assembled on the other side of the river, to welcome two poor pilgrims, who were just emerging from its depths. They were the same whom Apollyon and ourselves had persecuted with taunts, and gibes, and scalding steam, at the commencement of our journey—the same whose unworldly aspect and impressive words had stirred my conscience amid the wild revellers of Vanity Fair.

"How amazingly well those men have got on," cried I to Mr. Smooth-it-away. "I wish we were secure of as good a reception."

"Never fear, never fear!" answered my friend. "Come, make haste; the ferry boat will be off directly, and in three minutes you will be on the other side of the river. No doubt you will find coaches to carry you up to the city gates."

A steam ferry boat, the last improvement on this important route, lay at the river side, puffing, snorting, and emitting all those other disagreeable utterances which betoken the departure to be immediate. I hurried on board with the rest of the passengers, most of whom were in great perturbation; some bawling out for their baggage; some tearing their hair and exclaiming that the boat would explode or sink; some already pale with the heaving of the stream; some gazing affrighted at the ugly aspect of the steersman; and some still dizzy with the slumberous influences of the Enchanted Ground. Looking back to the shore, I was amazed to discern Mr. Smooth-it-away waving his hand in token of farewell.

"Don't you go over to the Celestial City?" exclaimed I.

"O no!" answered he with a queer smile, and that same disagreeable contortion of visage which I had remarked in the inhabitants of the Dark Valley. "O, no! I have come thus far only for the sake of your pleasant company. Good by! We shall meet again."

And then did my excellent friend Mr. Smooth-it-away laugh outright, in the midst of which cachinnation a smoke-wreath issued from his mouth and nostrils, while a twinkle of lurid flame darted out of either eye, proving indubitably that his heart was all of a red blaze. The impudent fiend! To deny the existence of Tophet, when he felt its fiery tortures raging within his breast, I rushed to the side of the boat, intending to fling myself on shore; but the wheels, as they began their revolutions, threw a dash of spray over me so cold—so deadly cold, with the chill that will never leave those waters until Death be drowned in his own river—that, with a shiver and a heartquake I awoke. Thank heaven it was a Dream!

16. The Bigelow Papers

JAMES RUSSELL LOWELL

The campaign against slavery paralleled the exposure of urban ills and came to overshadow it in the 1850's, in part because of the prolonged abolitionist stress on the immorality of slavery, in part because it was easier for the North to attack an external problem than to solve an internal one. Tacitly recognizing the South's right to retain its peculiar institution where it existed, the North broadly responded to antislavery appeals only when tied to the question of slavery expansion. The Mexican War crystallized much Northern feeling, and this Lowell exploited.

A Boston Brahmin of impeccable social and literary credentials, Lowell as a young man, perhaps influenced by his reform-minded wife, entered wholeheartedly into the antislavery fight. Perhaps his most important contribution was *The Bigelow Papers* (1848), where his use of the vernacular and humor, just as Mrs. Stowe's later use of sentiment, won an audience that wasn't predisposed to abolition. Lowell touched on deep chords in his audience by suggesting through his dialect the superior moral wisdom of the simple person— much as Twain was to do with Huck Finn later. And perhaps never did New England idiom better highlight New England character than in these poems:

> "An' you've gut to git up airly
> Ef you want to take in God."

A LETTER FROM MR. EZEKIEL BIGELOW OF JAALEM . . . INCLOSING A POEM OF
HIS SON, MR. HOSEA BIGELOW

> Thrash away, you'll *hev* to rattle
> On them kittle drums o' yourn,—
> 'Taint a knowin' kind o' cattle
> Thet is ketched with mouldy corn;

James Russell Lowell, "The Bigelow Papers," in *The Poetical Works* (Boston, 1869), 183–185, 207–208.

Put in stiff, you fifer feller,
  Let folks see how spry you be,—
Guess you'll toot till you are yeller
  'Fore you git ahold o' me!

'T would n't suit them Southern fellers,
  They're a dreffle graspin' set,
We must ollers blow the bellers
  Wen they want their irons het;
May be it 's all right ez preachin',
  But *my* narves it kind o' grates,
Wen I see the overreachin'
  O' them nigger-drivin' States.

Them thet rule us, them slave-traders,
  Haint they cut a thunderin' swarth,
(Helped by Yankee renegaders,)
  Thru the vartu o' the North!
We begin to think it 's nater
  To take sarse an' not be riled;—
Who'd expect to see a tater
  All on eend at bein' biled?

Ez fer war, I call it murder,—
  There you hev it plain an' flat;
I don't want to go no furder
  Than my Testyment fer that;
God hez sed so plump an' fairly,
  It 's ez long ez it is broad,
An' you 've gut to git up airly
  Ef you want to take in God.

'Taint your eppyletts an' feathers
  Make the thing a grain more right;
'Taint afollerin' your bell-wethers
  Will excuse ye in His sight;
Ef you take a sword an' dror it,
  An' go stick a feller thru,
Guv'ment aint to answer for it,
  God 'll send the bill to you.

Wut 's the use o' meeting-goin'
  Every Sabbath, wet or dry,
Ef it 's right to go amowin'
  Feller-men like oats an' rye?

I dunno but wut it 's pooty
        Trainin' round in bobtail coats,—
But it 's curus Christian dooty
        This ere cuttin' folks's throats.

They may talk o' Freedom's airy
        Tell they 're pupple in the face,—
It 's a grand gret cemetary
        Fer the barthrights of our race;
They jest want this Californy
        So 's to lug new slave-states in
To abuse ye, an' to scorn ye,
        An' to plunder ye like sin.

Aint it cute to see a Yankee
        Take sech everlastin' pains
All to git the Devil's thankee,
        Helpin' on 'em weld their chains?
Wy, it 's jest ez clear ez figgers,
        Clear ez one an' one make two,
Chaps thet make black slaves o' niggers
        Want to make wite slaves o' you.

Tell ye jest the eend I 've come to
        Arter cipherin' plaguy smart,
An' it makes a handy sum, tu,
        Any gump could larn by heart;
Laborin' man an' laborin' woman
        Hev one glory an' one shame,
Ev'y thin' thet 's done inhuman
        Injers all on 'em the same.

'Taint by turnin' out to hack folks
        You 're agoin' to git your right,
Nor by lookin' down on black folks
        Coz you 're put upon by wite;
Slavery aint o' nary color,
        'Taint the hide thet makes it wus,
All it keers fer in a feller
        'S jest to make him fill its pus.

Want to tackle *me* in, du ye?
        I expect you 'll hev to wait;
Wen cold lead puts daylight thru ye
        You 'll begin to kal'late;

'Spose the crows wun't fall to pickin'
    All the carkiss from your bones,
Coz you helped to give a lickin'
    To them poor half-Spanish drones?

Jest go home an' ask our Nancy
    Wether I 'd be sech a goose
Ez to jine ye,—guess you 'd fancy
    The etarnal bung wuz loose!
She wants me fer home consumption,
    Let alone the hay 's to mow,—
Ef you 're arter folks o' gumption,
    You 've a darned long row to hoe.

"I'll return ye good fer evil
    Much ez we frail mortils can,
But I wun't go help the Devil
    Makin' man the cus o' man;
Call me coward, call me traiter,
    Jest ez suits your mean idees,—
Here I stand a tyrant-hater,
    An' the friend o' God an' Peace!"

Ef I 'd *my* way I hed ruther
    We should go to work an' part,—
They take one way, we take t'other,—
    Guess it would n't break my heart;
Man hed ough' to put asunder
    Them thet God has noways jined;
An' I should n't gretly wonder
    Ef there 's thousands o' my mind.

FROM A CANDIDATE FOR THE PRESIDENCY IN ANSWER TO SUTTIN QUESTIONS
PROPOSED BY MR. HOSEA BIGELOW

DEAR SIR,—You wish to know my notions
    On sartin pints thet rile the land;
There 's nothin' thet my natur so shuns
    Ez bein' mum or underhand;
I 'm a straight-spoken kind o' creetur
    Thet blurts right out wut 's in his head,
An' ef I 've one pecooler feetur,
    It is a nose thet wunt be led.

So, to begin at the beginnin',
    An' come direcly to the pint,

I think the country's underpinnin'
    Is some consid'ble out o' jint;
I aint agoin' to try your patience
    By tellin' who done this or thet,
I don't make no insinooations,
    I jest let on I smell a rat.

Thet is, I mean, it seems to me so,
    But, ef the public think I 'm wrong,
I wunt deny but wut I be so,—
    An,' fact, it don't smell very strong;
My mind 's tu fair to lose its balance
    An' say wich party hez most sense;
There may be folks o' greater talence
    Thet can't set stiddier on the fence.

I 'm an eclectic; ez to choosin'
    'Twixt this an' thet, I 'm plaguy lawth;
I leave a side thet looks like losin',
    But (wile there 's doubt) I stick to both;
I stan' upon the Constitution,
    Ez preudunt statesmun say, who 've planned
A way to git the most profusion
    O' chances ez to *ware* they 'll stand.

Ez fer the war, I go agin it,—
    I mean to say I kind o' du,—
Thet is, I mean thet, bein' in it,
    The best way wuz to fight it thru;
Not but wut abstract war is horrid,
    I sign to thet with all my heart,—
But civlyzation *doos* git forrid
    Sometimes upon a powder-cart.

About thet darned Proviso matter
    I never hed a grain o' doubt,
Nor I aint one my sense to scatter
    So 's no one could n't pick it out;
My love fer North an' South is equil,
    So I 'll jest answer plump an' frank,
No matter wut may be the sequil,—
    Yes, Sir, I *am* agin a Bank.

Ez to the slaves, there 's no confusion
    In *my* idees consarnin' them,—
I think they air an Institution,
    A sort of—yes, jest so,—ahem:

Do *I* own any? Of my merit
   On thet pint you yourself may jedge;
All is, I never drink no sperit,
   Nor I haint never signed no pledge.

Ez to my principles, I glory
   In hevin' nothin' o' the sort;
I aint a Wig, I aint a Tory,
   I 'm jest a candidate, in short.

PART THREE

DEMOCRATIC TRAUMAS

17. Advice for the Home

Although notions about man's innate capacity for good were prominent, there was also a somewhat contradictory consensus that this good would triumph only if fostered by rigorous family training. Hordes of books were published offering advice on familial behavior and duties. If there was no generally recognized Dr. Spock, it was in part because of the intensity of the competition. Two popular advice tracts were Lydia Sigourney's *Letters to Mothers* and Heman Humphrey's *Domestic Education*. Both books suggest how stress on family training grew in part from fears engendered by uncertainties about aspects of American politics and society.

Mrs. Sigourney gained contemporary fame as a poetess, "the sweet singer of Hartford." She also wrote abundant sentimental essays, particularly for children, young girls, and women. She had no children herself. Humphrey, working in his early years as schoolteacher and farm laborer, entered Yale at twenty-five and became a Congregationalist minister of conservative bent. He was president of Amherst College between 1823 and 1845. Long a leader of the temperance crusade, Humphrey succeeded in pledging 80 per cent of his Amherst students to refrain from the use of liquor, tobacco, and opium.

Letters to Mothers
LYDIA SIGOURNEY

PRIVILEGES OF THE MOTHER

My Friend, if in becoming a mother, you have reached the climax of your happiness, you have also taken a higher place in the scale of being.

Lydia Sigourney, *Letters to Mothers* (New York, 1838), 9–15, 168–172; Heman Humphrey, *Domestic Education* (Amherst, Mass., 1840), 3–12.

A most important part is allotted you, in the economy of the great human family. Look at the gradations of your way onward,—your doll, your playmates, your lessons,—perhaps to decorate a beautiful person,—to study the art of pleasing,—to exult in your own attractions,—to feed on adulation,—to wear the garland of love;—and then to introduce into existence a being never to die;—and to feel your highest, holiest energies enlisted to fit it for this world and the next.

No longer will you now live for self,—no longer be noteless and unrecorded, passing away without name or memorial among the people. . . . In bequeathing your own likeness to the world, you will naturally be anxious to array it in that beauty of virtue, which fades not at the touch of time. What a scope for your exertions, to render your representative, an honour to its parentage, and a blessing to its country.

You have gained an increase of power. The influence which is most truly valuable, is that of mind over mind. How entire and perfect is this dominion, over the unformed character of your infant. Write what you will, upon the printless tablet, with your wand of love. Hitherto, your influence over your dearest friend, your most submissive servant, has known bounds and obstructions. Now, you have over a newborn immortal, almost that degree of power which the mind exercises over the body, and which Aristotle compares to the "sway of a prince over a bond-man." The period of this influence must indeed pass away;—but while it lasts, make good use of it. . . .

"A good mother, says the eloquent L'Aime Martin, will seize upon her child's heart, as her special field of activity. To be capable of this, is the great end of female education. I have shewn that no universal agent of civilization exists, but through mothers. Nature has placed in their hands, our infancy and youth. I have been among the first to declare the necessity of making them, by improved education, capable of fulfilling their natural mission. The love of God and man, is the basis of this system. In proportion as it prevails, national enmities will disappear, prejudices become extinguished, civilization spread itself far and wide,—one great people cover the earth, and the reign of God be established. This is to be hastened, by the watchful care of mothers over their offspring, from the cradle upwards."

What an appeal to mothers! What an acknowledgement of the dignity of their office! The aid of the "weaker vessel," is now invoked by legislation and sages. It has been discovered that there are signs of disease in the body politick, which can be best allayed, by the subordination taught in families, and through her agency to whom is committed the "moulding of the whole mass of mind in its first formation."

Woman is surely more deeply indebted to the government that protects her, than man, who bears within his own person, the elements of self-defence. But how shall her gratitude be best made an operative principle? Secluded as she wisely is, from any share in the administration of government, how shall her patriotism find legitimate exercise? The admixture of the female mind in the ferment of political ambition, would be neither safe if it were permitted, nor to be desired if it were safe. Nations who have encouraged it, have usually found their cabinet-councils perplexed by intrigue, or turbulent with contention. History has recorded instances, where the gentler sex have usurped the sceptre of the monarch, or invaded the province of the warrior. But we regard them either with amazement, as a planet rushing from its orbit, or with pity as the lost Pleiad, vanishing from its happy and brilliant sisterhood. . . .

It seems now to be conceded, that the vital interests of our country, may be aided by the zeal of mothers. Exposed as it is, to the influx of untutored foreigners, often unfit for its institutions, or adverse to their spirit, it seems to have been made a repository for the waste and refuse of other nations. To neutralize this mass, to rule its fermentations, to prevent it from becoming a lava-stream in the garden of liberty, and to purify it for those channels where the life-blood of the nation circulates, is a work of power and peril. The force of public opinion, or the terror of law, must hold in check these elements of danger, until Education can restore them to order and beauty. Insubordination is becoming a prominent feature in some of our principal cities. Obedience in families, respect to magistrates, and love of country, should therefore be inculcated with increased energy, by those who have earliest access to the mind. A barrier to the torrent of corruption, and a guard over the strong holds of knowledge and of virtue, may be placed by the mother, as she watches over her cradled son. Let her come forth with vigour and vigilance, at the call of her country, not like Boadicea in her chariot, but like the mother of Washington, feeling that the first lesson to every incipient ruler should be, *"how to obey."* The degree of her diligence in preparing her children to be good subjects of a just government, will be the true measure of her patriotism. While she labours to pour a pure and heavenly spirit into the hearts that open around her, she knows not but she may be appointed to rear some future statesman, for her nation's helm, or priest for the temple of Jehovah.

OPINION OF WEALTH

Earlier than we suppose, children form opinions of those who are around them. They are anxious to know who are good, and how they have earned that distinction. We should be ready to guide their first ideas of what is worthy of praise, or dispraise, for these are the germinations of principle. Let us not inoculate them with the love of money. It is the prevailing evil of our country. It makes us a care-worn people. "I know an American," said a satirical traveller, "wherever I meet him, by the perpetual recurrence of the word *dollar*. See, if you can talk with him one hour, and not hear him use it."

Not only does the inordinate desire of wealth, engross conversation, but turn thought from its nobler channels, and infect the mind as with an incurable disease. It moves the ambitious to jealous or fierce competition, and the idle to fraud, and the unprincipled to crime. Ask the keepers of our prisons, what vice peoples many of their cells? They will tell you, the desire to get money without labour. Ask the chaplain of yonder penitentiary, what crime that haggard man has committed, whom he is toiling to prepare for an ignominious death? He replies, "the love of money, led him to strike at midnight the assassin's blow."

The determination to be rich, when disjoined from honest industry, opens the avenues of sin, and even when connected with it, is dangerous, unless regulated by the self-denying spirit of religion. Allowed to overleap the limits of moderation, it becomes a foe to domestic enjoyment, and uproots the social pleasures and charities of life.

Since then the science of accumulation, is in its abuse destructive, and in its legitimate use unsafe, without the restraint of strict principle, let us not perplex the unfolding mind, with its precepts, or confound it with its combinations. The child hears perpetual conversation about the dearness or cheapness of the articles, with which he is surrounded. Perhaps, the associations which he forms, are not between the furniture and its convenience, between his apparel and its fitness or comfort, but between the quantity of money which they cost, or the adroitness with which the merchant was beaten down. He is interested by frequent remarks from lips that he revers, about how much, such and such a person is worth; and hears the gradation gravely settled, between neighbour and neighbour. "Does *worth* mean *goodness?*" inquires the child. "No. It means money." "*Worth makes the man, and want of it the fellow*," said the ethical poet. But the child coming with his privately amended dictionary, says, "*Money makes the man;*" of course, he whose purse is empty, is less than a man. Some person is spoken of, as possessing distinguished talents. The listening child is prepared to admire, till the clause, "he can never make a fortune," changes his respect to pity or indifference. The piety of another is mentioned, his love of doing good, his efforts to make others better and happier. "But he is poor." Alas, that the forming mind should be left to undervalue those deeds and motives, which in the sight of heaven, are the only true riches.

Possibly, in the freedom of domestic discourse, some lady is censured for vanity or ignorance, for ungrammatical language, or an ill-spelt epistle. But "she is rich," may be the reply, and he sees the extenuation accepted. If he is skillful at drawing inferences, or indisposed to study, he says "money is an excuse for ignorance, so if I have but little knowledge, it is no matter, if I can only get rich." He hears a man spoken of as unkind, or intemperate, or irreligious. He listens for the sentence of blame, that such conduct deserves. "He is worth five hundred thousand dollars," is the reply. And there is silence. "Can money excuse sin?" asks the poor child, in silent ruminations.

It is unwarily remarked at the table, "such a young man will be very rich when his father dies." Beware lest that busy casuist arrive at the conclusion, that a parent's death, is not a great affliction if he leaves something behind: that if his possessions are very large, the event may be both contemplated and borne with indifference. Now, though the long teaching of a selfish world may fasten this result on the minds of men, it should never enter the simple sanctuary of a child's heart, displacing the first, holiest affections of nature. . . .

Of what effect is it, that we repeat to them in grave lectures on Sundays, that they must "lay up for themselves treasures in heaven," when they can see us, the other six days toiling after, and coveting only "treasures on earth?" When we tell them that they must not "value the gold that perisheth," neither "love the world, nor the things of the world," if they weigh the precepts with our illustration of them, will they not think that we mean to palm on them, what we disregard ourselves, and despise our cunning? or else that we assert what we do not believe, and so distrust our sincerity?

Domestic Education
HEMAN HUMPHREY

Families, are so many divinely instituted and independent communities, upon the well ordering of which, the most momentous interests of the church and the state, of time and eternity are suspended. The relation between parents and children, and the obligations growing out of it, are elementary and fundamental. They lie, at the foundation of all virtue, of all social happiness, and of all good government. Were some great convulsion suddenly to subvert the political institutions of a state, without breaking up its families, those institutions might, under the same or modified forms, soon be re-established; but let the sacred ties of husband and wife, parent and child, brother and sister, once be severed; let these elements of social order be driven asunder and scattered, and it would be impossible, out of such materials, ever to re-construct any tolerable form of civil government. It would be like dissolving the attraction of cohesion in every substance upon the face of the earth. What human power and skill could ever, after that, build a city, or even erect the humblest human habitation?

Every family is a little state, or empire within itself, bound together by the most endearing attractions, and governed by its patriarchal head, with whose prerogative no power on earth has a right to interfere. Nations may change their forms of government at pleasure, and may enjoy a high degree of prosperity under different constitutions; and perhaps the time will never come, when any *one* form will be adapted to the circumstances of all mankind. But in the family organization there is but one model, for all times and all places. It is just the same now, as it was in the beginning, and it is impossible to alter it, without marring its beauty, and directly contravening the wisdom and benevolence of the Creator. It is at once the simplest, the safest and the most efficient organization that can be conceived of. Like everything else, it may be perverted to bad purposes; but it is a divine model, and must not be altered.

Every father is the constituted head and ruler of his household. God has made him the supreme earthly legislator over his children, accountable, of course, to Himself, for the manner in which he executes his trust; but amenable to no other power, except in the most extreme cases of neglect, or abuse. The will of the parent is the law to which the child is bound in all cases to submit, unless it plainly contravenes the law of God. Children are brought into existence and placed in families, not to follow their own wayward inclinations, but to look up to their parents for guidance; not to teach, but to be taught; not to govern but to be governed. . . .

Although, as I have already remarked, the state has no right to interfere with the domestic arrangements of families, except in extreme cases, it is nevertheless true, that in order to become good citizens in after life, children must be accustomed to cheerful subordination in the family, from their earliest recollection. I know that those who grow up without restraint by the fire-side, and whose youth is consequently as wild as the winds, *can* be governed afterwards by absolute power. The bayonet of the Czar and the scimitar of the Sultan, can tame them and keep them in subjection. But it may well be doubted, whether anything like a free constitutional government can ever be maintained over a people, who have not been taught the fifth commandment in their childhood. I do not believe it can. Children must be prepared to reverence the majesty of the laws, and to yield a prompt obedience to the civil magistrate, by habitual subjection to their parents. If they are not governed in the family, they will be restive under all the wholesome and necessary restraints of after life; and the freer the form of government is, in any state, the more necessary is it that parents should fit their children "to lead quiet and peaceable lives in all godliness and honesty" under it, by a proper course of domestic training. We cannot, in this country, hope to preserve and hand down our free and glorious institutions in any other way. To remain free, the mass of the people must be virtuous and enlightened; and to this end, domestic education, including all suitable restraints and discipline, must engage the earnest attention of heads of families throughout the land. It has been said a thousand times, that the practicability of maintaining a highly republican form of government has been *tried* and is *settled* in the United States, however it may have failed everywhere else. I wish it were so: but I am afraid the question is settled, so far *only* as we have gone. What the future may disclose, who can certainly tell? It is yet a grand desideratum, whether we have religion and virtue and intelligence enough to sustain our blessed institutions. The danger is, that our liberties will degenerate into licentiousness, and that the growing laxity of family government in this country will hasten on the fearful crisis. There is, if I am not deceived, a reaction in our unparalleled political freedom, upon our domestic relations. It is more difficult than it was, half, or even a quarter of a century ago, for parents to "command their household after them." Our children hear so much about liberty and equality, and are so often told how glorious it is to be "born free and equal," that it is hard work to make them understand for what good reason their liberties are abridged in the family; and I have no doubt this accounts, in multitudes of instances, for the reluctance with which they submit to parental authority. The boy wants to be "his own man," long before his wisdom teeth are cut; and the danger lies in conceding the point to him under the notion, that our fathers were quite too rigid and that a more indulgent domestic policy, corresponding with the "spirit of the age," is better. This may be the way to make *rulers* enough for a hundred republics; but not to make a single good *subject*. I repeat, therefore, that if it is important to secure a prompt obedience to the wholesome laws of the state, then is family government indispensably necessary, and the father who takes no care to control his own sons, is not himself a patriot, if he is a good citizen.

Moreover, without family government there will be very little *self-government* in any community. If you do not restrain the waywardness of your child, in its early developments, and thus assist him to get the mastery of it while yet the conquest is comparatively easy, it will be in vain for you to expect him ever to gain that self-control which is so essential to his happiness and safety. Nothing is better settled by the experience of all ages, than that the will grows stubborn—that evil passions become impetuous by indulgence; and that indulged they will be, by the child, if they are not held in check by parental authority. In this view, a greater misfortune can hardly befall a young person, than to be left to himself. The consequence is, that before reason and conscience can assert their supremacy, bad habits are formed, and his depraved inclinations have time to ripen into such maturity, that to bring them into subjection is infinitely more difficult than if the work had been commenced in the nursery. One in a hundred perhaps, may, without aid, learn to "rule his own spirit;" but it will cost him many a hard struggle; while the ninety and nine will never have resolution and perseverance enough to achieve any tolerable degree of self-control. How many slaves to an irascible temper have lamented to their dying day, that their fathers did so little to check its early growth! But what individual, in after life, was ever sorry for the aid which he received from his parents in mastering his own bad passions?

18. The Child's World

Illustrations

232

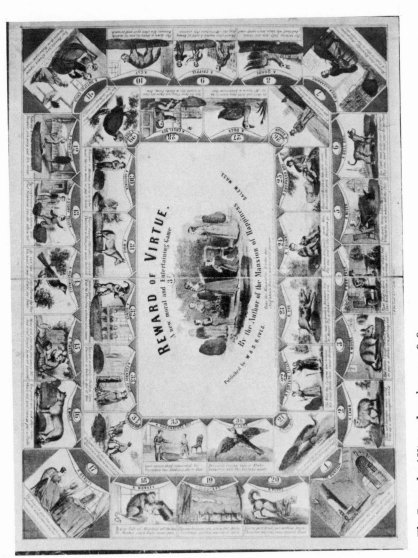

1. *The Rewards of Virtue, board game, 1838.*

2a—*Mrs. Slack's children pout about having to go to Sabbath School because they've been badly brought up.*

2. *The Bad Boy's Progress, 1835.*

2c—*The oldest Slack boy, Jesse, drowns while playing near the water when he should have been in Sabbath school.*

2f—*Samuel Slack, who liked to fight when he was a boy, kills a man in a street brawl.*

2e—*Joseph Slack, having robbed his employer to pay gambling debts, is sent to States Prison where "they shut them up each one alone, in a little room, all the time."*

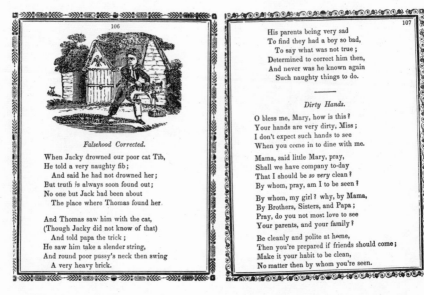

106

Falsehood Corrected.

When Jacky drowned our poor cat Tib,
He told a very naughty fib;
   And said he had not drowned her;
But truth *is* always soon found out;
No one but Jack had been about
   The place where Thomas found her.

And Thomas saw him with the cat,
(Though Jacky did not know of that)
   And told papa the trick;
He saw him take a slender string,
And round poor pussy's neck then swing
   A very heavy brick.

107

His parents being very sad
To find they had a boy so bad,
   To say what was not true;
Determined to correct him then,
And never was he known again
   Such naughty things to do.

Dirty Hands.

O bless me, Mary, how is this?
Your hands are very dirty, Miss;
I don't expect such hands to see
When you come in to dine with me.

Mama, said little Mary, pray,
Shall we have company to-day
That I should be *so very* clean?
By whom, pray, am I to be seen?

By whom, my girl? why, by Mama,
By Brothers, Sisters, and Papa;
Pray, do you not most love to see
Your parents, and your family?

Be cleanly and polite at home,
Then you're prepared if friends should come;
Make it your habit to be clean,
No matter then by whom you're seen.

3. *Rhymes for the Nursery,* 1837.

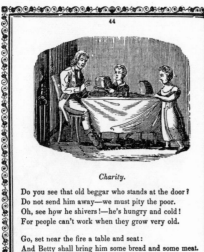

44

Charity.

Do you see that old beggar who stands at the door?
Do not send him away—we must pity the poor.
Oh, see how he shivers!—he's hungry and cold!
For people can't work when they grow very old.

Go, set near the fire a table and seat:
And Betty shall bring him some bread and some meat.
I hope my dear children will always be kind,
Whenever they meet with the aged and blind.

45

Miss Sophia.

Miss Sophy, one fine sunny day,
Left her work and ran away:
When soon she reach'd the garden gate,
Which finding lock'd, she would not wait,
But tried to climb and scramble o'er
A gate as high as any door!

Now little girls should never climb,
And Sophy won't another time
For when upon the highest rail
Her frock was caught upon a nail,
She lost her hold, and, sad to tell,
Was hurt and bruis'd—for down she fell.

THE VERY SAD STORY OF PAULINE AND THE MATCH BOX.

One day Pauline was all alone,
Her parents both from home had gone;
As round the room she lightly sprung,
And clapped her hands, and danced and sung,
She suddenly before her spied
A box of matches. Oh! she cried,
How glad I am this box to see!
Oh! what a pretty play 'twill be;
I'll light a little match or two,
Just as I've seen my mother do.

But Minz and Maunz, the little cats,
Held up their little paws,
"Miow, miow, miow!" they cried,
And threatened with their claws,
Don't touch it, or in flames thou'lt be,
Thy father has forbidden thee.

Pauline the kittens did not hear,
The little match burnt bright and clear,
It crackled, flickered prettily,
Just as you in the picture see.
Oh! never in her life before
Had any play-thing pleased her more.

But Minz and Maunz, the little cats,
Still raised their little paws,
"Miow, mio, miow!" they cried,
And threatened with their claws,
"Oh! put it down! in flames thou'lt be,
Thy mother has forbidden thee!"

4. *Very Sad Story of Pauline
and the Match Box, 1854.*

But dreadful, dreadful tale to tell,
The match upon her apron fell;
It kindled, burnt her hands, her head,
All over her the flames soon spread.

Then Minz and Maunz, those little cats,
Began to scream and cry,
"Help! fire! Oh who will quickly come,
The child will surely die;
She's all in flames from top to toe,
Miow! Mio! Miow! Mio!

Pauline now no more was there;
She burnt from pantalette to hair,
But in the place where she had been,
A heap of ashes could be seen;
And that with her dear little shoes,
Alone remained to tell the news!

And Minz and Maunz, the faithful cats,
Sat by the pretty shoes,
And cried, "Oh! to her parents, wao,
Oh! who shall tell the news?"
"Miow! Mio! Miow! Mio!"
Their tears like little brooks did flow.

5. *"Old Mother Hubbard," 1830*

6. *"Only A Penny,"* 1854.

19. Little Ferns for Fanny's Little Friends

SARA PAYSON PARTON ("FANNY FERN")

The 1850's revealed America's first batch of writers specializing in muckraking social criticism; even a whole class of juvenile literature developed out of it. One of the most popular of these works was *Little Ferns,* which sold fifteen thousand copies in its first year. It went through repeated editions.

"Fanny Fern" was one of that "tribe of female scribblers" who so irritated Nathaniel Hawthorne. Left a widow with two children to support, she began to write and soon supported them very well; by the late 1850's she was reportedly the best paid of American writers, particularly for her columns in the New York *Ledger.* Her sketches lack the proportions of classic schmaltz found in the philanthropist Charles Loring Brace's "Parable of the Rich Boy and the Poor Boy," in which a poor boy starves to death but goes to heaven while the rich boy, who refused him food, dies (vaguely of overeating) and goes elsewhere. But there is, gasping through Mrs. Parton's sentiment, a certain observational vitality and human responsiveness. Even in children's literature, a social sensitivity and explanation of evil were warring with the older moralism in the 1850's.

THE LITTLE "MORNING GLORY"

Dear little pet! She was going a journey in the cars with mamma; and her little curly head could not stay on the pillow, for thinking of it. She was awake by the dawn, and had been trying to rouse mamma for an hour. She had told her joy in lisping accents to "Dolly," whose stoical indifference was very provoking, especially when she knew she was going to see "her dear, white-haired old grand-papa," who had never yet looked upon her sweet face, although pen and ink had long since heralded her

Sara P. Parton, *Little Ferns for Fanny's Little Friends* (Auburn, N.Y., 1854), 33–37, 47–51, 157–161.

polite perfections. Yes, little pet must look her prettiest, for grand-papa's eyes are not so dim, that the sight of a pretty face does n't cheer him like a ray of glad sunlight; so the glossy waves of golden hair are nicely combed, and the bright dress put on, to heighten, by contrast, the dimpled fairness of the neck and shoulders; then, the little white apron, to keep all tidy; then the Cinderella boots, neatly laced. I can see you, little pet! I wish I had you in my arms this minute! . . .

Alas! poor little pet!

Grand-papa's eyes grow weary watching for you, at the little cottage window. Grand-mamma says, "the cakes will be quite spoiled;" and she "knits to her seam needle," and then moves about the sitting-room uneasily; now and then stopping to pat the little Kitty, that is to be pet's play-fellow. And now lame Tim has driven the cows home; and the dew is falling, the stars are creeping out, and the little crickets and frogs have commenced their evening concert, and *still* little pet has n't come! Where *is* the little stray waif?

Listen! Among the "unrecognized dead" by the late RAILROAD ACCIDENT, was a female child, about three years of age; fair complexion and hair; had on a red dress, green sack, white apron, linen gaiters, tipped with patent leather, and white woolen stockings.

Poor little pet! Poor old grand-papa! Go comfort him; tell him it was a *"shocking accident,"* but then *"nobody was to blame;"* and offer him a healing plaster for his great grief, in the shape of "damage" money.

THE CHARITY ORPHANS

"Pleasant sight, is it not?" said my friend, glancing complacently at a long procession of little charity children, who were passing, two and two —two and two—with closely cropped heads, little close-fitting sun-bonnets and dark dresses; "pleasant sight, is it not, Fanny?" Yes—no—*no*, said I, courageously, it gives me the heart-ache. "Oh, I see as you do, that their clothes are clean and whole, and that they are drilled like a little regiment of soldiers, (heads up,) but I long to see them step out of those prim ranks, and shout and scamper. I long to stuff their little pockets full of anything—everything, that other little pets have. I want to get them round me, and tell them some comical stories to take the care-worn look out of their anxious little faces. I want to see them twist their little heads round when they hear a noise, instead of keeping them straight forward as if they were "on duty." I want to know if anybody tucks them up comfortably when they go to bed, and gives them a good-night kiss. I want to know if they get a beaming smile, and a kind word in the morning. I want to know who soothes them when they are in pain; and if they *dare say so*, when they feel lonely, and have the heart-ache. I want to see the tear roll freely down the cheek, (instead of being wiped slyly away,) when they see happy little ones trip gaily past, hand in hand, with a kind father, or mother. I want to know if "Thanksgiving" and "Christmas" and "New Year's" and *"Home"* are anything but empty sounds in their orphan ears.

I know their present state is better than vicious poverty, and so I try to say with my friend, "it is a pleasant sight;" but the words die on my lip; for full well I know it takes something more than food, shelter and clothing, to make a child happy. Its little heart, like a delicate vine, *will* throw out its tendrils for something to *lean on*—something to *cling to;* and so I can only say again, the sight of those charity orphans gives me the heart-ache.

ONLY A PENNY

Now I am going to tell you a story about little Clara. Those of you who live in the city will understand it; but some of my little readers may live in the country, (or at least I hope they do,) where a beggar is seldom seen; or if he is, can always get of the good, nice, kind-hearted farmer, a bowl of milk, a fresh bit of bread, and liberty to sleep in the barn on the sweet-scented hay; therefore, it will be hard for you to believe that there is anybody in the wide world with enough to eat, and drink, and wear, who does not care whether a poor fellow creature starves or not; or whether he lives or dies.

But listen to my story.

One bright, sunny morning I was walking in Broadway, (New-York), looking at the ladies who passed, in their gay clothes—as fine as peacocks, and just about as silly—gazing at the pretty shop windows, full of silks, and satins, and ribbons, looking very much as if a rainbow had been shivered there—looking at the rich people's little children, with their silken hose, and plumed hats, and velvet tunics, tiptoeing so carefully along, and looking so frightened lest somebody should soil their nice clothes—when a little, plaintive voice struck upon my ear—

"Please give me a penny, Madam—*only* a penny—to buy a loaf of bread?"

I turned my head: there stood a little girl of six years,—so filthy, dirty —so ragged, that she scarcely looked like a human being. Her skin was coated with dust; her pretty curly locks were one tangled mass; her dress was fluttering in strings around her bare legs and shoeless feet—and the little hand she held out to me for "a penny," so bony that it looked like a skeleton's. She looked so very hungry, I would n't make her talk till I had given her something to eat; so I took her to a baker's, and bought her some bread and cakes; and it would have made you cry (you, who were never hungry in your life,) to see her swallow it so greedily, just like a little animal.

Then I asked her name, and found out 'twas "Clara;" that she had no papa; that while he lived he was very cruel, and used to beat her and her mother; and that now her mother was cruel too, and drank rum; that she sent little Clara out each morning to beg,—or if she couldn't beg, to steal,—but at any rate to bring home something, "unless she wanted a beating."

Poor little Clara!—all alone threading her way through the great, wicked city—knocked and jostled about,—*so* hungry—*so* tired—*so* frightened! Clara was afraid to steal, (not because God saw her—for she didn't know anything about *Him*,) but for fear of policemen and prisons— so she wandered about, hour after hour, saying pitifully to the careless crowd, "Only a penny—*please* give me a penny to buy a loaf of bread!"

Yes—Clara's mother was very cruel; but God forbid, my little innocent children, that you should ever know how hunger, and thirst, and misery, may sometimes turn even that holy thing—*a mother's love*—to bitterness.

Poor Clara! she had never known a better home than the filthy, dark cellar, where poor people in cities huddle together like hunted cattle. . . . Her little head often pained her. She was foot-weary and heart-sore; and what was worse than all, she had never heard of heaven, "where the weary rest." Wasn't it very pitiful?

Well, little Clara kissed my hand when she had eaten enough—(it was so odd for *Clara* to have *enough*)—and her sunken eyes grew bright, and she said—"Now I shall not be beaten, because I 've something left to carry home;" so she told me where she lived, and I bade her good bye, and told her I would come and see her mother to-morrow.

The next day I started again to find little Clara's mother. I was *very* happy going along, because I meant, if I could, to get her away from her cruel mother; to make her clean and neat; to teach her how to read and spell, and show to her that the world was not *all* darkness—not *all* sin, and tears, and sorrow; and to tell her of that kind God who loves *everything* that He has made. So as I told you I was very happy,—the sun looked so bright to me—the sky so fair,—and I could scarcely make my feet go fast enough.

Turning a corner suddenly, I met a man bearing a child's coffin. . . .

Yes—it was she! I was too late—*she* was in the little coffin! No hearse—
no mourners—no tolling bell! Borne along—unnoticed—uncared for—
through the busy, crowded, noisy, streets. But, dear children, kind Angels
looked pitying down, and Clara "hungers no more—nor thirsts any more—
neither shall the sun light on her, nor any heat."

A PEEP UNDER GROUND

THE RAFFERTYS AND THE ROURKES

I have made up my mind, that there is nothing lost in New-York. You
open your window and toss out a bit of paper or silk, and though it may
be no bigger than a sixpence, it is directly snatched up and carried off,
by a class of persons the Parisians call, "Chiffoniers" (rag-pickers)! You
order a load of coal or wood, to be dropped at your door;—in less than
five minutes a whole horde of ragged children are greedily waiting round
to pick up the chips, and bits, that are left after the wood or coal is
carried in and housed; and often locks of hair are pulled out, and bloody
noses ensue, in the strife to get the largest share. You will see these
persons round the stores, looking for bits of paper, and silk, and calico,
that are swept out by the clerks, upon the pavement; you will see them
watching round provision shops, for decayed vegetables, and fruits, and
rinds of melons, which they sell to keepers of pigs; you will see them
picking up peach stones to sell to confectioners, who crack them and use
the kernels; you will see them round old buildings, carrying off, at the
risk of cracked heads, pieces of decayed timber, and old nails; you will
see them round new buildings, when the workmen are gone to meals,
scampering off with boards, shingles, and bits of scaffolding. I thought I
had seen all the ingenuity there was to be seen, in picking up odds and
ends in New-York, but I had n't then seen Michael Rafferty!

Michael Rafferty, and Terence Rourke, who was a wood sawyer by
profession, lived in a cellar together; the little Raffertys, and little Rourkes,
with their mammas, filling up all the extra space, except just so much as
was necessary to swing the cellar door open. A calico curtain was swung
across the cellar for a boundary line, to which the little Rourkes and little
Raffertys paid about as much attention, as the whites did to the poor
Indians' landmarks.

At the time I became acquainted with the two families, quite a jealousy
had sprung up on account of Mr. Rafferty's having made a successful
butter speculation. Mrs. Rourke, in consequence, had kept the calico
curtain tightly drawn for some weeks, and boxed six of the little Rourkes'

ears (twelve in all,) for speaking to the little Raffertys through the rents in the curtain.

All this I learned from Mrs. Rafferty, as I sat on an old barrel in the north-west corner of her cellar. "It was always the way," she said, "if a body got up in the world, there were plenty of envious spalpeens, sure, to spite them for it;" which, I took occasion to remark to Mrs. Rafferty, was as true, as anything I had ever had the pleasure of hearing her say.

Just then the cellar door swung open, and the great butter speculator, Mr. Michael Rafferty, walked in. He nodded his head, and gave an uneasy glance at the curtain, as much as to say, "calicoes have ears." I understood it, and told him we had been very discreet. Upon which he said, "You see, they 'll be afther staling my thrade, your ladyship, if they know how I manage about the butther."

"Tell me how you do it, Michael," said I; "you know women have a right to be curious."

"Well," said he, speaking in a confidential whisper, "your ladyship knows there are plenty of little grocery shops round in these poor neighborhoods, where they sell onions, and combs, and molasses, and fish, and tape, and gingerbread, and rum. Most of them sell milk, (none of the best, sure, but it does for the likes of us poor folks.) It stands round in the sun in the shop windows, your ladyship, till it gets turned, like, and when they have kept it a day or two, and find they can't sell it," (and here Michael looked sharp at the calico curtain,) "I buys it for two cents a quart, and puts it in that churn," (pointing to a dirty looking affair in the corner,) "and my old woman and I make it into butter." And he stepped carefully across the cellar, and pulled from *under the bed*, a keg, which he uncovered with a proud flourish, and sticking a bit of wood in it, offered me a taste, "just to thry it."

I could n't have tasted it, if Michael had shot me; but I told him I dare say he understood his trade and hoped he found plenty of customers.

"I sell it as fast as I can make it," said he, putting on the cover and shoving it back under the bed again.

"What do you do with the buttermilk?" said I.

He looked at Mrs. Rafferty, and she pointed to the bright, rainbow ribbon on her cap.

"Sell it?" said I.

"Sure," said Michael, with a grin; "we are making money, your ladyship; we shall be afther moving out of this cellar before long, and away from the likes of them," (pointing in the direction of the curtain); "and, savin' your ladyship's presence," said he, running his fingers through his mop of wiry hair, "Irish people sometimes understhand dhriving a thrade as well as Yankees;" and Michael drew himself up as though General Washington could n't be named on the same day with *him*.

Just then a little snarly headed boy came in with two pennies and a cracked plate, "to buy some butther."

"Didn't I tell your ladyship so?" said Michael. "Holy Mother!" he continued, as he pocketed the pennies, and gave the boy a short allowance of the vile stuff, "how I wish I had known how to make that butther when every bone in me body used to ache sawin' wood, and the likes o' that,— to say nothing of the greater respictability of being in the mercantile profession."

20. The Almighty Dollar! or The Brilliant Exploits of a Killer

ANONYMOUS

While Fanny Fern told middle-class American children about disparities of wealth and the terror of poverty in the big city, another class of literature sprang up speaking more directly for the proletariat being created. Charles Godfrey Leland in his *Memoirs* claimed that in Philadelphia about 1850 a whole class of writing existed "in all of which there is a striving downwards into blackguardism and brutality, vileness and ignorance which has no parallel in literature" and which contributed to "a terrible and general growth and spread of turbulence and coarse vulgarity among youth."

"The Killers" were one of the many gangs of urban toughs, often connected with volunteer fire companies and political organizations, that gave social unity to poor young men in large cities. Whether these groups were as class-conscious and as powerful as the story suggests is dubious, but clearly there was a great deal of hatred for the "proud aristocrat." The hatred, however, much like the middle-class Jacksonian thrusts at aristocracy two decades earlier, seems much more rhetorical and personal than programmatic.

THE ALMIGHTY DOLLAR

What think you, kind reader, lends such a potent charm to a small coin, to a silver dollar, to a piece of UNCLE SAM'S *currency?*

Think you that it is on account of its snowy-white, dazzling brightness, and of its neat, workmanship aspect? or on account of the virginity of its metal, save the small portion of polluting copper unthought of by the mass?

The Almighty Dollar! or The Brilliant Exploits of a Killer, a Romance of Old Quakerdelphia (Philadelphia, 1847), 3–4, 9–18, 22–26, 48 (Courtesy of the Historical Society of Pennsylvania).

A dollar is certainly a coin of little value, a minim altar at whose shrine to worship; mankind have worshipped a golden calf with bitter regret, but for mankind at this enlightened day to reverence a small piece of money, appears mad and absurd in the extreme. But it is an undeniable fact, that the DOLLAR is ALMIGHTY, and that it is WORSHIPPED! Let us try to analize its virtues. . . .

Here is a boy of an amassive turn, fips and levies are now and than given to him, and he saves them, and looks at them with smiling lips and glistening eyes; all his mind centres there, and the idea of soon realizing a DOLLAR is a perfect Godsend, a heaven of bliss, a brimful cup of happiness, an object of heart and soul's adoration!

There is a man poverty-stricken, want-prostrated, borne down by worldly struggles to obtain a livelihood, honestly, of course; he is comfortless, friendless, homeless, and he drags out a wretched existence amidst scenes of joy and comfort, of plenty and extravagance; he sees money squandered to gratify a whim, that would make him light and happy as a lark for a whole year; and the want of the money which he curses, plunges him into the bitterest and most violent despair: a DOLLAR would transfer him to the realms of bliss, to the seventh paradise of Mahomet, to the vaunted Elysium Fields!

Then we see a man possessing an hundred thousand; truly a superb independence. But think you that he is an independent man? By no means. He is happiless, restless, *the* DOLLAR *is not a gilded idol but a* LIVING GOD! He kneels, he clings to its very shadow; he is its voluntary *slave,* and at its polluted altar he would lay down his *soul* to grasp one more *dollar:* exclaiming, gnashing his teeth, and with convulsive sobs: *thou only true and living god, with thee I will sway the world, and bring all creation at my feet, and though I govern like the cruellest Nero, not a whisper is heard! and with thee, omnipotent dollar, I am launched to heaven!*

O vilest of things! let us take leave of thee.

But we must own that we do not despise, nor should we wish to make the reader despise the dollar, the pure and honest dollar; for in its place, it is desirable and welcome, and we complain of the *abuse,* not of the *use.*

EMMA WILLDAY

It is Queen Street.

The street bears no inviting appearance; none but dull, dingy, dilapidated buildings are to be seen, and persons wretchedly clad, and of fierce and hyena like faces.

And this is Emma's residence, a truly gloomy and comfortless one, outside. Let us ascend a miserable, break-neck staircase, and enter Emma's room.

It was a room on the third floor, of small dimensions, with blackened walls, of a comfortless and dirty aspect, containing but few pieces of furniture, and those of the coarsest make; a low bed stood in a corner, a sheet-iron stove and a table covered with a scanty supply of household implements, stood in another.

Emma lies in bed, the victim of a withered heart and body, the prey of the devouring monster, consumption.

Beside the bed knelt Emma's child, in all the beauty of angelic earnestness. She was tall for her age, of a fine figure, beautiful features, though sad and fireless, and fair-haired. Her colorless cheek seemed like a rose-bud, sickly, odorless, and without beauty, from confinement and breathing in an impure atmosphere: she was a promising plant, but drooping, and unless she was transplanted into some more congenial clime, she must certainly be carried away as a prize by the arch-destroyer.

Robert, the oysterman, was by also. He was a young man of about twenty-five, with a robust and strong constitution, passable countenance, and unpolished gait and manners. Though he appeared of a benevolent turn, a deep-seated mischievousness lurked in his eye, uncontrollable when let loose.

"How do you feel now?" asked Robert.

"Bad, bad, Robert. I am quite confident that the light of day will soon close for me, I must soon quit this sad world. Don't weep, dear child; dear Emma, my only regret is to leave you in the midst of this cold, unfeeling world—to guide you I would have faced the world's torments, but it is not in my power. Robert, you have been kind to me, you have been kind to her, be so yet—you have my thanks and blessings for your noble conduct, may heaven reward you, Robert, you are the only true friend that I have in the world, promise me to look to Emma, to be kind to her. I know that it is a serious charge, but, oh God! to whom confide her! promise me, Robert, heaven *will* reward you; be kind to the orphan child, love her, even as a brother."

"I do," lisped Robert.

Emma was too much affected with joy to thank him. Little Emma wept bitterly.

"Thanks, Robert, you have made me happy, even at this hour; you were sent by Providence across my path."

"It's a bounden duty to help one another."

"Yes, but little practised in this cold, selfish age. Dear Emma, don't weep so, my child, you make me more sad."

"Ma, I can't help it when I see you so ill." . . .

Emma commenced:—"I was once beautiful and admired, I say it without vanity, for vanity, alas, has long departed from my breast; and it is not to be wondered at after the many privations and mortifications that I have been subjected to. At my father's house, in my blooming and happy days, I was courted and admired as *la belle Emma*, and as with all girls, it made me vain. I received homage and flatteries as due to me by right. Though light and vain, I was not cold and cruel; my heart felt the glow of love, and it bounded with joy at the knowledge of Cupid's visit. I loved a young gentleman, a gentleman by nature and in manners, but he was poor, being only a clerk, and possessing no influence. Though nurtured in the lap of luxury, I did not crave riches, I was ready and willing to share the fortunes of him I loved. But it is ever so, interest must thwart the finer feelings of our natures by bringing disparaging pictures. As soon as our attachment was noticed all the batteries that avarice and malevolence could invent were brought to bear; I was emphatically told, that if I married a poor young man dependent on his situation and salary, my accomplishments would be thrown away, I should be reduced to a state of servitude, going through all the drudgery of a menial. When I answered, that *for the one I would love such a task would be most sweet and agreeable,* I was called a silly, foolish girl, and if I dared to act like a fool I should be treated like a dog. On the other hand I was given to understand that if I wedded the merchant who was enamored of me, being gallant, handsome, young and wealthy, possessing *credit* and *influence,* I should be a *lady in the first circles, the queen of fashion, and commanding homage on all hands.* I had not yet broken the trammels of parental obedience, and the glowing picture dazzled my eyes, my self-love was flattered, and the thought of domineering, and at the same time of pleasing my parents, made me fall into the snare prepared to engulph me. *Why in matters of the heart are not the hearts alone left to decide, and not bring interest to subserve the feelings, bartering away happiness and life itself for* MONEY AND INFLUENCE!"—She fell, breathless.

After a pause she continued:—"I was forced to relinquish the love of the CLERK to marry the MERCHANT. The nuptials took place. It was not long before the veil of hypocrisy was torn, and the *man* appeared in his true light—*he was cold, indifferent, even cruel;* absenting himself till an early hour in the morning, with the most deadly indifference, filling me with alarm and anxieties. *I soon learned with horror that he indulged in the gaming table and in the cup!* The discovery was agonising, but I uttered no complaints to my relations, and when I proffered a few words of remonstrance to *him*, my husband, *he brutally repulsed them!* Emma was born, but his conduct remained unamended. In two years' time from my marriage my husband, the *gallant and princely merchant, was a bankrupt, a swindler, a forger,* A CRIMINAL! He had largely forged on my father, and successfully. *He was the most hellish villain that trod the earth!* and in that moment of trial, when I sought to be a soothing angel to him, he maltreated me unmercifully. He was, indeed, unworthy to enjoy the light of heaven, and he launched his demon soul into eternity by suicide! *I was the criminal's, the suicide's widow!* I who might have been the contented and happy wife! the thought was heart-rending! I bitterly reproached my relations with all this, but I received no aid or comfort, and I scorned them. I was an outcast from society, a beggar upon the world, I only clung to life for my child, and bitter and gloomy it has been. *Love and mere comforts would have made me happy, but an inordinate craving for wealth and an influential connection made me this!* Spare my feelings distracted as they are, you know the rest; I cannot go on, my breath—fails me!"

"Don't go on, rest yourself. Ma, how I do pity you."

"You do, my dear." Emma proceeded feebly. "Robert, by your advice and through your information I succeeded in my errand, and my last. A dandy Fairman who was at Miss Miffis', gave me five dollars, but it was a mockery, the deed of the hand, not of the heart; and a Mr. Mann gave a dollar, and this order, read it:

"*Mr. Mildew at Pennsylvania Bank—*

"Please pay the bearer ten dollars. EDWARD MANN."

"He gave it so feelingly and graciously, that truly his left hand knoweth not what his right hand giveth; and in these two actions was admirably exemplified *true and false generosity.* Emma, dear, keep that *dollar* sacredly; part not from it but to save life, and always remember Edward Mann with reverence, it is your mother's wish. Emma, say this:—Edward Mann, mother's dollar."

"Edward Mann—mother's dollar." . . .

Her countenance fell and her eyes closed in death!

"Ma! ma!" sobbed Emma, and she clasped her lifeless parent.

ROBERT THE KILLER

READER, it was in the neighborhood of Fifth and Shippen streets, but as to the precise house we are—mum; though not a Killer ourselves, nor are we courting the good graces or dreading the resentment of the Killers, but simply because we have not ascertained the exact locality.

It is well known, or be it well known, that the aforesaid locality bears no predisposing or inviting aspect; it is even shunned by grown people as is a spot by children said to be haunted.

Then, near Fifth and Shippen the promising *Killers' Club* held its head-quarters. Let us lift the veil and we are in the midst of the assembled Killers.

There were near a hundred present—but how describe them? *They were mostly under twenty, of the ragamuffin and utterly depraved order, and undoubtedly the hardest cases to be found within the precincts of Quakerdelphia county.*

They were seated on benches, the Secretary was seated by a desk, and the Vice-President occupied the chair.

The Secretary arose and said: "Brother Killers, I will arraign Robert Falsestep before your omnipotent bar for desertion of his post and the Club, if there's no objection."

No objection was made.

"The motion is unanimous; Robert Falsestep, appear."

Robert came forward.

"Robert Falsestep, you are accused of having given aid and comfort to an enemy of our race and of our Club."

"In what manner?"

"No bamboozling, d'ye hear?" grinned one.

"By harboring an ARISTOCRAT."

"An ARISTOCRAT! brother Killers, this is ridiculous; *an aristocrat, who ate the bran bread of poverty and drank the cold water of the outcast!* she was once an aristocrat, but became one of US, one of the SOVEREIGN PEOPLE."

Immense applause followed.

"Must we not rejoice *when we see an aristocrat by an aristocrat hurled from marbled and carpeted halls to dwell in an humble and comfortless hovel!"*

"Aye," rung a tremendous shout from an hundred throats.

"Brother Killers, judge if she could be an aristocrat by making for a living *shirts at ten cents and pants at twenty!"*

"No," was the universal response.

"Thus the rich will grind down the poor, and every one of their dollars is STAINED WITH THE BLOOD OF SOME OF US!"

"Down with the aristocrats! down with the rich! they're demons to torment the poor!" (Loud and long hissing.)

"Some heartless taskmasters killed the poor woman, she is dead, *may heaven have her soul!*" A profound silence reigned.

"When the poor woman died, she confided her daughter to my care, but a rich uncle soon came and took her away; he rewarded me liberally for my services towards his sister and niece."

"He's an *aristocrat*," shouted some.

"True; he helped me, I opened an oyster restaurant; you all, brother Killers, have been welcome, and all I made went to our cause; what can you complain of?"

"All right! and nothin' else," was heard all around.

Robert was the most intelligent of all the Killers, and he had been appointed to preside over them; he had also prepared a constitution.

"Now, brother Killers," continued Robert, "you've got my case, I await your verdict."

Deafening applause succeeded.

"I move that Robert Falsestep, our President, take the chair," said the Secretary.

"Aye," as one sound, rang through the room.

He took the chair.

Secretary. "The business before the meeting is the reading of the Constitution for adoption."

"Read;" "let's have it;" "let's have a constitution;" "I'll vote it down."

The President. "Rap, rap," with the hilt of his dagger.

The Secretary read—

THE CONSTITUTION

SECT. 1. Society is so framed, and the DOLLAR has become such a mighty engine, and those who have wealth have power, and those who have power will be sure to abuse it; and whereas, the poor are looked upon as so many dogs, unworthy to live, except it be to obey the will and whims of aristocrats, for the mere crumbs that fall from their tables, on penalty of the lash if the tyrants' commands are disobeyed. (*Hisses and groans long and tumultuous.*) Therefore, it is apparent that the rich want a signal estrangement from the people, and WE, the people, swear an eternal estrangement, *a deadly enmity, a war of extermination against the aristocrats, the plunder and burning of their property,* and all the mischief that can be concocted and executed against those overbearing and self-styled demigods. ("*We swear;*" "*good!*" "*even more, death!*" "*measure for measure;*" "*down with the aristocrats,*" *and tumultuous applause.*) We are bound to rise from our fallen state, to vindicate our wrongs, to assert and conquer our rights, to reassume our place in society, even if it were to be done with *the incendiary's torch, the assassin's knife, and the fiend's frenzy." ("Three cheers;" "serve 'em right, they'll come down," and vociferous applause.*)

SECT. 2. As a Tell and a Washington (*"three times three!" "three times three again!"*) have rescued their country from thraldom, let it be the aim, the never ceasing, never dying aim of the Killers to free their free and glorious land from *the scourge of vassalage, from the iron-sway of the rich, from the tyranny and grinding of lordly demagogues,* our motto being, LIBERTY, EQUALITY AND WASHINGTON. (*"He was one of the b'hoys!" Immense shouting and clapping.*)

SECT. 3. We are democrats, (*"Aye, to the core;" "We aint nothin' else!" and immense cheering,*) but we will not be the slaves nor the tools of the democratic party, nor of any party, but keeping aloof from all, we will remain a distinct organisation, free in our actions, in a word, NEUTRALS, (*"Who's the ballot box for;" "Where's our freedom?" "That's an aristocrat's move;" "Who wants to be a neutral?" "We all want to have a finger in the pie!" and hisses,*) when it will be to our interests, (*Cheering*) and to defeat measures not consonant with our views; (*immense cheering,*) our strength lies in the district of Moyamensing, and Moyamensing must be our stronghold; MOYAMENSING MUST BE OURS! (*"It must;" "It will;" "The Killers' own," and applause,*) we must control the votes of Moyamensing, and selling our influence to the highest party bidder, OUR EXISTENCE IS CERTAIN, WE WILL BE FEARED, (*tremendous shouting and howling,*) though not loved, WE WILL BE COURTED, *we will gain strength day by day, the ground down and oppressed will flock to our standard, the sovereign people will sway once more,* ("*They'll do nothin' else;" "Yes sir-ee!" and cheering,*) and like the Jacobin club in France, the Killers' Club, from a mere party organisation, *will sway parties and dictate to the whole country, putting down aristocrats, monopolies, and the* DOLLAR'S MISRULE, to plant in our land the GOLDEN AGE; but we look not toward the eruption of a volcano vomiting forth blood and flames, but toward A REIGN OF PEACE AND HAPPINESS; not towards a Robespierre, but a Washington. (*Prolonged and deafening applause.*)

SECT. 4. All brother Killers will be sworn in this wise: *I swear to uphold the Killers' Club by thought, word, and deed, to advance its interests by will, strength, and influence, and at the hazard of welfare, interest and life; not to betray its objects and purposes, and if I do, to be hunted down like a wild beast, until the dagger's point will pierce my heart,* EVEN IN THE SANCTUARY! (*"Serve him right!" "Who'd flinch in such a cause?" "We'll not be slaves but freemen!" "The Killers' forever;" "How'd a Killer look as Mayor of Quakerdelphia;" "Or as President of the United States;" with stunning cheering.)*

SECT. 5. Native and naturalized citizens may become members of the Killers' Club. (*"We're all brothers when oppressed."*)

SECT. 6. The usual mode of government will govern the Club; meetings semi-weekly, and a tax will be levied on the Killers' until the expenses of the Club shall be otherwise provided for. (*"All right," "I've got a fip," "Who's the treasurer," and cheering.*)

"That's all." (*Immense uproar and cheering.*)

Secretary. "It is moved and seconded that the Constitution be adopted; all who are in favor of it will signify it by saying aye."

"Aye;" with immense cheering.

"Contrary, no." Dead silence.

"Unanimously carried."

A Killer. "I'll move an amendment: that when a man'll be exposed, he'll resign the Constitution, and be expelled a member."

Another. "I object to it, it's too fairified, can't go to Fairmount."

"I move the amendment be laid on the table." And it was.

A knock was heard, and the door being opened, three Killers came in convoying a tip-top-dressed man, blindfolded.

"Who is he?" asked Robert, in an imperious tone.

"A spy," answered one of the captors.

"A SPY!" cried Robert in a voice of thunder, that made the man tremble from head to foot. "Let him see where, and in the midst of whom he stands."

The bandage was removed from his eyes, and he beheld, in stupid petrification, an hundred uplifted daggers directed to his heart. He stared wildly around; his impulse was to fly, but all the avenues presented steel defences.

"Stir not an inch for thy life," cried Robert. "Knowest thou in the midst of whom thou standest."

He shook his head.

"THOU ART IN THE KILLERS' CLUB, IN THE MIDST OF THE KILLERS!!!"

"KILLERS!" he muttered, and he felt a convulsive spasm all through his frame.

"It is well that thou shouldst not only dread the *name*, but fear the *arm* and the *might* of the Killers, if thou hast trespassed against them."

"I most solemnly protest."

"Thou art accused by three brother Killers with being *a spy!*"

"THEY LIE!"

The three Killers rushed towards him, daggers in hand, with the wrath of demons and the ferocity of tigers.

"Hold, Killers!" cried Robert, "but how darest thou, dog, give the lie to the word of three Killers?"

"Let me explain the affair."

"Go on."

"I have heard of your DAMNABLE CLUB—"

"DAMNABLE CLUB!" a fierce and blood-thirsty cry arose among the Killers.

"Let him go on."

Having mustered, or affecting great courage, he proceeded:

"Yes, *having heard of your* DAMNABLE CLUB, and hearing all say that they dare not face *a Killer in your* DOMINIONS, I said that *I would* and pledged my honor *to do it,* and to do it I should have faced the devil!" Though not brave nor chivalric, but thus hemmed in a tight corner, the dandy played the hero, and looked grand and sublime in that fit of valor.

"You defied the KILLERS' MIGHT AND POWER, but beware! thy skull is not in safety, *none are allowed to trespass in our dominions with impunity!*"

"He spied all the neighborhood of Fifth and Shippen streets, and coming up to us he stared at us with his glass saying: 'are you some of the Killing devils?' we ain't nothin' else, said we, and we nabbed him."

"THOU ART A SPY, but if it were thy intention to *inform against us,* BEWARE, TAKE HEED, *and though thy breast should be guarded by a coat of mail, and thy body be shielded by the law and its thousand minions, thou shouldst yet be* HURLED TO HELL!"

The dandy quailed under the awful threat.

"Thy name?"

"Fairman."

"What! DANDY FAIRMAN?"

He remained silent. Robert vacated the chair.

"Now, I've got something of a private nature against you. You know Miss Miffis?"

"I do."

"About two years ago you were at Miss Miffis', Edward Mann was also there, when a poor unfortunate woman came in, and you wanted to have her put out of doors."

"She was a miserable beggar," said Fairman.

"THOU LIEST! she was a poor, but an honest, industrious woman; *but who made her so?* A DANDY, A VILLAIN LIKE THOU ART, A CURSED DOG OF AN ARISTOCRAT! And though thou didst hear her sad tale of woe, *thou didst spurn her and gave her alms like a kick to a dog!* She was then in want and sick, but she soon died, and her daughter, Emma Wildday, is now under the protection and is the heiress of Jacob Snivell, her uncle."

"*The beggar's daughter an heiress!*" cried the dandy in amazement.

"YES, AN HEIRESS, *and may thou be called to account for her mother's wrongs!* KNOW THAT WE FEAR NO ONE, WE SET ALL LAWS AT DEFIANCE, *but lest thou shouldst do harm out of our club,* thou wilt leave thy money and valuables here, and then thou shalt be safely escorted to THE LIMITS OF OUR JURISDICTION!"

A Killer's command, in the Killers' Club, was more than LAW, and an INJUNCTION which no one would have dared disobey. So Fairman gave up watch, glass, rings and money.

"Edward Mann's generosity will serve my stars; I have made a splendid discovery; THE DOLLAR *will work like a* CHARM, THE HEIRESS MUST BE MINE!"

Having been blindfolded, he was led away wiser, if poorer.

THE CONFLAGRATION

LET us enter Robert's oyster cellar, in Third, near Chestnut street.

There stands Robert, busily attending on the comforts of his customers. It was quite a contrast to see so dangerous a man, of such wicked and revolutionising principles, the head of so unruly and disorganising a faction, carrying on such a quiet and peaceable occupation. His public character was cognizant to all, and his receipts were large in consequence; his place was orderly, for he had the *will* and the *power* to keep it quiet, and all knew the fact, therefore, no infringement happened; though he was the head of the Killers, and received his brother Killers with a hearty welcome, yet in business he always separated the chief from the business man; the authorities were well aware of his station at the head of the Club, but the man could not be touched until he flagrantly violated the law, and as the Club was located in Moyamensing, they could not take cognizance of a nuisance existing in that district.

Among other customers, sat a young gentleman at one of the tables reading a newspaper. On a sudden his attention was particularly attracted, and he called on the landlord:

"I say, landlord, what means this paragraph?"

Robert looked at it and read:

"ELOPEMENT EXTRAORDINARY! It appears that a dandy about town, named Fairman, had succeeded in engrafting himself into the good graces of Miss Emma Wildday, the rich heiress—"

"The villain! the dog! But this is a sad affair."

"The heartless, base villain! but go on, sir."

Robert proceeded—"with the aid of a magic dollar in the lady's possession—."

"He has imposed upon her; he has no claim to that dollar," said Robert, in a rage.

"It is a swindling affair," said the young gentleman; "but tell me, sir, how comes it that the little daughter of poor, unfortunate Emma Wildday is a rich heiress?"

"By a lucky turn of fortune, sir, Emma died shortly after her visit to Miss Miffis, and on her death-bed she confided her little Emma to my care."

"Then you are Robert of whom she spoke in such glowing terms at Miss Miffis'?" said the customer.

"I ain't anything else, at your service."

"Give me your hand, I am proud and happy to shake a good and humane man's hand."

"May not your name be Edward Mann, sir, as you seem to know all about the CHARMED DOLLAR?"

"It is, my friend."

"Give me your hand, I am happier than a king at this meeting; I owe you a service, and you have my word that I will serve you with all my power. . . ."

"Leave all to me and be easy."

Edward and Robert parted.

It must be conceded that the discovery of the extraordinary paragraph and the acquaintance of Edward and Robert, was the most fortunate event that could have happened for the benefit of all concerned, designed by a JUST and RULING PROVIDENCE.

Robert, intent on serving Edward and Emma, and on fulfilling his promise, went to the house of Mr. Twiddle, where Emma and her uncle resided. Inquiring for the gentleman, he was called and came.

"Good morning, sir," said Robert, bowing.

Mr. Twiddle but feebly inclined his head in return.

"Sir," added Robert, "I have an important message to deliver to Miss Wildday on pressing business."

"*You have!*" said the man, ironically.

" I have."

"Let me tell you, my friend, that Miss Wildday has no friend of your stamp, and no confidence to receive from a man such as you; you may leave your message."

"*I must see the lady,*" said Robert.

" Who are you?"

"*I! I am Robert the Killer!*"

"You! dog! leave my house!"

"I will; but mark me: *you are a* DAMNED ARISTOCRAT, *and this affront shall be fully repaid! You will yet hear of* ROBERT THE KILLER!"

"Go, dog! John, put this dog out of doors!"

"Don't take the trouble; but mind—ROBERT THE KILLER'S CURSE IS ON THEE AND ON THY HOUSE!"

Robert, wrathy against the purse-proud and overbearing man, was bent on being revenged, but he wished not that the innocent should suffer with the guilty, and he sent the following note to Emma's uncle:

"Mr. Jacob Snivell—*I hasten to pen these few lines to apprise you that a direful calamity is impending over* THE HEARTLESS ARISTOCRAT TWIDDLE'S HOUSE; *therefore be wise and leave it immediately with your niece Emma Wildday.*

A FRIEND."

On the evening of the following day, smoke and flames were seen issuing from Mr. Twiddle's house, in intense and violent columns. The alarm was given—loud cries of fire! fire! were heard in all directions. The State House bell, and all the surrounding bells tolled in a mournful manner, summoning the fire department to rescue the building from the devouring element.

The fire department was soon on the spot, also a vast multitude as spectators, but no assistance could be rendered to the burning building: the incendiary torch had been so well and skilfully applied, that the fire had spread with wonderful rapidity; the flames had communicated from room to room, allowing scarcely time for all the inmates to escape; the furniture, and all the house contained, became in a moment the prey of the flames, and the building became a compact and burning mass.

All exertions were bestowed on the surrounding buildings, which were saved; but Mr. Twiddle's house, with its sumptuous furniture, had disappeared, leaving as vestiges nothing but a blackened heap of bricks.

THE REVENGE WAS COMPLETE.

THE TRIAL FOR ARSON

THE burning of Mr. Twiddle's house under such suspicious circumstances, had caused a stir in the public mind, and the anxiety to discover the incendiary was intense; but of course no one knew, or suspected any one of the deed, except Mr. Twiddle himself, and in his steadfast belief of the guilt of the miscreant, he was eager to foster it on his shoulders, and to endorse it with his oath.

The term *iron-hand* has often been used in speaking of JUSTICE, but we think it admits of a more popular definition, and as it is human, it may well have TWO HANDS, the *iron-hand* and the *golden-hand.* It is a notorious fact that the *iron-hand of* JUSTICE *is only brought to bear on and to smite those persons who are poor and unfortunate,* therefore, unable TO FLATTER AND INTEREST ITS MINISTERS, and the consequence is, *that they are snarled and frowned into prison, while the influential and gold-ladened are certain of a triumphant acquittal and a signal vindication!* AND SUCH IS JUSTICE! *it smiles on the rich but frowns on the poor;* and whatever may be their claims, the two classes stand as far AS POLE TO POLE ASUNDER.

[Robert is convicted of arson, but at the end of the trial produces a pardon, and leaves a free man.]

DÉNOUEMENT

"Edward will have her, she can't say no, I know she won't," said the uncle in high glee.

"Emma, don't be silly; why, girl, the wedding day will be the happiest of your life; you ought to be proud to have such a fine fellow for a husband;" said Miss Miffis, and she placed Emma's hand in Edward's.

At this stage Robert came into the house, and the servant communicating the fact to Mr. Snivell, he gave orders to have him introduced into the parlor.

Mr. Snivell shook hands with him as he entered, and said:

"Miss Miffis, this is Robert, *Robert the Killer,* who was so good to Emma and her mother."

"Robert," said the respectable spinster, tendering her hand, "I am glad to see you; but why Robert *the Killer?* you don't *kill* for a living, I hope?"

"Only to oblige friends," chuckled the uncle.

Robert shook hands with Emma and Edward.

"Robert," said Mr. Snivell, "you must come to our wedding."

"Excuse me, sir," said Robert.

"Not to Edward and Emma's wedding?"

"Edward and Emma!" Robert was illumined with joy and happiness.

"But on one condition, that you'll *kill* nothing but oysters. Though old, we'll dance yet; won't we, Miss Miffis?"

"And drink Edward's and Emma's health and happiness!" said Miss Miffis.

Let us take our leave of the happy group.

Emma had soon forgot Fairman; or she remembered him with indignation, for the deception which he sought to practise was of the blackest character.

VIRTUE *and* HONESTY *are sure to meet with their just* REWARD, *as will* DECEPTION *and* DISSIPATION.

Before laying down the pen, let us mention that Fairman recovered, saw and amended the evil of his ways; he resolved to become a useful member of society and to gain the esteem of the world; he humbly apologized to Mr. Snivell, and Mr. Snivell in return took him under his protection.

Having *said* all that we think we *ought* to say, we rest, bidding the reader who has kindly followed us, an affectionate ADIEU.

21. Things in the Saddle

Illustrations

1. *Mormon 3-Dollar Anti-Bank Note, 1837.*

2. *"The Yankee Pedlar," by John W. Enninger, 1853.*

3. *"Factory Town,"* 1845.

4. *"Railroad Suspension Bridge Near Niagara Falls,"* 1856.

5. "*The Dreadful Accident on the North Pennsylvania Railroad,*" 1857.

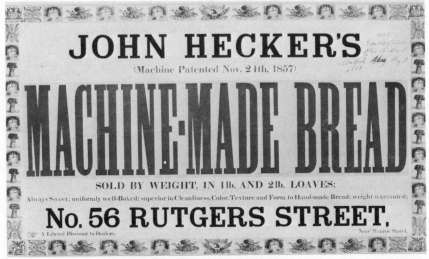

6. *John Hecker's Machine-Made Bread, 1857.*

SELF-PROTECTORS TO TRAVELLERS AND PLANTERS.

THE greatest modern improve-ment in Fire-arms---SELF-COCKING REPEATING PISTOL.

This Pistol can be discharged six times with almost the rapidity of thought. The pistol cocks, the barrel revolves and discharges merely by pulling the trigger. The chamber and barrel are in one piece, and therefore cannot blow apart like some repeating pistols. The construction of the pistol is perfectly simple—they can be drawn from the pocket and used with one hand without the loss of a moment's time in cocking; six shots can be fired as fast as a man can crook his finger. They are no larger than an ordinary pocket pistol.

For travellers, housekeepers, captains, planters, and others, they are an indispensable article, as persons, both male and female, can with this pistol protect their lives or property if attacked by many persons, as one of them is equal to near a dozen of the common kind.

Gentlemen are invited to call at the store of the advertiser and examine the same, as their simplicity, perfect safety, and non-liability to get out of order, will certainly recommend them over all others. For sale wholesale and retail by J. G. BOLEN,
[Feb. 5.] 104 Broadway, between Wall and Pine-streets.

7. *Self Protectors for Travellers and Planters, 1842.*

8. *"The Young Merchants," by William Page.*

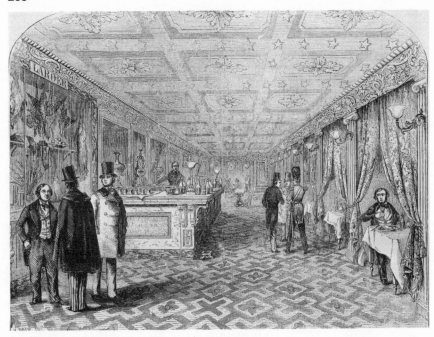

9. *A Broadway, New York, Refreshment Salon, 1854.*

10. *"The Sick Women in Bellevue Hospital, New York,"* 1860.

22. Diary

GEORGE TEMPLETON STRONG

Strong noted in his diary that all of New York was in a dither about the great match race between Fashion and Boston, but that he had no intention of attending.

He was not the sort. A member of a prominent New York family, Strong became a successful Wall Street lawyer, who devoted much of his time to serving on the boards of his alma mater, Columbia College, of Trinity Episcopal Church, of various classical music societies, and, during the Civil War, of the important Sanitary Commission. From his days as a college student to the end of his life, he kept a diary which has become the major source both of what day-to-day life was like for the wealthy classes in America's burgeoning metropolis and of their complex reaction to the increasingly disturbing quality of American life. Perceptive, intelligently opinionated, verbally agile, the diary not only mirrors life in New York, but also demonstrates how concern for urban ills in the early 1850's was overshadowed by growing antislavery sentiment—or, more accurately, by growing animosity toward what was considered Southern aggression.

October 7, 1836

By the way, speaking of *ultraism*, who, in the name of wonder, would have suspected Henry J. Anderson, the upright, steady, stiff, immutable, cool, cautious, rational, judgmatical, reasoning, accurate, mathematical, matter-of-fact, sober, anti-enthusiastic, clear-headed, moneymaking, real-estate-buying, demonstrating Prof. Harry—that incarnation of a right angle—*who* would ever have suspected him of being a furiously enthusiastic Democrat? No—not a Democrat, the expression's certainly too tame,

George Templeton Strong, *Diary*, eds. Allan Nevins and Milton H. Thomas (New York, 1952), Vols. I and II.

but a *"Pas eauto*-crat" (the word's coined for the occasion), an "every man himself-ocrat"—a man who believes in the utter perfectibility of the human race, and regards all law as an encumbrance, a shackle on that freedom which is the birthright of all mankind? Yet such he is—on the very best authority. Trevett has heard him argue on it; he grows perfectly rabid the moment he gets into the subject, e.g., "The fire laws are nuisances—every man has a right to have his house burnt down, and himself in it, if he likes"; "The laws prohibiting omnibusses from Wall Street are atrocious—shameful—*infernal*—" (on this topic he was particularly indignant, and in Trevett's hearing) "a shameful infringement on our liberties." Agrarianism, too, he supports. In religion no one knows his sentiments—they are not far from Deism—though he always speaks with respect of the Bible, and lives a moral life. Who would have thought it of Harry Anderson! ! . . .

April 27, 1837

Matters very bad out of doors. Confidence annihilated, the whole community, big and little, traveling to ruin in a body. Strong fears entertained for the banks, and if they go, God only knows what the consequences will be. Ruin here, and on the other side of the Atlantic, and not only private ruin but political convulsion and revolution, I think. . . .

May 2, 1837

Workmen thrown out of employ by the hundred daily. Business at a stand; the coal mines in Pennsylvania stopped and no fuel in prospect for next winter—delightful prospects, these.

May 3, 1837

Went up to the office at six. Fresh failures, Talbot Olyphant & Co., among them. So they go—smash, crash. Where in the name of wonder is there to be an end of it? Near two hundred and fifty failures thus far! . . .

Locofoco meeting in the Park this morning—and such a meeting! It looked like a convention of loafers from all quarters of the world.

May 4, 1837

Terrible news in Wall Street. [John] Fleming, late president of the Mechanics Bank, found dead in his bed this morning. Some say prussic acid; others (and the coroner's jury) say "mental excitement" and apoplexy.

Anyhow there's a run on the bank—street crowded—more feeling of alarm and despondency in Wall Street than has appeared yet. . . .

May 8, 1837

This affair of the Dry Dock Bank has gone better than I expected, but I fear it will prove the entering wedge to split up all Wall Street. The other banks are generally blamed for not sustaining it, and justly so.

Only imagine that [Uncle Benjamin] should actually have come to such a situation as to be afraid of personal insult if he go into the street! Yet so it is. What can be more dreadful? I can scarcely realize it—as kind and good-hearted and benevolent a man as ever breathed, his character unimpeached and unimpeachable, yet obliged to secure his house from attack and afraid of showing himself. These wretched banks and credit systems and paper wealth; they have done all this.

May 10, 1837

Extensive news in this morning's paper. The banks (except three) have concluded to stop specie payment! ! ! Glory to the Old General! Glory to little Matty, second fiddler to the great Magician! Glory—ay, and double patent glory—to the experiment, the specie currency, and all the glorious humbugs who have inflicted them on us.

Commerce and speculation here have been spreading of late like a card house, story after story and ramification after ramification till the building towered up to the sky and people rolled up their eyes in amazement, but at last one corner gave way and every card that dropped brought down a dozen with it, and *sic transit gloria mundi!*

November 5, 1838

Two things I'm sorry to see in this election: one, the introduction of abolitionism into politics, which may play the devil with our institutions and which is at any rate a new force brought into the system, with an influence now almost inappreciable, but which may grow greater and greater till it brings the whole system into a state of discord and dissension, from which heaven preserve it! The other is the increasing tendency of the Whig party to absorb all the wealth and respectability, and of the Democratic (so called) to take in all the loaferism of the nation, a tendency which may bring us finally to be divided into two great factions, the rich and the poor; and then for another French Revolution, so far as American steadiness and good sense can imitate French folly and bloodthirstiness.

June 30, 1839

Got into Stonington bright and early—and whizzed off in style. . . .
It wasn't altogether pleasant, though, for I contrived to get my eyes full
of sparks from the engine and I never suffered more in that way in my life.
Didn't get rid of the trespassers till after dinner, just as I had made up
my mind to go to Dr. Somebody—and recover his fee by a suit against the
company. It's wonderful that such a nuisance isn't stopped.

July 1, 1839

Mary and *pater meus* left [for New York] this afternoon. Saw 'em
comfortably off. It's a great sight to see a large train get under way. I
know of nothing that would more strongly impress our great-great-
grandfathers with an idea of their descendants' progress in science. As to
the engine, the most pithy and expressive epithet I ever heard applied to
it is "Hell-in-Harness." Just imagine such a concern rushing unexpectedly
by a stranger to the invention on a dark night, whizzing and rattling and
panting, with its fiery furnace gleaming in front, its chimney vomiting
fiery smoke above, and its long train of cars rushing along behind like
the body and tail of a gigantic dragon—or like the d——l himself—and all
darting forward at the rate of twenty miles an hour. Whew!

February 3, 1840

This was not one of the gunpowdery, irregular, flashy fires that have
been so common of late, governed by none of the acknowledged rules of
the art, but a good, steady, old-fashioned conflagration, in which the
dramatic interest was well sustained throughout, and fire and water were
"head and head" till the grand finale when the walls tumbled down in
various directions with a great crash, and then fire triumphed, which as
the hero of the piece it was very proper and perfectly regular that it
should do. On the whole, this was a very fair fire. I'm getting quite a
connoisseur.

It's very amusing to notice the view the loaferage (i.e., the majority
of the lookers-on at fires) take of the subject. They consider it a sort of
grand exhibition (admission gratis) which they have a perfect right to
look at from any point they like and to choose the best seats to see the
performance; the interests of the owners never seem to enter their heads,
and any attempt to keep them back, or to keep a passage open, or any
other effort to save property by which their freedom of locality or locomotion is impaired, they consider an unwarrantable interference, of
course. . . .

But the state of things is really too bad. Here, in the two first days of last week $2,500,000 of property were destroyed by fire. Now comes another, the loss of which can't be under $80,000, and as to the little fires that have taken place during the interval, I don't take count of them. One committee, appointed by the merchants on Saturday, at their meeting, to devise means for stopping this extraordinary inflammability, don't seem yet to have done much. From all I've seen of fires of late, I'm fully convinced that our fire department is utterly and shamefully incompetent. The engines are not powerful enough to throw water to any considerable height, the hose are so full of rips and holes that a third of the water must be lost, the hydrants never seem to have any water in them, a large part of the firemen do nothing but bustle about in their caps, swear at everybody and try to look tremendous, the engines are never worked for five minutes in succession, and everything in short is as badly conducted as possible. It's a wonder to me at every large fire that half the city don't burn up; some night it will, and then they'll get to work to reform in earnest.

May 8, 1840

Tonight is the anniversary of that greatest military operation of the present age, that most heroic achievement of ancient or modern warfare— surpassing all "affairs" on record from the siege of Troy down to the Battle of Brokow—to wit, the raising of the siege of Fort Meigs, when the Britishers were smitten hip and thigh by the immortal Harrison. Candidly, I never heard of the affair till the last three months. But that only shows what ignoramuses we are. Just to think of the besieging army's firing some two hundred and fifty shot in one day—and actually killing one man and wounding ten! What a regular fire-eater the old Hero must be!

However, the loaferage of New York not being particularly well versed in the history of this or any other age, the Battle of Fort Meigs does as well to tickle them with as anything else, and to be sure the procession and fuss tonight surpassed in spirit and numbers anything of the sort that I ever saw here—except during the excitement of election. The procession seemed interminable. I thought as the Irishman did that somebody must have cut off the other end of it. Banners, log cabins on wheels, barrels supposed to be full of hard cider, and all sorts of glories adorned its march. Getting into Niblo's wasn't to be thought of; not more than a third of the procession accomplished it. The Locos, of course, disgraced themselves as usual, by a fierce attack on one banner in particular—representing Matty shinning away from the White House with O. K. under it, i.e., "Off to Kinderhook." Brick bats were thrown and heads broken and an attack was made on the Garden (subsequently), but the siege was raised by a few sticks and stones dropped on the heads of the assailants from above. Altogether it was a grand affair—Harrison forever!

October 11, 1840

I took a walk up to Eighth Street and down again. It's a pity we've no street but Broadway that's fit to walk in of an evening. The street is always crowded, and whores and blackguards make up about two-thirds of the throng. That's one of the advantages of uptown; the streets there are well paved, well lighted, and decently populated.

March 28, 1841

Went to church. Heard [the Reverend John Murray] Forbes this morning. Matty Van Buren was there, in the pew of his brother president, Duer of Columbia College, and by a curious coincidence the subject of the sermon was the spiritual blessings that flow from retiracy and seclusion for a season from the busy world and the cares of active life. If I wasn't nearsighted I've no doubt I should have observed Matty wince considerably.

April 5, 1841

Mournful news this morning. General Harrison died on Saturday night, a few hours less than one month from his inauguration. The news was most unexpected to me, for I didn't suppose him very seriously ill, and he was said on Saturday to be recovering. I confess I never was so sincerely sorry for the death of any one whom I knew of merely as a *public* character. Though not possessed of any great talent, I believe he was a good, honest, benevolent, right-minded man—qualities far more rare among our political people.

September 23, 1842

Left for the Yankee Metropolis Saturday afternoon in the *Cleopatra.* Beautiful evening, and I smoked cigars on deck during the greater part of it. They burn anthracite coal on board that boat—it's dangerous but cheap, and that's the main point. I didn't like it a bit, for we went off at near twenty miles an hour (we were abreast of the *Oldfield* at eight o'clock), and with two great flickering, waving streams of pale yellow fire pouring out of flues it looked downright awful.

June 22, 1843

Entered into conversation with a man who told me he'd never been on board a steamboat before—rather an intelligent person, too, from Delaware county. Hitherto "father had gone down to York, but father was gittin' old." Such greenness in an enlightened American I'd never dreamed possible and I involuntarily felt my pockets, in doubt whether he wasn't a wolf in sheep's clothing, bent on abstracting my valuables. Had a curiosity to ascertain the sensations of the subject on first experiencing this novel kind of locomotion. He said it made him kind o' dizzy. Considering our nomadic habits as a people, I regard this person as a curiosity deserving the attention of the scientific world.

November 18, 1843

Took tea in Murray Street and went with Templeton to the *First Philharmonic*.

Great crowd: all the aristocracy and "gig respectability" and wealth and beauty and fashion of the city there on the spot an hour beforehand. For myself, being superior to such vanities I selected the little side gallery where I could look down in a calm and philosophical manner on the splendors below, and especially upon George Anthon making very strong love apparently to one of the ——s! and upon Schermerhorn making himself generally ornamental, and Fanning Tucker trying to devise outlets for his legs and barking his knees on the bench next in front of him, and Mr. Wilmerding dozing off regularly at the soft passages and waking up with a jump at the loud ones, and so forth.

Beethoven's Symphony in A was the *opus magnum* of the evening. . . . I hold this the finest symphony I've heard yet.

February 2, 1844

Read the article attributed to Dickens in the *Foreign Quarterly* on American poets, over which all the papers are going into severe paroxysms of patriotic wrath. Don't see why they can't keep cool. That we have no national school of poetry is very true, but it's our misfortune and not a fault, for we've no materials to make one out of. We've neither a legendary past nor a poetic present. Large mountains, extensive prairies, tall cataracts, long rivers, millions of dirty acres of every cosmographical character don't "constitute a state" for purposes of poetry; but "men, high-minded men" and their memories.

May 11, 1844

The City of Brotherly Love is reduced to a state of quietude by dint of hostile demonstrations from the Governor of the Commonwealth and eloquent appeals to the public by the Fathers of the City. Such a pitiable scene of feebleness, irresolution, and old-grannyism in general as the civic potentates of that place have enacted for the amusement of posterity isn't to be found anywhere. . . . An amusing commentary on the whole affair is the resolution adopted by acclamation at the grand meeting held after all the damage had been done, that the majority of rioters consisted of small boys too young to know how naughty they were; and that all parents and guardians were requested to keep said small boys at home, send 'em early to bed or hide their stockings. Doubtless it was a sensible practical person that moved that resolution.

May 12, 1844

Walked uptown tonight. Looked at Grace Church. They won't consecrate it this fall, I think, from present appearances. [James] Renwick [Jr.] is a clever fellow and his church looks very well on paper, but I fear the practical embodiment of his conception, the church itself, will be a botch. He's hampered for money and the plan's an ambitious one and the effect of the structure will probably be that of an attempt at the sumptuous on slender means, which is always undignified, and generally unsuccessful.

May 27, 1844

The sole shadow of a chance of nomination that John Tyler ever possessed is gone. Don't much care; "country's risin', Clay and Frelinghuysen, quite surprizin', give the Loco pisen," and so on. It don't matter much which Loco is selected to be made a martyr of. . . .

Whether the jacobinical spirit and the antipathy to law and order and the overthrow of everything worth preserving, which is the unconscious principle of the one party, and the temper and final result of its unchecked development, be worse than commercial, speculating, bank-swindling, money-worshipping *primum mobile* of the other is a question.

Certainly since the downfall of Federalism there has been no conservative party in the country which has ventured to avow any higher aim than the cultivation of tariffs and credit systems, trade and manufactures.

Its unchecked development would make us a commercial aristocracy which is mean enough everywhere, but here 'twould be a fluctuating mushroom aristocracy and the meanest the world has seen yet.

November 8, 1844

. . . the illustrious Pork is President-Elect.

And the Whig Party is defunct, past all aid from warm blankets, galvanic batteries, and the Humane Society; it's quite dead and the sooner it's buried the better. What form of life will be generated from its decomposition remains to be seen.

Two causes have mainly brought all this to pass: Native Americanism, and the great difference between the candidates in conspicuousness and vulnerability. Everybody could talk about Clay's long career as a prominent politician and find something in it to use against him fairly or falsely, while his opponent was impregnable from the fact that he'd never done or said anything of importance to anybody. . . .

Henceforth I think political wire-pullers will be careful how they nominate prominent and well-known men for the Presidency; they'll find it safer to pick up the first man they may find in the street. . . .

March 31, 1845

Somebody was recommending . . . to get out a Greek Testament with English notes mainly for the benefit of Harper's friends of the Methodist clerical corps, who, being generally men of rather limited education, would find it much more convenient than the Latin notes and commentaries that belong to most standard editions. "Don't," said Harper; "they're nice people, they are—but they all think the New Testament was written in English, and it would only unsettle their minds and throw them into horrid perplexities to be undeceived; they do very well as they are—let 'em alone."

December 23, 1845

Well, last night I spent . . . at Mrs. Mary Jones's great ball. Very splendid affair—"the ball of the season," I heard divers bipeds more or less asinine observe in regard to it. Two houses open—standing supper table—"dazzling array of beauty and fashions." Polka for the first time brought under my inspection. It's a kind of insane Tartar jig performed to a disagreeable music of an uncivilized character. Everybody was there and I loafed about in a most independent manner and found it less of a bore than I had expected. Mrs. Jones, the hostess, is fat but comely; indeed, there's enough of her to supply a small settlement with wives.

December 24, 1845

The practical lesson I've learned from my experience of the last two nights is that if this be "going out," I shall come in again and stay in; that if going into Society consists in habitually participating in such comfortless, joyless, insipid exhibitions of extravagance without results and folly without amusement, I have shewn more wisdom in staying at home hitherto than I gave myself credit for. Dissipation it is in the strictest sense of the word. Rational speech there is none, and none is expected; people leave their common sense in the dressing rooms with their cloaks and hats, and one finds himself the next day unfit for business and wholly stupified and done up without having had anything in the way either of amusement or edification to show for it. So I'll go to no more balls. May people who give them bear the painful announcement with resignation!

September 20, 1848

At Niblo's last night (Astor Place). *London Assurance,* clever comedy, played middling well. Driven nearly desperate by the mosquitoes all the rest of the night as the small hours drew on. I commenced promenading the room with my eyeglass on my nose, candle in one hand and handkerchief in the other, "deer stalking" on a small scale. Game shy—bagged three mosquitoes and one cockroach and finally sunk into slumber a little before four. Desperately tired and altogether good for nothing all today.

May 11, 1849

Row last night at the Opra House, whereof I was a spectator. Mob fired upon, some twelve or fifteen killed and four times as many wounded, a real battle, for the b'hoys fought well and charged up to the line of infantry after they had been fired upon. Prospect of a repetition of the performances tonight on a larger scale, for the blackguards swear they'll have vengeance. The houses of the gentlemen who signed the invitation to Macready to perform last night threatened. Judge [William] Kent and Mr. Ruggles and some six or seven others of them live on Union Square and that will, therefore, very probably be a scene of disturbance. I'm going up now to clean my pistols, and if possible to get my poor wife's portrait out of harm's way.

May 12, 1849

Mrs. Ruggles was brought up to our front parlor, where an extempore bed was rigged for her. She hadn't left her room for two or three months before. Poor Ellen's portrait and some other precious things were sent up.

Spent the night till about one partly with Mr. Ruggles and Judge Kent and partly in reconnoitering the view of operations at Eighth Street and Astor Place. Everything looked much in earnest there—guns loaded and matches lighted—everything ready to sweep the streets with grape at a minute's notice, and the police and troops very well disposed to do it whenever they should be told. The mob were in a bitter bad humor but a good deal frightened, and the only overt acts that were committed, on the Bowery side, were met by prompt measures and with instant success. Some of the cavalry were badly hit with paving stones, but as soon as the Unwashed were informed that unless they forthwith took themselves off they'd be treated with a little artillery practice, they scampered. . . .

June 15, 1849

There's that prodigious Twenty-first Street house staring me in the face, and saying from every one of its drawing rooms and boudoirs: "We shall have to be furnished next fall." . . .

It's a terrible daily source of anxiety and depression. . . . Ruskin is right—no man's happiness was ever promoted by the splendors of rosewood and brocatelle and ormolu and tapestry carpets; they never give pleasure to their possessor or to those who come and see them. . . . It is a slavery to which we submit in the meekest silence, though it darkens life with needless cares and shuts us out from other and real enjoyments that might be purchased with the wasted cost of this pernicious trumpery. . . .

July 31, 1849

A terrible business will be the tottle of the bills growing out of that charming specimen of domestic architecture. The primal curse that condemned man to earn his bread by the sweat of his brow was heavy, but far heavier is the curse that man has laid upon himself by the artificial habits and conventional necessities and social fictions of the system of luxury and extravagance and ostentation to which he has bound himself in these latter days. Toil and labor may be happiness; they are so to a healthy mind; but there never is aught but wretchedness in the bitter, corrosive cares and sickening anxieties of debt, of position too expensive for the real abilities of its occupant.

July 11, 1850

The President died at half-past ten Tuesday evening. A very unhappy event, not only because he was a good and upright man, such as is uncommon in high office, but because everybody North and South had a vague sort of implicit confidence in him, which would have enabled him to guide us through our present complications much better than his "accidental" successor, of whom nobody knows much, and in whom no party puts any very special trust or faith.

September 2, 1850

Jenny Lind has arrived, and was received with such a spontaneous outbreak of rushing, and crowding, and hurrahing, and serenading as this city has never seen before. The streets round the Irving House blocked up with a mob night and day; horses hardly permitted to carry her through the streets, so vehemently did the mob thirst for the honor of drawing her carriage, and so on. Really it's very strange—Miss Jenny is a young lady of very great musical taste, and possessed of a larynx so delicately organized that she can go up to A *in alto* with brilliancy and precision, and sing with more effect than any other living performer. Furthermore, she is a good, amiable, benevolent woman, fully equal, I dare say, to the average of our New York girls; and having in her vocal apparatus a fortune of millions, she devotes a liberal share of it to works of charity. But if the greatest man that has lived for the last ten centuries were here in her place, the uproar and excitement could not be much greater and would probably be much less. . . .

January 8, 1851

Henry Long, the interesting black representative of the Rights of Man, adjudged this morning to be lawfully held to service and delivered up to the Philistines of Virginia, notwithstanding the rhetoric of John Jay. . . .

January 16, 1851

Bad accident in this street between Fifth and Sixth Avenues yesterday. The houses Tom Emmet and Ferris Pell (or rather his widow) were putting up and on which the Bank has a rather large loan, tumbled down spontaneously, killing or mangling and mutilating some two dozen people. Cause, the criminal economy of the contractor. Saw some of the *mortar*, a greasy, pulverulent earth or clay, apparently far less tenacious than an average specimen of Broadway mud. The contractor, who certified to the sufficiency of his work three hours before the crash, has discreetly run away.

May 27, 1851

Tremendous row at Hoboken yesterday; a battle of the peoples, like Leipzig. German loaferism warring with the Aaron Burrs of New York, the gutterhorn soaplocks and shortboys of the wharves and their Irish allies. Some lives lost, and strong possibility that the fight may be renewed here.

Mr. Ruggles's affairs worse and worse and worse and worse, and as he falls he will propagate ruin and spread desolation and devastation around him. I wish some new nineteenth century saint would arise and preach a curse upon all credit systems, a crusade against negotiable paper, and proclaim all the woes of the Apocalyptic Babylon against that complex work of devilish ingenuity whereby ruin, bankruptcy, and dishonor are made so fearfully familiar to this enlightened age; the system that makes the utmost fruit of steady industry vulgar and cheap when compared with the glittering results that form exceptions only to its legitimate and usual result, but yet occur often enough to lure the multitude and make us a nation of gamblers, easily classified as a minority of millionaires sprinkled through a majority of bankrupt beggars.

God deliver me from *debt!* Yet the insolvent debtor, I suppose, cares but little for the incubus, as a general rule, after he has become resigned to the conviction that it can't be thrown off, and that he must live under it as he best may. That is the worst of our wretched "financial" system. It degrades, debases, demoralizes its victims. They look men in the face whom they have ruined by breaking their promises, and have nothing to say but that it was a "business transaction." It dissolves out all the sterling integrity there may be in the great mass of people, and leaves the dross and dirt behind. . . .

July 7, 1851
Talk of the ennobling pursuits of literature, historic research, art, music, the elevating influence of investigations into natural science, the noble object of reviving a fit and reverent style of church architecture, and the other subjects which the better class of cultivated men select as their business or their relaxation—they are all good. But . . . it strikes me that most "liberal pursuits," no matter how purifying to the tastes and invigorating to the intellect, are something like a wretched waste of time and perversion of talent and an insane misapplication of energy and industry, while men and women and children in multiplying thousands lie rotting alive, body and soul at once, in those awful catacombs of disease and crime, and even the question how to save them is yet unsolved.

We have our Five Points, our emigrant quarters, our swarms of seamstresses to whom their utmost toil in monotonous daily drudgery gives only bare subsistence, a life barren of hope and of enjoyment; our hordes of dock thieves, and of children who live in the streets and by them.

No one can walk the length of Broadway without meeting some hideous troop of ragged girls, from twelve years old down, brutalized already almost beyond redemption by premature vice, clad in the filthy refuse of the rag-picker's collections, obscene of speech, the stamp of childhood gone from their faces, hurrying along with harsh laughter and foulness on their lips that some of them have learned by rote, yet too young to understand it; with thief written in their cunning eyes and whore on their depraved faces, though so unnatural, foul, and repulsive in every look and gesture, that that last profession seems utterly beyond their aspirations. On a rainy day such crews may be seen by dozens. They haunt every other crossing and skulk away together, when the sun comes out and the mud is dry again. And such a group I think the most revolting object that the social diseases of a great city can produce. A gang of blackguard boys is lovely by the side of it.

Meantime, philanthropists are scolding about the fugitive slave law, or shedding tears over the wretched niggers of the Carolinas who have to work and to eat their victuals on principles inconsistent with the rights of man, or agitating because the unhanged scoundrels in the City Prison occupy cells imperfectly ventilated. "Scholars" are laboriously writing dissertations for the Historical Society on the First Settlement of the Township of Squankum. . . . And what am I doing, I wonder? I'm neither scholar nor philanthropist nor clergyman, nor in any capacity a guide or ruler of the people, to be sure—there is that shadow of an apology for my sitting still. But if Heaven will permit and enable me, I'll do something in the matter before I die—to have helped one dirty vagabond child out of such a pestilential sink would be a thing one would not regret when one came to march out of this world—and if one looks at FACTS, would be rather more of an achievement than the writing another *Iliad*.

May 15, 1852

Thursday evening, Charles and Eleanor and James Lydig and Lydig Suydam, Walter Cutting and Ellie and I went off to 78 Twenty-sixth Street and had a private interview with Mrs. Fish and her knocking spirits, and then came back here and had some supper. The knockers are much talked of now, from Edmonds' extraordinary publications in the *Shekinah*. One . . . is meant to be a statement of facts, a vision of Heaven and Hell in which Benjamin Franklin and William Penn and Sir Isaac Newton and the late Mrs. Edmonds appear and express their views. Sir Isaac informs the Judge that he made a great mistake about the Law of

Gravitation and the Judge adds a note stating that he had been convinced that it was so for a great many years. . . . There is a stout little duodecimo volume consisting of "communications" from George Washington, Jefferson, Andrew Jackson, Margaret Fuller, and a great many other people, all of them writing very remarkably alike, and most of them very questionable grammar. People publish statements of extraordinary visitations made them by six individuals "in ancient costume," who promenade about for a long while and finally disappear, leaving Hebrew and Sanscrit MSS behind them, not specially relevant to anything. Edgar A. Poe spells out bad imitations of the poetry he wrote while in the flesh. Tables loaded with heavy weights are made to dance vigorously. . . . It is a strange chapter in the history of human credulity at all events, and as such worth investigating.

July 2, 1852
    We shall have to get up a volunteer force in this city before long, a sort of Holy Vehm or Vigilance Committee, if rowdyism continues to grow on us at its present rate. The Common Council is notoriously profligate and corrupt; the police force partly awed by the blackguards of the brothel and groggery, partly intimate with them. And if some drunken ruffian is arrested, he's sure to be discharged by some justice or alderman, who feels that it won't do to lose the support of the particular gang to which he belongs. An organized amateur society of supporters of law would be wholesome, an association that should employ agents to prosecute violence and corruption vigorously, and to follow up with the penalties of the law those of its ministers who are too timid or dishonest to enforce it. It might not effect a cure, though, unless it went further and took the law into its own hands. . . .

July 29, 1852
    Heard that the *Henry Clay* had been burnt. . . .
    The loss of life seems to have been fearful, and the transaction a case of wholesale murder. Reckless racing leading to mischief, and then panic and frenzy among the passengers, imbecility in the officers, and murderous absence even of *boats* to save a dozen or two.
    July 30. Went up by railroad last night. The funeral took place this morning, attended by nearly every one on the Point; a melancholy business it was. I shall never forget poor Bailey's figure, and look of apathy— almost of stupor; and the three little boys clinging round him and crying, unnoticed; the still sunlight on the cemetery, the burial service, the multi-

tude of sad faces, the two coffins with which we all felt that all the life and hope and heart of one man were sinking into the earth to wither into dust. And all this and so much beside, *that the Henry Clay might beat the Armenia.*

It is time that this drowning and burning to death of babies and young girls and old men to gratify the vanity of steamboat captains were stopped. I would thank God for the privilege of pulling the cap over the eyes of the captain and owners of this boat, and feel as I completed my hangman's office that I had not lived utterly in vain. . . .

The scene at the wreck yesterday morning was hideous: near thirty bodies exposed along the shore—many children among them.

And some enterprising undertakers from Yonkers and New York had sent up their stock of coffins on speculation.

"Looking for deceased friend, sir?" "Buying a coffin, sir?" "Only five dollars, sir, and warranted."

Public feeling is very strong now. But it will die out within the week. These scoundrels will never be punished, not even indicted. *Damn them!* No, I retract that, for God knows we all stand in need of something less than the rigor of justice. But a thousand years or so of fire and brimstone after hanging in this world, would be a moderate award of retribution. . . .

September 27, 1852

Count Sartiges is married to a Miss Thorndike of Boston, or rather a minister plenipotentiary is married to $100,000. He's a beast, and proposed "an intrigue" to Mrs. H., at Newport, pending this engagement, and apologized on being called to account, and pleaded ignorance of the usages of the country.

February 16, 1853

Visit from Edward A. Strong this morning, discussing the drunkenness, whoremongering, insubordination, and total worthlessness of poor Bob [Strong], and with much feeling and distress. Poor Bob!—and poor young America generally, from Jem Pendleton and the "Pup-Club" down. Was there ever among the boys of any city so much gross dissipation redeemed by so little culture and so little manliness and audacity even of the watchman-fighting sort? It has grown to be very bad, the tone of morals and manners has, even among the better class of young men about town.

March 11, 1853

Stocks down. Wonder whether I'd better invest some loose savings in another Erie bond at present prices, or wait for a farther depression?

Alas, alas, alas, for all the dreams of former times, the dreams to which this journal bears witness! Is it the doom of all men in this nineteenth century to be weighed down with the incumbrance of a desire to make money and save money, all their days? I suppose if my career is prosperous, it will be spent in the thoughtful, diligent accumulation of dollars, till I suddenly wake up to the sense that the career is ended and the dollars dross. So are we gradually carried into the social currents that belong to our time, whether it be the tenth century, or this cold-blooded, interest-calculating age of our own. . . .

May 7, 1853

Another murderous *noyade* on the New Haven Railroad yesterday. More than fifty lives lost; a car full of people pitched over an open draw into the Norwalk River, as a trap with its rats is soused into a wash-tub, by the brute stolidity of the engineer, who didn't see the appointed signal that told him to pull up. Or quite as truly by the guilty negligence of the directors who reappointed this man after he'd been dismissed two years ago for causing an accident by some piece of gross recklessness. What is to be done? . . . I should have thought the surviving passengers and the good people of Norwalk far from clearly unjustifiable in this case had they administered Lynch Law to the criminal on the spot. . . .

July 6, 1854

Wall Street all agog with the fraud on the New Haven Railroad Company by its President Robert Schuyler, whose failure was announced last week. A swindle of near two millions, by no nameless money-making speculator, but by one of our "first" people in descent and social position and supposed wealth.

October 8, 1855

Ellie has heard Rachel tonight in *Les Horaces*. Unlike most people, she is able to retain some appearance, at least, of moderation and sense, in speaking of that artiste. For polite society generally the sound of her name is the signal for a display of mental alienation; persons generally discreet and accustomed to use language with ordinary accuracy babble the ecstatic exaggerations of very green school-girls and excited chambermaids.

May 28, 1856

Never was the country in such a crazy state as just now. Civil war impending over Kansas. . . . I believe civilization at the South is retrograde and that the Carolinas are decaying into barbarism. Brooks comes on Sumner at his desk unawares, stuns him with a cudgel, and belabors the prostrate orator till the cudgel breaks and splinters, and Southern editors and Congressmen talk about the "chivalry," "gallantry," and manliness of the act, and they're getting up a testimonial for Brooks in Charleston.

May 29, 1856

No new vagaries from the wild men of the South since yesterday. The South is to the North nearly what the savage Gaelic race of the Highlands was to London *tempore* William and Mary, *vide* Macaulay's third volume; except that they've assumed to rule their civilized neighbors instead of being oppressed by them, and that the simple, barbaric virtues of their low social development have been thereby deteriorated.

A few fine specimens have given them a prestige the class don't deserve. We at the North are a busy money-making democracy, comparatively law-abiding and peace-loving, with the faults (among others) appropriate to traders and workers. A rich Southern aristocrat who happens to be of fine nature, with the self-reliance and high tone that life among an aristocracy favors, and culture and polish from books and travel, strikes us (not as Brooks struck Sumner but) as something different from ourselves, more ornamental and in some respects better. He has the polish of a highly civilized society, with the qualities that belong to a ruler of serfs. Thus a notion has got footing here that "Southern gentlemen" are a high-bred chivalric aristocracy, something like Louis XIV's noblesse, with grave faults, to be sure, but on the whole, very gallant and generous, regulating themselves by "codes of honor" (that are *wrong*, of course, but very grand); not rich, but surrounded by all the elements of real refinement. Whereas I believe they are, in fact, a race of lazy, ignorant, coarse, sensual, swaggering, sordid, beggarly barbarians, bullying white men and breeding little niggers for sale.

May 30, 1856

On my way up at eight, I stopped at the Tabernacle, where the citizens of New York were summoned to meet and declare their sentiments about Sumner and the South. A vast crowd, earnest, unanimous, and made up of people who don't often attend political gatherings. Significant that John A. Stevens called the meeting to order and old Griswold presided; men not given to fits of enthusiasm or generous sympathy, unlike to be prominent in anything wherein the general voice of the community does not sustain them. Evarts read the resolutions, which seemed discreetly framed and not intemperate. The meeting was prepared to swallow much stronger language. The roar of the great assemblage when Sumner's name occurred, and its spontaneous outburst of groaning and hissing at the sound of "Preston S. Brooks" impressed me. They seemed expressions of deep and strong feeling. I guess the North is roused at last.

23. Memoirs and Writings

CASSIUS MARCELLUS CLAY

As Southern aristocrat, deist, and practicing politician, Clay was an anomalous abolitionist, but abolition had no doughtier—and in some ways no more embarrassing—a champion. Clay's position, complex and atypical but not contradictory, was based on a sense of the practical economic hardships that slavery brought to most Southerners and on a rationalistic moral condemnation of slavery. He was quite willing to brawl and fight duels—he always wore a bowie knife and two pistols—to protect his right to be heard, but he staunchly denied that one could espouse a "higher law doctrine" on slavery and expect the protection of the state. When the United States declared war against Mexico, he went to fight for patriotic and political reasons, though he had determinedly opposed the annexation of Texas as slave state. A wealthy planter, he early aimed his political appeal to the small farmer and workingman he saw victimized by slavery. Admitting his own repugnance to racial amalgamation, he insisted that full social and political equality must be given blacks. Returning to the United States after serving as Lincoln's ambassador to Russia, his later years had a real-life Faulknerian Gothic quality: progressively deserted by family and friends and burdened with fits of insanity, he turned his decaying plantation into a fortress against the enemies by whom he felt surrounded. At eighty-four he married a fifteen-year-old poor white girl who soon deserted him; on his deathbed he used his pistol to shoot flies off his bedroom wall.

Clay published his antislavery opinions in 1844 in *The True American* in Lexington, Kentucky. A "gentlemanly mob" took advantage of Clay's illness

Cassius M. Clay, *The Life of Cassius Marcellus Clay, Memoirs, Writings and Speeches* (Cincinnati, 1886), 78–85. *The Writings of Cassius Marcellus Clay, including Speeches and Addresses*, edited with a Preface and a Memoir, Horace Greeley, ed. (New York, 1848), 203–206, 221–224, 256–258, 284–285.

in 1845 to pack his presses and type off to Cincinnati from where the paper continued to be published for a few months. The *Memoirs* were written in Clay's late years and published in 1886. In them he remembered with pride and amusement how he had once been introduced at a banquet of Philadelphia Negroes: "Cassius Clay—Liberator: Though he has a white skin he has a very black heart."

MEMOIRS BY CASSIUS M. CLAY

When I was in the Legislature of Kentucky, Sprigg was an old representative from Shelby County—"a good fellow," as the phrase goes, but quite quarrelsome, and the hero of many fights. He seemed to think himself called upon to have a "muss" with me especially. For, as my mother says in one of her letters to me, I was not always mild in my mode of statement. Some words passed in the House, and it was thought that Sprigg would challenge me. As other fights of mine were tragic, so this one was quite comic. Sprigg was a dear lover of the State beverage—"old Bourbon"—which, as elsewhere, here was apt to loosen the tongue. So, on one occasion, he revealed to me, confidentially, how he had always been triumphant in personal rencounters. He approached his antagonist, when a fight was inevitable, in a mild and conciliatory manner, dealt him a sharp blow, and followed that up with unrelenting severity till he was whipped. "Thus," said he, "size and strength amount to nothing against mind!" Sprigg had no doubt forgotten that he had ever revealed to me his system of tactics. So, when the House adjourned, as we both boarded at the same hotel, and the weather was cool, I found Sprigg sitting on the far side of the fire-grate, and several members of the Legislature present in the same room. As soon as Sprigg, who was evidently awaiting my arrival, saw me, he advanced past all these gentlemen toward me, with a pleasant look, without speaking. I remembered his methods; and, when he got within reach, without a word on either side, I gave him a severe blow in the face, and brought him staggering to the floor. As fast as he would rise—for I played with him as a cat with a mouse—I repeated my blows; allowing him always to rise, as I felt myself greatly an overmatch for him, and would not strike him when down. When the bystanders saw the unequal fight, and felt that Sprigg, who was a notorious bully, was fully punished, one of them caught him by the coat-tail (fine delicate broad-cloth was then fashionable), and tearing his coat to the very collar, pulled him away; and thus ended the set-to. The upshot was that Sprigg, the aggressor, was severely punished—eyes blacked, nose bleeding, and coat torn; whilst I stood smiling, without a touch.

Sprigg laid by for several days; and all thought now, at least, a duel was inevitable. After a while he ventured out, with his eyes marked with wide black rings. Approaching me, smiling, with outstretched hand to show peace, he said: "Clay, old fellow, here's my hand. I taught you my tactics, and you have beaten your master at his own game." Of course, I accepted his hand, and we remained good friends. Poor Sprigg! he was elected to Congress—that school of demoralization—still patronized "old Bourbon;" and, in a fight with an Irishman, lost his eye, or his nose, I do not remember which, and that was the last I have ever heard of him. . . .

Of course, what influence I had with my compact body of personal friends—among laboring men mostly—went with me for Davis. Wickliffe, in canvassing, was in the habit of reading a "hand-bill" in his own behalf, without naming another "hand-bill" which refuted his friend's statement. In Garrett Davis's absence, I took the liberty to interrupt him, and, by his permission, to say: "That hand-bill," which he had just read, "was proven untrue by another of good authority." He then would resume his remarks. After this had occurred several times, he sent for Samuel M. Brown, late of New Orleans, who was post-office traveling-agent under Charles A. Wickliffe, his relative, then Postmaster-General under John Tyler. Brown was soon on the ground. He was an old Whig, of social character, strong physique, and, in a word, a political bully. He it was who had the fight with Thos. Moore, the Democratic Congressman at Harrodsburg; and of whom it was said that he had "forty fights, and never lost a battle." At Russell's Cave, in Fayette County, when Mr. Wickliffe repeated the usual rôle, I interrupted him again, as before, saying: "That hand-bill has been proven untrue." At the moment, Brown gave me the "damned lie," and struck me simultaneously with his umbrella. I knew the man, and that it meant a death-struggle. I at once drew my Bowie-knife; but, before I could strike, I was seized from behind, and borne by force about fifteen feet from Brown, who, being now armed with a Colt's revolver, cried: "Clear the way, and let me kill the damned rascal." The way was speedily cleared, and I stood isolated from the crowd. Now, as Brown had his pistol bearing upon me, I had either to run or advance. So, turning my left side toward him, with my left arm covering it, so as to protect it to that extent, I advanced rapidly on him, knife in hand. Seeing I was coming, he knew very well that nothing but a fatal and sudden shot could save him. So he held his fire; and, taking deliberate aim, just as I was in arm's reach, he fired at my heart. I came down upon his head with a tremendous blow, which

Memoirs and Writings ★ 289

would have split open an ordinary skull; but Brown's was as thick as that of an African. This blow laid his skull open about three inches to the brain, indenting it, but not breaking the textures; but it so stunned him that he was no more able to fire, but feebly attempted to seize me. The conspirators now seized me, and held both arms above my elbows, which only allowed me to strike with the fore-arm, as Brown advanced upon me. I was also struck with hickory sticks and chairs. But, finding I was likely to get loose, they threw Brown over the stone-fence. This fence, which inclosed the yard near the steep descent to the cave and spring, was built of limestone, about two feet high on the upper side, but perhaps seven or eight on the lower side. So Brown had a terrible fall, which ended the contest.

Raising my bloody knife, I said: "I repeat that the hand-bill was proven a falsehood; and I stand ready to defend the truth." But, neither Mr. Wickliffe nor any of the conspirators taking up my challenge, some of my friends, recovering from their lethargy, took me by the arm (seeing where Brown's bullet had entered,) to the dwelling-house; and, on opening my vest and shirt-bosom, found only a red spot over my heart, but no wound. On examination it was found that the ball, as I pulled up the scabbard of my Bowie-knife, in drawing the blade, had entered the leather near the point, which was lined with silver, and was there lodged.

Thus Providence, or fate, reserved me for a better work. And when I look back to my many escapes from death, I am at times impressed with the idea of the special interference of God in the affairs of men; whilst my cooler reason places human events in that equally certain arrangement of the great moral and physical laws, by which Deity may be said to be ever directing the affairs of men. Certain it is that he who stands on the right may often hold his own against hosts in arms. . . .

Brown had his skull cut to the brain in several places; one ear cut nearly off, his nose slit, and one eye cut out; and many other wounds. Had the rencounter taken place between two ordinary citizens, no notice whatever would have been taken of it by the grand jury; but, as I was odious to the slave-holders, they improved all the chances to weaken and ruin me. I was indicted for *mayhem*. Henry Clay and John Speed Smith were my counsel and defenders; both volunteering their services. Brown, outraged at his being thrown over the fence, and deserted, was my principal witness. He proved that there was a consultation at Ashton's (hotel-keeper,) between himself, Wickliffe, Prof. J. C. Cross of the Transylvania Medical School, Jacob Ashton, and Ben. Wood, a police bully; that the pistol with which I was shot was loaded in advance; that he was to bring on the affray, and they were to aid; that they four went in the same hack to Russell's Cave, and there all took part in the fight.

SLAVERY: THE EVIL—THE REMEDY

Thomas Jefferson never thought of the absurdity of debating the question, whether slavery be an evil, nor was he indulgent to the delusive idea that it would be perpetual. He reduced the subject to its certain elements: the master must liberate the slave, or the slave will exterminate the master. This conclusion is not weakened by the history of the past. The same color in the ancient republics enabled the state to use emancipation as a safety valve; yet notwithstanding the thorough amalgamation of the freed man with the free born, servile wars nearly extinguished by violence the noblest nations of antiquity: while no man dare say that slavery was not the secret cause of their ultimate ruin. But if "His justice" should "sleep for ever," and the tragedy so awfully predicted should never occur, still must we regard slavery as the greatest evil that ever cursed a nation.

Slavery is an evil to the slave, by depriving nearly three millions of men of the best gift of God to man—liberty. I stop here; this is enough of itself to give us a full anticipation of the long catalogue of human woe, and physical and intellectual and moral abasement, which follows in the wake of slavery.

Slavery is an evil to the master. It is utterly subversive of the Christian religion. It violates the great law upon which that religion is based, and on account of which it vaunts its pre-eminence.

It corrupts our offspring by necessary association with an abandoned and degraded race, ingrafting in the young mind and heart all the vices and none of the virtues.

It is the source of indolence, and destructive of all industry, which in times past among the wise has ever been regarded as the first friend of religion, morality, and happiness. The poor despise labor, because slavery makes it degrading. The mass of slaveholders are idlers.

It is the mother of ignorance. The system of common schools has not succeeded in a single slave state. Slavery and education are natural enemies. In the free states one in fifty-three, over twenty-one years, is unable to read and write; in the slave states one in thirteen and three tenths is unable to write and read!

It is opposed to literature, even in the educated classes. Noble aspirations and true glory depend upon virtue and good to man. The conscious injustice of slavery hangs as a mill-stone about the necks of the sons of genius, and will not let them up!

It is destructive of all mechanical excellence. The free states build ships and steam cars for the nations of the world; the slave states import the handles for their axes—these primitive tools of the architect. The educated population will not work at all; the uneducated must work without science, and of course without skill. If there be a given amount of mechanical genius among a people, it is of necessity developed in proportion as a whole or part of the population are educated. In the slave states the small portion educated is inert.

It is antagonistic to the fine arts. Creations of beauty and sublimity are the embodiments of the soul's imaginings: the fountain must surely be pure and placid whence these glorious and immortal and lovely images are reflected. Liberty has ever been the mother of the arts.

It retards population and wealth. Compare New York and Virginia, Tennessee and Ohio—states of equal natural advantages, and equal ages. The wealth of the free states is in a much greater ratio even superior to that of the slave states, than the population of the free is greater than that of the slave states. The manufactures of the slave as compared to those of the free states, are as one to four nearly, as is shown by statistics. I consider the accumulation of wealth in a less ratio.

It impoverishes the soil and defaces the loveliest features of nature. Washington advises a friend to remove from Pennsylvania to Virginia, saying, that cheap lands in Virginia were as good as the dear lands in Pennsylvania, and, anticipating the abolition of slavery, would be more productive. His anticipations have perished; slavery still exists; the wild brier and the red fox are now there the field-growth and the inhabitants!

It induces national poverty. Slaves consume more and produce less than freemen. Hence illusive wealth, prodigality, and bankruptcy, without the capability of bearing adversity, or recovering from its influence: then comes despair, dishonor, and crime.

It is an evil to the free laborer, by forcing him by the laws of competition, supply, and demand, to work for the wages of the slave—food and shelter. The poor, in the slave states, are the most destitute native population in the United States.

It sustains the public sentiment in favor of the deadly affray and the duel—those relics of a barbarous age.

It is the mother and the nurse of *Lynch law,* which I regard as the most horrid of all crimes, not even excepting parricide, which ancient legislators thought too impossible to be ever supposed in the legal code. If all the blood thus shed in the South could be gathered together, the horrid image which Emmett drew of the cruelty of his judges would grow pale in view of this greater terror.

Where all these evils exist, how can liberty, constitutional liberty, live? No indeed, it cannot and has not existed in conjunction with slavery. We are but nominal freemen, for though born to all the privileges known to the Constitution and the laws, written and prescriptive, we have seen struck down with the leaden hand of slavery, the most glorious banner that freedom ever bore in the face of men; "Trial by Jury, Liberty of Speech and of the Press." The North may be liable to censure in congress for freedom of speech; may lose the privileges of the post office, and the right of petition, and perhaps yet be free; but we of the land of slavery, are ourselves slaves! Alas for the hypocritical cry of liberty and equality, which demagogues sound for ever in our ears! The Declaration of Independence comes back from all nations, not in notes of triumph and self-elation, but thundering in our ears the everlasting *lie*—making us infidels in the great world of freedom—raising up to ourselves idols of wood and stone, inscribed with the name of Deity, where the one invisible and true God can never dwell. . . .

If the Union should not be perpetual, nor the American name be synonymous with that of liberty in all coming time, slavery is at once the cause, the crime, and the avenger!

THE TRUE AMERICAN, TUESDAY, JUNE 10, 1844

PROGRESS

Revelation, as well as natural philosophy, teach us that creation itself has been progressive; organism, both vegetable and animal, has slowly reached its present perfection; history confirms the combined evidence of the anterior theory, till speculation has subsided into fact. . . .

From the earliest time man has been improving in his social condition, or advancing in those complicated developments and relations which are understood by the term civilization. We dare say that our race is better guarded against natural evils than ever before; better housed, better clothed, better fed, and better provided with medicines against disease and casualties. . . . The intellect has not fallen behind the physical part in its progress. Men no longer bow down to sticks and stones, and shed each other's blood in submissive sacrifice to wooden gods. . . . The angry voice of an avenging Deity is no more heard in the midst of the storm. . . .

The reformation was as much a political as a religious renovation. The independence of the English Church and the emigration of the Puritans, were but the results of a progression of the democratic principle. The declaration of American independence was not so much the work of the profound reflections of particular men, as the exponent of the spirit of the age, and the sum of the freedom of the world. The enunciation of the political equality of man was in politics, what the great law of love was in religion; both the eternal rocks of man's best happiness and highest glory—imperishable elements in progressive civilization. The sacrilegious hand of political tyranny and priestly superstition have in vain essayed their demolition.

For the first time in the history of nations was the conservative principle of *mutual interest, equality*—absolute equality, so far as God by the inequality of organization would allow—distinctly avowed. There was force in it, tremendous, irresistible force, the force of truth and justice. All human obstacles fell before it like the bent reed before the whirlwind. The most venerable monarchies, with their prestige of antiquity and Divine right, crumbled into dust: the dark veil of political Jesuitism was rent for ever; the priesthood, who wielded the thunders of usurped Divinity for long centuries, crushing the body and soul, were spit upon in their sanctuaries. The bent oak, grown to maturity, shivered with its rebound the mad hands who thought to trail it in the dust. No! Americans; the spirit of liberty, though seemingly retarded and turned back, is *onward.* Like as on the fabled wandering Jew, the hand of destiny is on the nations of the world; they shall *not rest;* the great, the wealthy, the refined, cut off from all physical pressure, are touched with drowsy lids; they would sleep, and be at peace, but labor, and famine, and woe, and contempt, are crushing the hearts, extinguishing the immortal aspirations of God's creatures; a voice which walls of chiselled marble cannot shut out, bids them awake—*"March! march!"* till justice be no more "compromised," and man's political redemption shall come.

JULY 1, 1844

SIX HUNDRED THOUSAND FREE WHITE LABORERS OF KENTUCKY—MEN, WOMEN, AND CHILDREN

If slavery deprives us of political and social equality; if it impoverishes us by the ruinous competition of unpaid wages; if it fails to educate our children, and places large farms between us, so that we can't get our own schools; if it degrades labor, so that slaveholders rank us below slaves— some of whom play idlers in the houses of the rich—if, above all, after suffering all these curses, we and ours are to be involved in the common ruin, which as sure as fate awaits the catastrophe which follows the violation of the laws of God and nature—shall we any longer support it, by our countenance, or our votes? No! Let us say, with one loud and unanimous voice, *slavery shall die!* and the Heavens and the earth shall respond, *amen!*

LIBERTY?—OR SLAVERY?

The Governor of South Carolina, in his correspondence with the venerable Thomas Clarkson, the pioneer of British emancipation, takes McDuffie's ground, that slavery is the corner-stone of liberty! How? by excluding *"poor white folks"* from power in the government! This head of the *"democracy,"* also *denies and ridicules the declaration of American independence!* Democrats, all over the Union, do you hear? Whigs, North and South, do you hear? Americans, awake! the time has come; take your ground. LIBERTY? or SLAVERY? *"Under which king, Bezonian? speak or die!"*

NON-RESISTANCE—OUR FIRST NUMBER—THE NORTHERN PRESS

Whilst we have the greatest respect for non-resistants, we beg leave to think and act for ourselves. If Washington and his compatriots had relied upon *"moral power" only,* the paw of the huge lion of Britannia would be now quietly resting upon the necks of the American people. . . . We say, that when *society fails to protect us,* we are authorized by the laws of God and nature to defend ourselves; based upon *the right,* "the pistol and Bowie knife" are to us as sacred as the gown and the pulpit; and the Omnipotent God of battles is our hope and trust for victorious vindication. "Moral power" is much; with great, good, true-souled men, it is stronger than the bayonet! but with the cowardly and the debased it is an "unknown God." Experience teaches us, common sense teaches us, virtue teaches us, justice teaches us, the right teaches us, instinct teaches us, *religion* teaches us, that it loses none of its force by being backed with "cold steel and the flashing blade," "the pistol and the Bowie knife." Without these, "moral power" has been and will be again, ridden on a rail; it will be graced with a plumigerous coat of less enviable colors than that of Joseph of old, and not so easily torn off! Moral power stands by and sees men slain in Vicksburg; Catholic churches plundered in Massachusetts; good citizens murdered in the defence of the laws in Philadelphia; public meetings broken up in New York; the envoys of Massachusetts mobbed in the South; United States citizens imprisoned in Charleston and New Orleans; men hung to the limbs of trees in the Southern states for exercising the "liberty of speech;" Lovejoy murdered in Illinois; Joe Smith assassinated in the sanctuary of the law. She stood by in Paris, during the French revolution, and saw the peasant and the prince, male and female, "the young, the beautiful, the brave," brought to the block. She looked coldly on when Christ himself was crucified in Judea! We say, then, she is powerless of herself. Meet mobs with "moral power!" not so thought the "little corporal" of Corsica; they are to be met (when will the American people learn it?) with "round and grape—to be answered by Shrapnel and Congreve; to be discussed in hollow squares, and refuted by battalions four deep." Yes, they must be met with "cold steel" and ball, the "pistol, and Bowie knife," and subterranean batteries, for they will never come to their senses while the ground is firm beneath their feet! Let us hear no more of this sickly cant, and mawkish sensibility. People at home and abroad greatly underrate *Kentuckians* if they suppose them capable of lawless outbreaks; the *few assassins,* who infest the best of communities, we thoroughly understand; and we must be allowed to deal with *them* as they deserve, *and after our own manner.*

FOSTER'S POWER PRESS

We invite our *pro-slavery* friends—for we are the enemies of *slavery,* not of *slaveholders*—to come and see this beautiful piece of mechanism, the product of *free labor.* If any man is proud of mental achievement let him look on this and reflect that slavery deprives us of such as these. If any one is covetous of wealth, let him see this, and reflect that slavery has sent millions of our money to *free states, to purchase machinery,* that ought to have been made at home. If any body is fond of the *"toiling millions,"* let him show his faith by his works, and see to it that our own money shall be spent among our own "people." Let those men who have spent the people's school fund in building locks, and dams, and turnpike roads, over which there is nothing to be carried, remember that there are thousands of Fosters in Kentucky, who for the want of proper education and encouragement, are lost to the world.

TUESDAY, AUGUST 12, 1844

Our leader to-day is from one of the very first intellects in this nation; and as he is a large slaveholder, we allow him to speak his sentiments in his own language. We shall give our plan of emancipation in our next.

We are called once more to our hard and responsible task from a bed of long and painful illness. The inquiry has been frequently made, we are told, whether we were living or dead, with hopes for the worst, in the bosoms of some. . . .

We had hoped to see on this continent, the great axiom, that man is capable of self-government, amply vindicated. We had no objections to the peaceable and honorable extension of empire over the whole continent, if equal freedom expanded with the bounds of the nation. Gladly would we have seen untold millions of freemen, enjoying liberty of conscience and pursuit. . . .

But we are told the enunciation of the great and soul-stirring principles of Revolutionary patriots was a lie; as a dog returns to his vomit we are to go back to the foul and cast off rags of European tyranny to hide our nakedness. Slavery, the most unmitigated, the lowest, basest that the world has seen, is to be substituted for ever for our better, more glorious, holier aspirations; the constitution is torn and trampled under foot; justice and good faith in a nation are derided; brute force is substituted in the place of high moral tone. All the great principles of national liberty which we inherited from our British ancestry are yielded up; and we are left without God or hope in the world. When the great hearted of our land weep, and the man of reflection maddens in the contemplation of our national apostacy; there are men pursuing gain and pleasure, who smile with contempt and indifference at their appeals. But remember, you who dwell in marble palaces, that there are strong arms and fiery hearts and iron pikes in the streets, and panes of glass only between them and the silver plate on the board, and the smooth skinned woman on the ottoman. When you have mocked at virtue, denied the agency of God in the affairs of men, and made rapine your honeyed faith, tremble! for the day of retribution is at hand, and the masses will be avenged.

24. The Face of America

Illustrations

298

1. *"The York Family,"* 1837.

2. *"Fanny Kemble," by Thomas Sully, 1833.*

3. *"Mrs. William Cornee," by Deacon Robert Peckham, 1836.*

4. *"Portrait of the Prophet's Mother," by Lucy Mack Smith, c. 1843.*

5. *"Negro Child."*

6. *"Caesar, New York's Last
    Slave,"* 1850.

7. *"Peter and Susan Palmer," c. 1855.*

8. *"Two Washington, D. C., Firemen," c. 1855.*

9. *The Woodsawyers' Mooning,"* 1855.

25. Autobiography of a Fugitive Negro

SAMUEL RINGGOLD WARD

A number of able blacks were prominent in the abolitionist crusade. Most famous and perhaps influential was Frederick Douglass, but when he came North to freedom and prominence in the 1840's other Negro leaders had prepared the way for some measure both of acceptance by abolitionist groups and tolerance by society at large. One of the most capable of these early leaders was Samuel Ringgold Ward, who escaped with his parents from a plantation in Maryland in 1820. Growing up in New York City, he managed to get enough education to be ordained in 1839, although the school he had gone to in Canaan, New Hampshire, in 1835 was destroyed by an orderly mob organized at a town meeting.

A brilliant orator, Ward was called to minister in 1841 by a white church in upstate New York who heard him lecture under Anti-Slavery Society auspices. Despite unbroken cordial relations between minister and congregation, Ward remained bitterly aware of the racist attitudes of American society, and left the country in 1851, after helping rescue a fugitive slave in Buffalo, to spend the rest of his life in Canada, Great Britain, and Jamaica.

THE WHITE CHURCH AND COLOURED PASTOR

It was while journeying through Western New York . . . that I went by appointment to the township of Butler, in the county of Wayne, on a certain Saturday in February, 1841. The meeting was attended by some steady honest farmers and others, with their wives and daughters. It was holden in the Congregational Church. As was and still is the custom in that region, the lecturer was invited to tea by a gentleman of prominence

Samuel Ringgold Ward, *Autobiography of a Fugitive Negro: His Anti-Slavery Labours in the United States, Canada, and England* (London, 1855), 79–100.

in the neighbourhood—George Candee, Esq., who had a heart warm in the anti-slavery cause. At the invitation of several members of the Church, I remained and preached the following day in the forenoon, having an engagement seven miles distant in the evening.

As they were without either a pastor or a supply, several members of the Church accompanied me to Wolcott in the evening. On the way, one of the number said something about my settling with them. Thinking it a matter which would not survive the excitement of the moment, I simply gave them liberty to write to me at Peterborough, my residence. In a few days a letter came; and shortly after, another, from Clarendon Campbell, Esq., M.D., the postmaster, one of the most pious and intelligent members of the Church, inviting me formally and officially to settle.

I went to visit them in April, and a series of meetings began which was not discontinued until several persons were converted to God, through Christ's redemption, and I had been called and had agreed to become their pastor.

The Church and congregation were all white persons save my own family. It was "a new thing under the sun" to see such a connection. The invitation was unanimous and cordial; and not one incident occurred during my settlement, on the part of any of the *living* members, to make it even seem to be otherwise. . . . I understood it to be a matter of vast importance, how I should demean myself in so responsible a position; for I felt it to be such, in two very important points of view—first, in regard to the anti-slavery cause generally; and secondly, in reference to the coloured people especially. If I should acquit myself creditably as a preacher, the anti-slavery cause would thereby be encouraged. Should I fail in this, that sacred cause would be loaded with reproach. So, if I were successful or unsuccessful in this charge would *encouragement* or *discouragement* come to the people of colour. . . . If I did succeed, some other young black would feel encouraged to qualify himself for a position of usefulness among his own people; but while appropriately serviceable to them, he might also be so situated as to do good *to* others and *for* his own class. I was not willing to do mischief to the dear anti-slavery cause, nor to that of my beloved people. I hope God spared me from either—from both. Or, at any rate, among the many things wherewithal I have been reproached, this is not one of them. . . . My own people were honest, straightforward, God-fearing descendants of New England Puritans. Living in the interior of the State, apart from the allurements and deceptions of fashion, they felt at liberty to hear, judge, and determine for themselves, and to act in accordance with what the Bible, as they understood it, demanded of them. They heard a preacher: they supposed and believed that he preached God's truth. That was what they wanted, and all they wanted. The mere accident of the *colour* of the preacher was to them a matter of small consideration. Some might ridicule: indeed, some did. But what of that? They received the truth, and it was of sufficient value to enable them to endure ridicule for its sake. Anti-slavery doctrines were unpopular; anti-slavery practice was still more so. But what said the Bible about these doctrines? Did they agree with the law of love? Were they in agreement with—or, what is more to the point, part and parcel of—what Jesus taught? If so, let rectitude take the place of popularity. They could afford to do without the latter. So this honest, right-hearted people loved—so they stood by the pastor—so their influence spread abroad—and so the Lord God of Jacob blessed them, according to his gracious promise.

When in South Butler, also, the people of my own colour called upon me not unfrequently to visit and labour among them. They seemed inclined to take advantage of my position, to make it serviceable; and I was but too happy to accede to their wishes.

In doing so, I always sought to inculcate some truth which would have a direct influence on our character and our condition. Being deprived of the right of voting upon terms of equality with whites—being denied the ordinary courtesies of decent society, to say nothing of what is claimed for every man, especially every freeborn American citizen—I very well know, from a deep and painful experience, that the black people were goaded into a constant temptation to hate their white fellow-citizens. I know, too, how natural such hatred is in such circumstances: and all I know of the exhibition of vindictiveness and revenge by the whites against *their* injurers—and the most perfect justice of the Negro regarding the white man according to daily treatment received from him—caused me to see this temptation to be all the stronger: and convinced me also, that the white had no personal claim to anything else than the most cordial hatred of the black.

How frequently have I heard a Negro exclaim, "I cannot like a white man. He and his have done so much injury to me and my people for so many generations." How difficult, how impossible, to deny this, with all its telling force of historical fact! How natural is such a feeling, in such circumstances! How richly the whites deserved it!

My course was, however, to remind them of the manner in which Christ had been treated by those for whom he died, *ourselves included*. . . . I urged that, as Christ forgave, so should we; and that he made our being forgiven depend upon whether we forgave our enemies; that just as surely as the whites were our enemies—a most palpable fact, of every-day illustration—just so surely we must forgive them, or lie down for ever with them, amid the torments of the same perdition! What an aggravation of our temporal torments, to be obliged to be associated with our injurers, and to be partakers with them in an unrepented, unsanctified, more fiendish state, in the pangs of an endless perdition!

I beg to state, that I never taught on this subject what I did not then, and do not now, believe. I seriously believe that the prejudice of the whites against Negroes is a constant source of temptation to the latter to hate the former. I also believe that that same prejudice will aggravate the perdition of both: and I pray, therefore, that my people may be saved from that hatred, and made forgiving; and for the whites of America, my highest wish is that they may all become like the people of South Butler, thus removing danger from themselves, and, by doing justly, remove the most insidious of temptations from my people, whom, God knows, they have injured enough already.

In pleading the cause of the blacks before the whites, while I tried faithfully to depict the suffering of the enslaved, and the injustice done to the nominally free, I never stooped to ask pity for either. Wronged, outraged, "scattered, peeled, killed all the day long," as they are, I never so compromised my own self-respect, nor ever consented to so deep a degradation of my people, as to condescend to ask pity for them at the hands of their oppressors. I cast no reflections upon, and certainly utter no censures against, those who do; but I never did, and God forgive me when I ever shall. Justice, "even-handed justice," for the Negro—that which, according to American profession, is every man's birthright—*that* I claimed, nothing less. The most savage of our tormentors could now and then shed a tear, or at least heave a sigh of pity, and go out and remain the same savage tormentor still; unchanged, only a little—a very little—softened, to harden again upon the earliest opportunity. Those who have done us the worst injuries think it a virtue to express sympathy with us—a sort of arms'-length, cold-blooded sympathy; while neither of these would, on any account, consent to do towards us the commonest justice. What the Negro needs is, what belongs to him—what has been ruthlessly torn from him—and what is, by consent of a despotic democracy and a Christless religion, withholden from him, guiltily, perseveringly. When he shall have that restored, he can acquire *pity* enough, and all the sympathy he needs, cheap wares as they are; but to ask for them instead of his rights was never my calling.

Nor could I degrade myself by arguing the equality of the Negro with the white; my private opinion is, that to say the Negro is equal morally to the white man, is to say but very little. . . .

The cool impudence, and dastardly cowardice, of denying a black a seat in most of their colleges and academies, and literary and scientific institutions, from one end of the republic to the other; and, in like manner, shutting him out of most of the honourable and lucrative trades and professions, dooming him to be a mere "hewer of wood and drawer of water"—discouraging every effort he makes to elevate himself—and then declaring the Negro to be naturally, morally, intellectually, or socially, inferior to the white—have neither parallel nor existence outside of that head-quarters of injustice to the Negro, the United States of America.

The coloured people of New York, Philadelphia, Boston—and, I may as well add, all other cities and towns in the American Union—bear themselves as respectably, support themselves as comfortably, maintain as good and true allegiance to the laws, make as rapid improvement in all that signifies real, moral, social progress, as any class of citizens whatever. They do not so rapidly acquire wealth, but it must be remembered that the avenues to wealth are not open to them. The French of Lower Canada —the Irish, the Welsh, the Jews, throughout continental Europe—the Poles—no people in a state of entire or partial subjection—ever bore subjection so well, or improved so rapidly in spite of it, as this very much abused class. During the past thirty years, they have furnished their full quota of doctors, lawyers, divines, editors, orators, and poets; these in their spheres compare most triumphantly with their countrymen, of whatever colour. With facts of this sort before me, how could I ask pity, sympathy, reason about equality, or anything short of justice, for my own people? . . .

The coloured people who are intelligent and prominent make friends for themselves among the very best classes of Americans; and the same is true, in its degree, of black men in inferior positions. I have known a black man to move into a neighbourhood where it was difficult for him to rent a house to live in, because of his colour; but edging his way in, and proving himself as good a mechanic, farmer, labourer, or artisan, as anyone else, he was sure to be patronized and respected by the very best customers. I have known whites to go to hear a Negro lecture, or preach, just for the fun of the thing: they have come away saying the most extravagant things in his favor. My advice to our people always was, Do the thing you do in the best possible manner: if you shoe a horse, do it so that no white man can improve it; if you plough a furrow, let it be ploughed to perfection's point; if you make a shoe, make it to bespeak further patronage from the fortunate wearer of it; if you shave a man, impress him with the idea that *such* shaving is a rare luxury; if you do no more than black his boots, send him out of your boot-black shop looking towards his feet, divided in his admiration as between the blacking and the perfection of its application. As one of our own poets hath it,

"Honour and fame from no distinction rise:
Act well your part—*there* all the honour lies."

I am happy to say, such is the good sense and honourable manly ambition of my people, that such advice was always approved and followed: indeed, it was seldom needed. . . .

The coloured people in the United States are in no hopeless circumstances. It has already ceased to be a marvel, that a coloured man can do certain things denied to be within his power thirty years ago. A State or a National Convention of black men is held. The talent displayed, the order maintained, the demeanour of the delegates, all impress themselves upon the community. All agree, that to keep a people rooted to the soil, who are rapidly improving, who have already attained considerable influence, and are marshalled by gifted leaders (men who show themselves qualified for legislative and judicial positions), and to doom them to a state of perpetual vassalage, is altogether out of the question. They cannot be turned back, they cannot be kept stationary; they must and they will advance. Then, it is well known that social progress is made with gigantic strides, when once a movement is made in a right direction. That impulse, a mighty impetus, has been given; and already signs of vigorous and hopeful advance have been developed as the result. Then look at the materials which the blacks have at command. They have the world's history before them. They are *Americans;* they are well taught in the history of their native country; they know the avenues to, and springs of, the most important and characteristic feelings of the American heart. They know what to say, to whom to say it, and at what time. They are wronged: their wrongs are violations of American profession, and what they know ought to be American principle. They are connected socially, by choice and by force, with the subjects of the most cruel oppression on the face of the earth. The more highly they are cultivated, the more keenly they feel their wrongs. . . . Already has the anti-slavery advocacy, for all effective purposes, passed into their hands: and America now stands in the position of a great country, nominally free, depriving one sixth of her citizens of freedom, and robbing those not actually enslaved of an equality which God has given to all nations of men, denying them even the title to it and fitness for it; while these *coloured men,* armed with the panoply of American birth, feelings, and history—gifted with talents surpassed by none—burning with an indignant sense of their own wrongs, and the enslavement of their brethren—highly skilled in the use of their powers and talents, and having gained the ears of their fellow citizens—are demonstrating the injustice of the position which they occupy, and the arrogant hypocrisy of that of their enemies.

Now, when it is considered that (with perhaps the exception of the Welsh) the Negroes are, in feeling, the most *religious* people in the world, and that in all they do they are guided, restrained, but made the more ardent, by the religious passion within them, you cannot imagine that this people will or *can* eventually fail in either recovering their rights, or attracting the thunderbolts of divine vengeance upon their oppressors. What says all past history, upon this subject? When did God cease to hear the cry of the oppressed? What, in history, is the final result of the upward struggles of an oppressed but advancing, praying, God-fearing people? But, to do as our American brethren like to do—leave out all considerations of divine interpositions, or to calculate upon indefinite forbearance of Deity—neither of which is admissible—any one can tell that, left to themselves, these causes must produce one or two important results. The young blacks of the Republic are everywhere acquiring a love for martial pastimes. Their independent companies of military are becoming common in many of the large towns. This, with other things, shows that they aspire to anything and everything within the reach of man. And as their fathers fought bravely in the former wars of the Republic, who can deny them the use of arms? Having almost everything to contend for, it is easy to see, that what wrongs they and their brethren suffer will so stimulate them as to draw out energies which not only would not be exhibited, in other circumstances, but which even themselves would scarcely believe to be theirs. The whites have all they want, and are satisfied. They are already most rapidly degenerating: they are given almost solely to the acquisition of money and the pursuit of pleasure. They will therefore become less and less active, more and more lethargic, while in their very midst the blacks will become less lethargic, and more energetic; until the latter, for all practical purposes, will exhibit, and wield too, more of the real American character, its manliness, its enterprise, its love of liberty, than the former. I speak not as a prophet: I only speak of causes now existing and in active operation, already producing some of their inevitable results. I illustrate my idea by a fact. In 1849 I introduced a young lady into my family, intending that she should teach my children, for which she was then qualified, being older and far better educated than they. In 1851 she recited in the same class with them; in 1853 she was the pupil of one of them, and lagging behind the other. Thus will it be, in my opinion, as between the blacks and the whites in America. They are now in the relation of teacher and taught, in the matter of liberty and progress; they will reverse positions ere the struggle be over, unless some sudden unforeseen changes occur.

26. Debate on John P. Hale's Bill to Outlaw Rioting

CONGRESSIONAL GLOBE

Mrs. John P. Hale, wife of the first avowedly antislavery man in the U.S. Senate, wrote her children that she had recently met Cassius Clay, whose picture hung in their parlor back in New Hampshire and had found him much handsomer than she'd expected. He would have been pleased.

The handful of abolitionists in Congress, who generally had stressed their commitment to legal process in the ending of slavery, faced a dilemma when a ship piloted by Jonathan Drayton was captured while taking a cargo of some forty runaway slaves north to freedom. Unwilling to condemn the attempt, they were also wary of openly condoning it, which would have injured the movement with most moderate Northerners. When a Washington, D.C., mob threatened Gamaliel Bailey's antislavery paper, the *National Era* (soon to begin serial publication of *Uncle Tom's Cabin*), Hale saw his political opportunity.

In his personal letters to his children, Hale expressed sentimental grief about the loss of freedom and the breakup of families among the returned captives; his public action was brilliantly pragmatic rather than moralistic. He simply introduced a perfectly unobjectionable bill against rioting in the District, which in context was interpreted as a defense of Drayton's action and an attack on the proslavery forces. It served as a red flag to Southerners, and they charged. There ensued the most spontaneous and frankest public debate on slavery that occurred. When it was over, Northern public opinion was diverted from slave-stealer Drayton to "Hangman" Foote.

Hale was a genial, joking Yankee lawyer, personally well-liked by even his bitterest political enemies, including Foote. He became the Free Soil candidate for President in 1852. Henry S. Foote was a Mississippi Democrat of

Congressional Globe, 30th Congress, 1st Session, Appendix (Washington, D.C., 1848), 500–508.

strongly Unionist feelings who refused to support secession. John C. Calhoun of South Carolina and Jefferson Davis of Mississippi were the old and the young leaders of proslavery Democrats; Stephen Douglas of Illinois was rising toward leadership of Northern Dmeocrats. Arthur Pendleton Bagby of Alabama and Andrew P. Butler of South Carolina were Democrats; Willie P. Mangum of North Carolina, John J. Crittenden of Kentucky, and Reverdy Johnson of Maryland were Whigs.

April 20, 1848
On the Bill introduced by Mr. Hale,
relating to Riots, and for the Protection
of Property in the District of Columbia.
[*See* Congressional Globe, *page 566.*]

MR. HALE. I wish to make a single remark, in order to call the attention of the Senate to the necessity of adopting the legislation proposed by this bill. The bill itself is nearly an abstract of a similar law now in force in the adjoining State of Maryland, and also in many other States of the Union. The necessity for the passage of the bill will be apparent to the Senate from facts which are probably notorious to every member of the body. Within the present week large and riotous assemblages of people have taken place in this District, and have not only threatened to carry into execution schemes utterly subversive to all law, with respect to the rights of property, but have actually carried these threats into execution, after having been addressed, upheld, and countenanced by men of station in society, whose character might have led us to suppose that they would have taken a different course, and given wiser counsels to those whom they addressed. It seems to me, then, that we have approached a time when the decision is to be made in this Capitol, whether mob-law or constitutional law is to reign paramount. The bill which I now propose to introduce simply makes any city, town, or incorporated place within the District liable for all injuries done to property by riotous or tumultuous assemblages. Whether any further legislation on the part of Congress will be necesary, time will determine. But I may be permitted to say, that at the present moment we present a singular spectacle to the people of this country and to the world. The notes of congratulation which this Senate sent across the Atlantic to the people of France on their deliverance from thraldom, have hardly ceased, when the supremacy of mob-law and the destruction of the freedom of the press are threatened in this capital of the Union. Without further remark, I move that this bill be referred to the Committee on the Judiciary.

MR. BAGBY. I rise for the purpose of giving notice that whenever that bill shall be reported by the committee—if it ever should be—I shall propose to amend it by a section providing a sufficient penalty for the crime of kidnapping in this District. I was struck by a remark made by the Senator from New Hampshire. He adverts to the rejoicing of the people of this country at the events now in progress in Europe, and thence infers that the slaves of this country are to be permitted to cut the throats of their masters. I shall certainly, sir, attend to this subject.

MR. HALE. To avoid misapprehension, I purposely abstained from saying a word in regard to anything that might even be supposed to lie beyond the case which it is the object of this bill to meet. I did not make the most distant allusion to slavery. I refrained from it purposely, because I wanted to present to the consideration of the Senate the simple question of the integrity of the law and the rights of property unembarrassed by considerations of the character alluded to by the honorable Senator from Alabama. . . .

MR. CALHOUN. I suppose no Senator can mistake the object of this bill, and the occurrence which has led to its introduction. Now, sir, I am amazed that even the Senator from New Hampshire should have so little regard for the laws and the Constitution of the country, as to introduce such a bill as this, without including in it the enactment of the severest penalties against the atrocious act which has occasioned this excitement. Sir, gentlemen, it would seem, have at last come to believe that the southern people and southern members have lost all sensibility or feeling upon this subject. I know to what this leads. I have known for a dozen years to what all this is tending. When this subject was first agitated, I said to my friends, there is but one question that can destroy this Union and our institutions, and that is this very slave question, for I choose to speak of it directly. I said further, that the only way by which such a result could be prevented was by prompt and efficient action; that if the thing were permitted to go on, and the Constitution to be trampled on; that if it were allowed to proceed to a certain point, it would be beyond the power of any man, or any combination of men, to prevent the result. We are approaching that crisis, and evidence of it is presented by the fact that such a bill upon such an occurrence should be brought in to repress the just indignation of our people from wreaking their vengeance upon the atrocious perpetrators of these crimes, or those who contribute to them, without a denunciation of the cause that excited that indignation. I cannot but trust that I do not stand alone in these views.

I have for so many years raised my voice upon this subject that I have been considered almost the exclusive defender of this great institution of the South, upon which not only its prosperity but its very existence depends. . . . If you do not regard the stipulations of the Constitution in our favor, why should we regard those in your favor? If your vessels cannot come into our ports without the danger of such piratical acts; if you have caused this state of things by violating the provisions of the Constitution and the act of Congress for delivering up fugitive slaves, by passing laws to prevent it, and thus make it impossible to recover them when they are carried off by such acts, or seduced from us, we have the right, and are bound by the high obligation of safety to ourselves, to retaliate, by preventing any of your sea-going vessels from entering our ports. That would apply an effectual remedy, and make up the issue at once on this, the gravest and most vital of all questions to us and the whole Union. . . .

MR. DAVIS, of Mississippi. . . . Is this District to be made the field of abolition struggles? Is this Chamber to be the hot-bed in which plants of sedition are to be nursed? Why is it that in this body, once looked to as the conservative branch of the Government—once looked to as so dignified that it stood above the power of faction—that we find the subject of this contest so insulting to the South—so irritating always when it is agitated—introduced on such an occasion? Is this debatable ground? No! It is ground upon which the people of this Union may shed blood, and that is the final result. If it be pressed any further, and if this Senate is to be made the theatre of that contest, let it come—the sooner the better. We who represent the southern States are not here to be insulted on account of institutions which we inherit. And if civil discord is to be thrown from this Chamber upon the land—if the fire is to be kindled here with which to burn the temple of our Union—if this is to be made the centre from which civil war is to radiate, here let the conflict begin. I am ready, for one, to meet it with any incendiary, who, dead to every feeling of patriotism, attempts to introduce it. . . .

MR. FOOTE. I undertake to say that there is not a man who has given his countenance to this transaction in any shape, who is not capable of committing grand larceny; or, if he happened to be a hero, as such men are not, of perpetrating highway robbery on any of the roads of this Union. He is not a gentleman. He would not be countenanced by any respectable person anywhere. He is amenable to the law. I go further— and I dare say my sentiments will meet the approbation of many even who do not live in slave States—and I maintain, that when the arm of the law is too short to reach such a criminal, he may be justly punished by a sovereignty not known to the law. Such proceedings have taken place, and there are circumstances which not only instigate, but justify such acts. I am informed, upon evidence on which I rely, that this very movement out of which the bill originates, has been instigated and sanctioned by persons in high station. It is even rumored, and it is believed by many —I am sorry for the honor of this body to say so—that a Senator of the United States is concerned in the movement. Certain it is, that a member of another body, meeting in a certain Hall not far distant, was yesterday morning engaged in certain reprehensible contrivances, and that but for his abject flight from the place of his infamous intrigues, he would have been justly punished, not by the mob, but by high-spirited citizens convened for the purpose of vindicating their rights, thus unjustly assailed.

Why is it that this question is continually agitated in the Senate of the United States—that it is kept here as the subject of perpetual discussion? Is it simply that gentlemen wish to be popular at home? I suppose so. Is it because of their peculiar sympathies for that portion of the population which constitutes slavery as recognized in the South? What is the motive? Is the object to attain popularity? Is it to gain high station? Is it to keep up a local excitement in some portions of the North, with the view of obtaining political elevation as the reward of such factious conduct? But I care not for the motives of such acts. I undertake to say that in no country where the principles of honesty are respected, would such a movement as that now attempted be promoted, or even countenanced for a moment. . . . The Senator from New Hampshire is evidently attempting to get up a sort of civil war in the country, and is evidently filled with the spirit of insurrection and incendiarism. He may bring about a result which will end in the spilling of human blood. I say to him, however, let him come forward boldly, and take the proper responsibility. Let him say, "Now I am ready to do battle in behalf of the liberties of my friends, the blacks—the slaves of the District of Columbia." Let him buckle on his armor; let him unsheath his sword, and at once commence the contest, and I have no doubt he will have a fair opportunity of shedding his blood in this holy cause on the sacred soil of the District of Columbia. If he is really in earnest, he is bound, as a conscientious man, to pursue his course, which cannot be persevered in, without all those awful scenes of bloodshed and desolation long anticipated by good men in every part of this Republic. . . .

All must see that the course of the Senator from New Hampshire is calculated to embroil the Confederacy—to put in peril our free institutions—to jeopard that Union which our forefathers established, and which every pure patriot throughout the country desires shall be perpetuated. Can any man be a patriot who pursues such a course? Is he an enlightened friend of freedom, or even a judicious friend of those with whom he affects to sympathize, who adopts such a course? Who does not know that such men are practically the worst enemies of the slaves? I do not beseech the gentleman to stop; but if he perseveres, he will awaken indignation everywhere: and it cannot be, that enlightened men, who conscientiously belong to the faction of the North, of which he is understood to be the head, can sanction or approve everything that he may do, under the influence of excitement, in this body. I will close by saying, that if he really wishes glory, and to be regarded as the great liberator of the blacks; if he wishes to be particularly distinguished in this cause of emancipation, as it is called, let him, instead of remaining here in the Senate of the United States, or, instead of secreting himself in some dark corner of New Hampshire, where he may possibly escape the just indignation of good men throughout this Republic—let him visit the good State of Mississippi, in which I have the honor to reside, and no doubt he will be received with such hosannas and shouts of joy as have rarely marked the reception of any individual in this day and generation. I invite him there, and will tell him beforehand, in all honesty, that he could not go ten miles into the interior, before he would grace one of the tallest trees of the forest, with a rope around his neck, with the approbation of every virtuous and patriotic citizen; and that, if necessary, I should myself assist in the operation.

MR. HALE. I beg the indulgence of the Senate for a few moments. Though I did not exactly anticipate this discussion, yet I do not regret it. Before I proceed further, as the honorable Senator from Mississippi has said that it has been asserted, and he thinks on good authority, that a Senator of the United States connived at this kidnapping of slaves, I ask him if he refers to me?

MR. FOOTE. I did.

MR. HALE. I take occasion, then, to say, that the statement that I have given the slightest countenance to the procedure is entirely without the least foundation in truth. I have had nothing to do with the occurrence, directly or indirectly, and I demand of the honorable Senator to state the ground upon which he has made his allegation.

MR. FOOTE. It has been stated to me, and I certainly believed it; and believing it, I denounced it. I did not make the charge directly. My remarks were hypothetical. I am glad to hear the Senator say that he has had no connection with the movement; but whether he had or not, some of his brethren in the great cause in which he was engaged no doubt had much to do with it.

MR. HALE. The sneer of the gentleman does not affect me. I recognize every member of the human family as a brother; and if it was done by human beings, it was done by my brethren. Once for all, I utterly deny, either by counsel, by silence, or by speech, or in any way or manner, having any knowledge, cognizance, or suspicion of what was done, or might be done, until I heard of this occurrence as other Senators have heard of it. . . .

MR. FOOTE. I ask the Senator—and beg to remind him that twenty millions of people are listening to his answer—in the circumstances of the case, evidently known to him, does he suppose that this occurrence could have taken place without extensive countenance and aid from men of standing in this District, whether members of Congress or others?

MR. HALE. I have no doubt that those persons could not have got away without some aid. It is enough that I have disclaimed all knowledge of it. I thought that when the honorable Senator was speaking, more than twenty millions of people were listening. He invites me to visit the State of Mississippi, and kindly informs me that he would be one of those who would act the assassin, and put an end to my career. He would aid in bringing me to public execution—no, death by a mob. Well, in return for his hospitable invitation, I can only express the desire that he would penetrate into some of the dark corners of New Hampshire, and if he do, I am much mistaken if he would not find that the people in that benighted region would be very happy to listen to his arguments, and engage in an intellectual conflict with him, in which the truth might be elicited. . . .

I think, if I did not misunderstand the honorable Senator from South Carolina, that he is surprised at the temerity of the Senator from New Hampshire in introducing this bill. Let me ask, what is this bill? What is this incendiary bill that has elicited such a torrent of invective? Has it been manufactured by some "fanatical abolitionist?" Why, it is copied, almost word for word, from a law on the statute-book which has been in operation for years, in the neighboring State of Maryland. It has no allusion, directly or indirectly, to the subject of slavery. Yet I am accused of throwing it in as a firebrand, and in order to make war upon the institutions of the South! How? In God's name, is it come to this, that the American Senate, and in the year of grace one thousand eight hundred and forty-eight, the rights of property cannot be named but the advocates of slavery are in arms, and exclaim that war is made upon their institutions; because it is attempted to cast the protection of the law around the property of an American citizen, who appeals to an American Senate! It has long been held by you that your peculiar institution is incompatible with the right of speech; but if it be also incompatible with the safeguards of the Constitution being thrown around property of American citizens, let the country know it! If that is to be the principle of your action, let it be proclaimed throughout the length and breadth of the land, that there is an institution so omnipotent—so almighty—that even the sacred rights of life and property must bow down before it!

Do not let it be said that I have introduced this subject. I have simply asked that the plainest provisions of the common law—the clearest dictates of justice—shall be extended and exercised for the protection of the property of citizens of this District; and yet, the honorable Senator from South Carolina is shocked at my temerity!

MR. BUTLER. Allow me to ask one question with perfect good temper. The Senator is discussing the subject with some feeling; but I ask him whether he would vote for a bill, properly drawn, inflicting punishment on persons inveigling slaves from the District of Columbia?

MR. HALE. Certainly not, and why? Because I do not believe that slavery should exist here.

MR. CALHOUN, (in his seat.) He wishes to arm the robbers, and disarm the people of the District.

MR. HALE. The honorable Senator is alarmed at my temerity—

MR. CALHOUN, (in his seat.) I did not use the word, but did not think it worth while to correct the Senator.

MR. HALE. The Senator did not use that term?

MR. CALHOUN. No. I said brazen, or something like that.

MR. HALE. The meaning was the same. It was brazen then, that I should introduce a bill for the protection of property in this District—a bill perfectly harmless, but which he has construed into an attack upon the institutions of the South. I ask the Senator and the country wherein consists the temerity? I suppose it consists in the section of the country from which it comes. He says that we seem to think that the South has lost all feeling. Ah! there is the temerity. The bill comes from the wrong side of a certain parallel! Why, did the honorable Senator from South Carolina imagine that we of the North, with our faces bowed down to the earth, and with our backs to the sun, had received the lash so long that we dared not look up? Did he suppose that we dared not ask that the protection of the law should be thrown around property in the District to which we come to legislate? . . .

And here let me tell the Senator from Alabama, that he will have my full cooperation in any measure to prevent kidnapping. I shall expect him to redeem his pledge. Again: I am shocked to hear the honorable Senator from South Carolina denounce this bill as a measure calculated to repress those citizens from the expression of their just indignation.

MR. CALHOUN. If the Senator will allow me, I will explain. I said no such thing. But I will take this occasion to say, that I would just as soon argue with a maniac from bedlam, as with the Senator from New Hampshire, on this subject.

SEVERAL SENATORS. "Order, order."

MR. CALHOUN. I do not intend to correct his statements. A man who says that the people of this District have no right in their slaves, and that it is no robbery to take their property from them, is not entitled to be regarded as in possession of his reason.

MR. HALE. It is an extremely novel mode of terminating a controversy by charitably throwing the mantle of maniacal irresponsibility over one's antagonist! . . .

MR. FOOTE. The Senator seems to suppose that I wanted to decoy him to the State of Mississippi. I have attempted no such thing. I have thought of no such thing. I have openly challenged him to present himself there or anywhere uttering such language and breathing such an incendiary spirit as he has manifested in this body, and I have said that just punishment would be inflicted upon him for his enormous criminality. I have said further, that, if necessary, I would aid in the infliction of the punishment. My opinion is, that enlightened men would sanction that punishment. But, says the Senator, that would be assassination! I think not. I am sure that the Senator is an enemy to the Constitution of his country —an enemy of one of the institutions of his country which is solemnly guaranteed by the organic law of the land—and in so far he is a lawless person. I am sure, if he would go to the State of Mississippi, or any other slave State of this Confederacy, and utter such language, he would justly be regarded as an incendiary in heart and in fact, and as such, guilty of the attempt to involve the South in bloodshed, violence, and desolation; and if the arm of the law happened to be too short, or the spirit of the law to be slumberous, I have declared that the duty of the people whose rights were thus put in danger would be to inflict summary punishment upon the offender. But, says the Senator, victims have been made, and there are other victims ready. I am sure that he could not persuade me that he would ever be a victim. I have never deplored the death of such victims, and I never shall deplore it. Such officious intermeddling deserved its fate. I believe no good man who is not a maniac, as the Senator from New Hampshire is apprehended to be, can have any sympathy for those who lawlessly interfere with the rights of others. He, however, will never be a victim! He is one of those gusty declaimers—a windy speaker —a—

MR. CRITTENDEN. If the gentlemen will allow me, I rise to a question of order. Gentlemen have evidently become excited, and I hear on all sides language that is not becoming. I call the gentleman to order for his personal reference to the Senator from New Hampshire.

MR. FOOTE. I only said, in reply to the remarks of the Senator from New Hampshire—

MR. CRITTENDEN. I did not hear what the Senator from New Hampshire said, but the allusion of the gentleman from Mississippi I consider to be contrary to the rules of the Senate.

MR. FOOTE. I am aware of that. But such a scene has never occurred in the Senate—such a deadly assailment of the rights of the country.

MR. JOHNSON, of Maryland. Has the Chair decided?

MR. FOOTE. Let my words be taken down.

THE PRESIDING OFFICER. In the opinion of the Chair, the gentleman from Mississippi is not in order.

MR. FOOTE. I pass it over. But the Senator from New Hampshire has said, that if I would visit that State, I would be treated to an argument. Why, I would not argue with him. What right have they of New Hampshire to argue upon this point? It is not a matter in which they stand in the least connected. . . .

His sentiments will find no response or approval in any enlightened vicinage in New England, and therefore he has no right to say that those who are faithful to the principles of the Constitution, and fail to re-echo the fierce, fanatical, and factious declarations of the Senator, are "cravens" in heart, and deficient in any of the noble sentiments which characterize high-spirited republicans. . . .

The declarations of the Senator from New Hampshire just amount to this: that if he met me on the highway and addressing me gravely or humorously—for he is quite a humorous personage—should say, I design to take that horse which is now in your possession; and then announce that he wished to enter into an argument with me as to whether I should prefer that the animal should be stolen from the stable or taken from me on the road; how could I meet such a proposition? Why, I should say to him, either you are a maniac, or, if sane, you are a knave. . . .

How are we to understand the Senator? He will not acknowledge that his object is to encourage such conduct, and he shuns the responsibility. When we charge upon him that he himself has breathed, in the course of his harangue this morning, the same spirit which has characterized this act, he says most mildly and quietly, "by no means—I have only attempted to introduce a bill corresponding substantially with the law on the statute books of most of the States of this Confederacy." And the Senator supposes that all of us are perfectly demented, or do not know the nature of the case, the circumstances, or the motives which have actuated the Senator. . . .

I trust that the indignation of the country will be so aroused, that even in the quarter of the country from which he comes, the Senator from New Hampshire, although his sensibilities are not very approachable, will be made to feel ashamed of his conduct. . . .

MR. MANGUM. Why should we pursue this discussion? Is it believed that we are to be reasoned out of our rights? Are we to be reasoned out of our convictions? No, sir. Then why discuss the subject? Why not stand upon our rights; upon our constitutional compromises? Why not stand thus perfectly passionless, but prepared to defend them when they shall be assailed? But are they to be assailed? Sir, nothing has occurred during this session that has afforded me more satisfaction than to hear from some of the ablest and most distinguished men in this Union, the declaration that whilst they are opposed to an extension of the area of slavery, they are not disposed to trample upon the compromises of the Constitution. This is our strength. It is to be found in the patriotism of those who love the institutions of our country better than party. I believe the great body of the people are prepared to stand upon the compromises of the Constitution. It is upon this ground that I stand content and passionless, and if I know myself I shall ever continue to do so.

Sir, no good can result from this discussion. . . .

MR. FOOTE. Will the honorable Senator allow me to ask him whether, in the case of a conspiracy to excite insurrection among the slaves, it would not, in his opinion, justify mob proceedings?

MR. MANGUM. Oh! my dear sir, in former years we had a compendious mode of disposing of such cases. We have now a mode equally certain, though not so compendious. Upon a matter of that nature we take a strong ground. But I am not to be driven hastily into legislation that is proposed by gentlemen who entertain extreme opinions on either side.

MR. CALHOUN. I disagree with my worthy friend, the Senator from North Carolina, in several particulars. I do not look upon a state of excitement as a dangerous state. On the contrary, I look upon it as having often a most wholesome tendency. The state to be apprehended as dangerous in any community is this, that when there is a great and growing evil in existence, the community should be in a cold and apathetic state. Nations are much more apt to perish in consequence of such a state than through the existence of heat and excitement. . . .

I differ also from my honorable friend from North Carolina in this respect: he seems to think that the proper mode of meeting this great question of difference between the two sections of the Union is to let it go on silently, not to notice it at all, to have no excitement about it. I differ from him altogether. . . . The very inaction of the South is construed into one of two things—indifference or timidity. And it is this construction which has produced this bold and rapid movement towards the ultimate consummation of all this. And why have we stood and done nothing? I will tell you why. Because the press of this Union, for some reason or other, does not choose to notice this thing. One section does not know what the other section is doing. . . . I do not stand here as a southern man. I stand here as a member of one of the branches of the Legislature of this Union—loving the whole, and desiring to save the whole. How are you to do it? . . . Sir, I hold equality among the confederated States to be the highest point, and any portion of the confederated States who shall permit themselves to sink to a point of inferiority—not defending what really belongs to them, as members, sign their own death warrant, and in signing that, sign the doom of the whole.

MR. DOUGLAS. On the occurrence I desire to say a word. In the first place, I must congratulate the Senator from New Hampshire on the great triumph which he has achieved. He stands very prominently before the American people, and is, I believe, the only man who has a national nomination for the Presidency. I firmly believe that on this floor, to-day, by the aid of the Senator from Mississippi, he has more than doubled his vote at the Presidential election, and every man in this Chamber from a free State knows it! . . . If they had gone into a caucus with the Senator from New Hampshire, and after a night's study and deliberation, had devised the best means to manufacture abolitionism and abolition votes in the North, they would have fallen upon precisely the same kind of procedure which they have adopted to-day. It is the speeches of southern men, representing slave States, going to an extreme, breathing a fanaticism as wild and as reckless as that of the Senator from New Hampshire, which creates abolitionism in the North. The extremes meet. It is no other than southern Senators acting in concert, and yet without design, that produces abolition.

MR. CALHOUN. Does the gentleman pretend to say, that myself, and southern gentlemen who act with me upon this occasion, are fanatics? Have we done anything more than defend our rights, encroached upon at the North? Am I to understand the Senator that we make abolition votes by defending our rights? If so, I thank him for the information, and do not care how many such votes we make.

MR. DOUGLAS. Well, I will say to the Senator from South Carolina, and every other Senator from the South, that far be it from me to entertain the thought, that they design to create abolitionists in the North, or elsewhere. Far be it from me to impute any such design. Yet I assert that such is the only inevitable effect of their conduct.

MR. CALHOUN, (in his seat.) We are only defending ourselves.

MR. DOUGLAS. No, they are not defending themselves. . . . My friend from Mississippi, [Mr. Foote,] in his zeal and excitement this morning, made a remark, in the invitation which he extended to the Senator from New Hampshire to visit Mississippi, which is worth ten thousand votes to the Senator, and I am confident that that Senator would not allow my friend to retract that remark for ten thousand votes.

MR. FOOTE. Will you allow me?

MR. DOUGLAS. Certainly.

MR. FOOTE. If the effect of that remark will be to give to that Senator all the abolition votes, he is fairly entitled to them. Had the Senator from Illinois lived where I have resided—had he seen insurrection exhibiting its fiery front in the midst of the men, women, and children of the community—had he had reason to believe that the machinery of insurrection was at such a time in readiness for purposes of the most deadly character, involving life, and that dearer than life, to every southern man—had he witnessed such scenes, and believed that movements like that of this morning were calculated to engender feelings out of which were to arise fire, blood, and desolation, the destruction finally of the South, he would regard himself as a traitor to the best sentiments of the human heart, if he did not speak out the language of manly denunciation. I can use no other language. I cannot but repeat my conviction, that any man who dares to utter such sentiments as those of the Senator from New Hampshire, and attempts to act them out anywhere in the sunny South, will meet death upon the scaffold, and deserves it.

MR. DOUGLAS. I must again congratulate the Senator from New Hampshire on the accession of five thousand votes! Sir, I do not blame the Senator from Mississippi for being indignant at any man from any portion of this Union, who would produce an incendiary excitement— who would kindle the flame of civil war—who would incite a negro insurrection, hazarding the life of any man in the southern States. The Senator has, I am aware, reason to feel deeply on this subject. . . .

MR. DAVIS, of Mississippi. I do not wish to be considered as participating in the feeling to which the Senator alludes. I have no fear of insurrection; no more dread of our slaves than I have of our cattle. Our slaves are happy and contented. They bear the kindest relation that labor can sustain to capital. It is a paternal institution. They are rendered miserable only by the unwarrantable interference of those who know nothing about that with which they meddle. I rest this case on no fear of insurrection; and I wish it to be distinctly understood, that we are able to take care of ourselves, and to punish all incendiaries. It was the insult offered to the institutions which we have inherited, that provoked my indignation. . . .

MR. DOUGLAS. All that I intended to say was, that the effect of this excitement—of all these harsh expressions—will be the creation of abolitionists at the North.

MR. FOOTE. The more the better!

MR. DOUGLAS. The gentleman may think so; but some of us at the North do not concur with him in that opinion. Of course the Senator from New Hampshire will agree with him, because he can fan the flame of excitement so as to advance his political prospects. And I can also well understand how some gentlemen at the South may quite complacently regard all this excitement, if they can persuade their constituents to believe that the institution of slavery rests upon their shoulders—that they are the men who meet the Goliath of the North in this great contest about abolition. It gives them strength at home. But we of the North, who have no sympathy with abolitionists, desire no such excitement.

MR. CALHOUN. I must really object to the remarks of the Senator. We are merely defending our rights. Suppose that we defend them in strong language; have we not a right to do so? Surely the Senator cannot mean to impute to us the motives of low ambition. He cannot realize our position. For myself, (and I presume I may speak for those who act with me,) we place this question upon high and exalted grounds. Long as he may have lived in the neighborhood of slaveholding States, he cannot have realized anything on the subject. I must object entirely to his course, and say that it is at least as offensive as that of the Senator from New Hampshire. . . .

MR. FOOTE. . . . I would say with all possible courtesy to the Senator from Illinois, for whom I entertain the highest respect, and whose general feelings of justice for us in the South we all understand and appreciate, he will permit me to say to him, in a spirit of perfect courtesy, that there are various ways of becoming popular. Our constituents will have confidence in us, if they see we are ready here to maintain their interests inviolate. And it may be, also, that the Senator from New Hampshire will strengthen himself in proportion as his conduct is denounced. But I beg the Senator from Illinois to recollect, that there is another mode of obtaining that popularity, which is expressed in the adage—*"in medio tutissimus ibis,"* and that there is such a thing as winning golden opinions from all sorts of people; and it may be that a man of mature power— young and aspiring as he may be to high places—may conceive that, by keeping clear of all union with the two leading factions, he will more or less strengthen himself with the great body of the American people, and thus attain the high point of elevation to which his ambition leads. But if the Senator from Illinois thinks that a middle course in regard to this question is best calculated to serve his purpose, he is mistaken.

MR. DOUGLAS.   The Senator has hit it precisely when he says that sometimes the course advised in the familiar adage which he has quoted, is, indeed, the course of duty and of wisdom. I do believe that upon this question that is the only course which can "win golden opinions" from reflecting men throughout the country.

MR. FOOTE, (in his seat.) "Golden opinions from all sorts of people."

MR. DOUGLAS.   In the North it is not expected that we should take the position that slavery is a positive good—a positive blessing. If we did assume such a position, it would be a very pertinent inquiry, Why do you not adopt this institution? We have moulded our institutions at the North as we have thought proper; and now we say to you of the South, if slavery be a blessing, it is your blessing; if it be a curse, it is your curse; enjoy it—on you rest all the responsibility! . . . But my object was to inform the people of the South how it is that gentlemen professing the sentiments of the Senator from New Hampshire, get here; how it is that they will see others coming here with similar sentiments, unless they reflect more calmly and coolly, and take a different course; and how this imprudent and violent course is calculated to crush us who oppose abolitionism. If any unpleasant feeling has been excited by these remarks of mine, I regret it. I know that it is not always pleasant to tell the truth plainly and boldly, when it comes home to an individual. But what I have said is the truth, and we all know it and feel it. . . .

MR. BUTLER.   From the course which this discussion has taken, is clearly indicated the approaching storm which will ere long burst upon this country. I am persuaded that the part of the country which I represent is destined to be in a minority—a doomed minority. . . .

27. The Valley of the Shadows

FRANCIS GRIERSON

History depends always upon what, for one reason or another, has survived from earlier periods, particularly upon what was written down or pictured. Hence the great majority of people become historically voiceless, because few leave remains of their ideas. And even what diaries or letters or wills do last are likely to cling close to the surface of life rather than exploring the quality of existence. In a democracy the historically silent majority matters, and the historian must often reconstruct his picture of it from the descriptions of intellectuals who sought words to give voice to otherwise unremembered parts of society. Grierson's memoir does a rare thing: evokes rather than merely explains or describes the scene and the language, the humor and pathos, the loneliness and kindliness and beauty, the religious intensity of remembered rural middle Americans as they drew the country toward Civil War.

Grierson was born in England in 1848, but came as a baby to the Illinois prairie with his parents. His "recollections of the Lincoln country" begin in 1858 when he was ten years old and continues through 1863 during which years the family moved first to Alton, Illinois, and then to St. Louis. When he was twenty-one, Grierson went to Paris, and almost immediately became a musical sensation by playing and singing improvised and highly evocative music for small groups. His career as pianist continued to the end of his life—he died at the piano at the end of one of his concerts—but in the 1880's he turned also to literature. His *La Révolte Idéaliste* in 1889 was a statement of his mysticism that influenced writers such as Maurice Maeterlinck, a mysticism that Grierson always associated with his boyhood Illinois.

Francis Grierson, *The Valley of the Shadows: Recollections of the Lincoln Country, 1858–1863* (Boston, 1909), 1–30.

PROEM

In the late 'fifties the people of Illinois were being prepared for the new era by a series of scenes and incidents which nothing but the term "mystical" will fittingly describe.

Things came about not so much by preconceived method as by an impelling impulse. The appearance of "Uncle Tom's Cabin" was not a reason, but an illumination; the founding of the Republican party was not an act of political wire-pulling, but an inspiration; the great religious revivals and the appearance of two comets were not regarded as coincidences, but accepted as signs of divine preparation and warning.

The settlers were hard at work with axe and plough; yet, in spite of material pre-occupation, all felt the unnameable influence of unfolding destiny. The social cycle, which began with the Declaration of Independence, was drawing to a close, and during Buchanan's administration the collective consciousness of men—that wonderful prescience of the national soul—became aware of impending innovation and upheaval.

It was impossible to tell what a day might bring forth. The morning usually began with new hope and courage; but the evening brought back the old silences, with the old, unsolved questionings, strange presentiments, premonitions, sudden alarms. Yet over and around all a kind of sub-conscious humour welled up, which kept the mind hopeful while the heart was weary. Dressed in butter-nut jeans, and swinging idly on a gate, many a youth of the time might have been pointed out as a likely senator, poet, general, ambassador, or even president. Never was there more romance in a new country. A great change was coming over the people of the West. They retained all the best characteristics of the Puritans and the settlers of Maryland and Virginia, with something strangely original and characteristic of the time and place, something biblical applied to the circumstances of the hour.

Swiftly and silently came the mighty influences. Thousands laboured on in silence; thousands were acting under an imperative, spiritual impulse without knowing it; the whole country round about Springfield was being illuminated by the genius of one man, whose influence penetrated all hearts, creeds, parties, and institutions. . . .

The prairie was an inspiration, the humble settlers an ever-increasing revelation of human patience and progress. There was a charm in their mode of living, and real romance in all the incidents and events of that wonderful time.

THE MEETING-HOUSE

All through the winter the meeting-house on Saul's Prairie had stood deserted and dormant, its windows rattling in the bleak winds, perhaps longing for the coming revivals and the living, vital sympathy of beings "clothed in garments divine"; but now, how different it looked on this wonderful Sunday morning, with its door and windows wide open, the flowers in bloom, and the birds perched on the tallest weeds pouring forth their song! The fleckless sky, and soft, genial atmosphere had made of the desolate little meeting-house and its surroundings a place that resembled a second Garden of Eden.

How calm and beautiful was the face of Nature! The prairie here in Illinois, in the heart of Lincoln's country, had a spirit of its own, unlike that of the forest, and I had come to look upon the meeting-house as a place possessing a sort of soul, a personality which made it stand out in my imagination as being unique among all the meeting-houses I had ever seen. It must, I thought, feel the states of the weather and the moods of the people.

The settlers made their way to meeting in wagons, on horseback and on foot; and for nearly an hour people straggled in. They came in family groups, and a moment of excitement would be followed by a period of impatient waiting. They came from the west, where a faint column of smoke rose in a zig-zag in the warm, limpid atmosphere; from the north, where houses and cabins were hidden in groves or in hollows; from the south, where a forest of old oaks and elms bordered the horizon with a belt of dark green; and from the east, where the rolling prairie spread beyond the limits of vision, a far-reaching vista of grass and flowers.

I had arrived early on my pony. Our neighbours would be here, and I should see some of them for the first time.

Silas Jordan and his wife, Kezia, were among the first to arrive. He, small, thin, and shrivelled, with wiry hair and restless nerves, had a face resembling a spider's web; cross-bars of crow's feet encircled two small, ferret-like eyes, sunk deep in their sockets, out of which he peered with eager suspicion at the moving phenomena of the world. She, with that deep glow that belongs to the dusk of certain days in autumn, had jet-black hair, smoothed down till it covered the tops of her ears; her neck rose in a column from between two drooping shoulders, and her great languid eyes looked out on the world and the people like stars from a saffron sunset. Dark and dreamy, she seemed a living emblem of the tall, dark flowers and the willows that bordered the winding rivers and creeks of the prairies.

Then came the Busbys on a horse that "carried double," Serena Busby wearing a new pink calico dress and sun-bonnet, the colour clashing with her reddish hair and freckled face.

When these had settled in their seats there came one of those half-unearthly spells of silence and waiting not unlike those moments at a funeral just before the mourners and the minister make their appearance.

I had taken a seat inside for a while, but I slipped out again just in time to see a man come loping along on a small, shaggy horse, man and animal looking as if they had both grown up on the prairie together. It was Zack Caverly, nicknamed Socrates. Zack was indeed a Socrates of the prairie as well in looks as in speech, and the person who first called him after the immortal sage had one of those flashes of inspiration that come now and then to the scholar whose cosmopolitan experience permits him to judge men by a single phrase or a gesture. He tied his horse to a hitching-post, then stood at the door waiting to see what new faces would appear at the meeting. Here he met his old acquaintance Silas Jordan.

The talk soon turned to personalities.

"Have ye heerd who them folks is down yander in the Log-House?" began Silas, alluding to the new home of my parents.

"They air from the old kintry," Socrates answered, his round eyes blinking in a manner not to be described.

"Kinder stuck up for these diggin's, I'm thinkin'."

"I 'low they ain't like us folks," was the careless response. "They hed a heap o' hired help whar they come from."

"The Squar tole me hisself what kyounties he hez lived in sence he came from the old kintry. He hez lived in two kyounties in Missouri en in four kyounties in Illinois, and now I reckon it's root hog or die ez fur ez these diggins goes. It's his second trial on prairie land. He 'lows it'll be the last if things don't plough up jest ez he's sot his mind te havin' 'em. He's a-layin' in with the Abolitionists, and he voted oncet fer Abe Lincoln, en he sez he air ready te do it ag'in."

Socrates looked down the road, and exclaimed:

"Bless my stars! if thar ain't Elihu Gest! He's got a stranger with him."

When Elihu Gest hitched his horse to the fence Socrates greeted him:

"Howdy, howdy, Brother Gest. I war wonderin' what hed become o' ye. Ain't seen ye in a coon's age."

Elihu Gest was known as the "Load-Bearer." He had earned this nickname by his constant efforts to assume other people's mental and spiritual burdens. The stranger he brought with him was the preacher.

"I war jes' wonderin' ez I come along," said the Load-Bearer, "what the Know-nothin's en sech like air a-goin' te do, seein' ez how Lincoln en Douglas air dividin' the hull yearth a-twixt 'em."

"Providence created the Know-nothin's te fill up the chinks," answered Zack Caverly, "en ye know it don't noways matter *what* ye fill 'em up with."

"I 'low the chinks hez to be filled up somehow," replied the Load-Bearer, "en a log-cabin air a mighty good place te live in when a man's too pore te live in a frame house."

"Thet's it; them thar politicioners like Abe Lincoln en Steve Douglas hev quit livin' in log-cabins, en thar ain't no chinks fer the Know-nothin' party te fill," said Socrates.

He had taken out a big jack-knife and was whittling a stick.

"'Pears like thar's allers three kyinds o' everything—thar war the Whigs, the Demicrats, en the Know-nothin's, en thar air three kyinds o' folks all over this here kintry—the Methodists, the Hard-shells, en them thet's saft at feedin'-time, plumb open fer vittles en dead shet agin religion. Ez I war explainin' te Squar Briggs t'other day, in the heavings thar air the sun, the moon, en the stars; thet air three kyinds agin. En whar hev ye ever see a kivered wagin 'thout hosses, creaturs, en yallar dogs? The yaller dogs air steppin'-stones te the hosses, the hosses comin' in right betwixt the varmints en human bein's, which the Scriptur' sez air jest a leetle below the angels. But ye'd never guess 'thout a heap o' cute thinkin' thet a yaller dog could make hisself so kinder useful like ez wal ez pertickler. Ez fer folks gen'ly, thar air three kyinds—Yankees, niggers, en white people."

"Ye don't calc'late te reckon niggers ez folks!" ejaculated Silas Jordan.

"They air folks jes like we air," said the Load-Bearer, "en they hev souls te save. They air bein' called on, but somehow the slave-owners ain't got no ears fer the call."

"Wal," chimed in Socrates, "I ain't agin th' Abolitionists, en up te now I ain't tuck much int'rest in the argiments fer en ag'inst. I ain't called on fer te jedge noways." He looked about him and continued: "They air talkin' 'bout freein' the niggers, but some o' these here settlers ain't got spunk 'nough te choose thar partner fer a dance, ner ile 'nough in thar j'ints te bow in a ladies' chain. Mebbe arter all the niggers air a sight better off 'n we uns air. They ain't got no stakes in the groun'."

At this point there was a shuffling of feet and spitting. Then his thoughts turned to the past.

"Afore Buchanan's election I hed all the fiddlin' I could do, but when Pete Cartwright come along he skeered 'em, en when the Baptists come they doused 'em in p'isen cold water, en now folks air predictin' the end o' the world by this here comet.* I'll be doggoned if I've drawed the bow oncet sence folks got skeered plumb te thar marrer-bones! T'other night when I heerd sunthin' snap I warn't thinkin' o' the fiddle, en when I tuck it down the nex' day jes' te fondle it a leetle fer old times' sake I see it war the leadin' string; en good, lastin' catgut air skase ez crowin' hens in these 'ere parts."

Silas Jordan, returning to the subject of my parents, remarked:

"I reckon them Britishers at the Log-House 'll hev te roll up en wade in if they want te git on in this here deestric'."

Just then the talk was interrupted by the appearance of the persons in question, and the crowd at the door stared in silence as they walked in. When Silas recovered his wits he continued his remarks:

"She's got on a store bunnit en he's got on a b'iled shirt." To which Socrates replied, without evincing the least surprise:

"Tallest man I've seed in these parts 'cept Abe Lincoln."

There was a pause, during which the two men gazed through the open door at the tall man who had passed in and taken a seat.

There was something strangely foreign and remote in the impression my parents produced at the meeting. My mother wore a black silk gown and a black bonnet with a veil; the tall, straight figure of my father appeared still taller with his long frock coat and high collar, and his serious face and Roman nose gave him something of a patriarchal look, although he was still in the prime of life. The arrival of the family from the Log-House caused a flutter of curiosity, but when it was seen that the new-comers were devout worshippers the congregation began to settle down to a spirit of religious repose.

It was a heterogeneous gathering: humorists who were unconscious of their humour, mystics who did not understand their strange, far-reaching power, sentimental dreamers who did their best to live down their emotions, old-timers and cosmopolitans with a marvellous admixture of sense and sentiment, political prophets who could foresee events by a sudden, illuminating flash and foretell them in a sudden, pithy sentence. It was a wonderful people, living in a second Canaan, in an age of social change and upheaval, in a period of political and phenomenal wonders.

A vague longing filled the hearts of the worshippers. With the doubts

* Donati's great comet.

and misgivings of the present, there was a feeling that to-morrow would bring the realisation of all the yearnings and promises, and when the preacher rose and announced that wistful old hymn:

"In the Christian's home in glory
There remains a land of rest,"

an instant change was produced in the faces of the people. Silas Jordan led the singing in a high, shrill voice which descended on the meeting like a cold blast through a broken window, but Uriah Busby, always on the look-out for squalls, neutralised the rasping sounds by his full, melodious waves. His voice gave forth an unctuous security, not unmixed with a good part of Christian gallantry. In it there was something hearty and fraternal; it leavened conditions and persons, and made the strangers feel at home.

If Uriah Busby's singing gave substance to the meeting, that of Kezia Jordan gave expression to its soul. In the second line her voice rose and fell like a wave from the infinite depths, with something almost unearthly in its tones, that seemed to bring forth the yearnings of dead generations and the unfulfilled desires of her pioneer parents.

A voice had been heard from behind the thin veil that separates the two worlds.

My mother felt somewhat timid among so many strangers. As she looked down at the hymn-book in her hands, her brows, slightly elevated, gave to her face an expression of pensive reverence. Kezia Jordan had noticed two things about the new-comer: her wonderful complexion and her delicate hands. Kezia had as yet only glanced at the stranger; had she heard her speak, she would have remembered her voice as an influence going straight to the soul, touching at the heart's secrets without naming them—a voice that enveloped the listener as in a mantle of compassion, with intonations suggestive of unaffected sympathy for all in need of it.

My mother had often heard the old Methodist hymns, but now for the first time she felt the difference between the music of a trained choir and the effects produced by the singing of one or two persons inspired by the spirit of the time, hour, and place. Never had sacred song so moved her. Kezia Jordan had infused into two lines something which partook of revelation. The words of the hymn, then, were true, and not a mere juggling with sentiment. Here was an untrained singer who by an unconscious effort revealed a truth which came to the listener with the force of inexorable law, for the words, "there remains a land of rest," came as a decree as well as a promise; and my mother now realised what life in the Log-House would be for her.

A glance at the singer confirmed the impression created by her singing. There, in her strange prophetic features, shone the indelible imprints made by the lonely years in the long and silent conflict; there, in Kezia Jordan's eyes, shone the immemorial mementoes of the ages gone, while the expression of her face changed as the memories came and went like shadows of silent wings over still, clear waters.

Prayers had been offered with more or less fervour; and now with awkward demeanour the preacher stood up, his pale face and half-scared expression arousing in the minds of many of the people no little curiosity and some apprehension.

"Brethering and sistering," he began, in a rambling way, "ye hev all heerd the rumours thet hez been passed from mouth te mouth pertainin' te the signs and wonders o' these here times. Folks's minds is onsettled. But me en Brother Gest hev been wrastlin' with the Sperit all night yander at his God-fearin' home; we were wrastlin' fer a tex' fittin' this here time en meetin', en it warn't till sommairs nigh mornin' thet Brother Gest opened the Good Book, en p'intin' his finger, sez: 'I hev found it! Hallelujer!' It war Isaiah, nineteenth chapter, twentieth verse."

Here the preacher opened the Bible. He read slowly, emphasising certain words so that even the most obtuse present might catch something of the meaning.

" 'En it shell be *fer* a sign, en *fer* a witness unto the Lord of hosts in the land of Egypt: fer they shell cry unto the Lord bekase of the oppressors, en he *shell* send them a saviour, en a *great* one, en he shell deliver them.' "

He stopped a moment to let the congregation muse on the text, and then proceeded:

"It looked like when he put his finger on thet tex' Brother Gest war changed ez in a twinklin', en our watchin' en prayin' war over fer thet night. Brethering, with the findin' o' thet tex' our troubles war gone, en in thar place thar come te our innermost feelin's a boundin' joy sech ez on'y them thet hez faith kin know.'

Here he lost himself; then, like a drowning man who clutches at a straw, he seized hold of an old hackneyed text, the first that came into his mind, and continued regardless of consequences:

"Fer ez the Scriptur' sez, 'What came ye out fer te see? A reed shaken by the wind?' I 'low most o' ye hez plenty reeds if ye're anywhars near a snipe deestric', but I reckon ye ain't troubled much by seein' 'em shake."

He began to regain confidence, and leaving reeds he grappled with the earth and the heavens in periods which carried everybody with him.

"But thar ain't a sinner here, thar ain't no Christian here to-day thet warn't plumb shuck up by thet yearthquake t'other night thet rocked ye in yer beds like ye were bein' rocked in a skiff in the waves behind one o' them Mississippi stern-wheelers. No, brethering, the Lord hez passed the time when He shakes yer cornfields en yer haystacks by a leetle puff o' wind. He hez opened the roof o' Heaven so ye can all see what's a-comin'. He hez made it so all o' ye, 'cept them thet's blind, kin say truly, 'I hev seen it.' Under ye the yearth hez been shuck, over ye the stars air beginnin' te shift en wander. A besom o' destruction 'll overtake them thet's on the wrong side in this here fight!"

He eyed the people up and down on each side, and then went on:

"But the tex' says, 'He shell send them a saviour, en a *great* one, en he shell deliver them.' Now it air jest ez plain ez the noonday sun thet the Lord God app'ints His own leaders, en it air jest ez plain thet His ch'ice ain't fell on no shufflin' backslider. Ye kin bet all yer land en yer cattle en yer hosses on this one preposition, en thet is ye cain't git away from fac's by no cross-argimints thet many air called but mighty few air chosen; en thet means thet on'y one man is 'p'inted te lead."

At this there was a visible change in the attitude of many of the listeners.

"What air he a-comin' to?" whispered old Lem Stephens to Uriah Busby.

It was a bold stroke; but Elihu Gest, the Load-Bearer, had won over the preacher to speak out, and he was coming to the main point as fast as an artless art and blunt but effective rhetoric would let him.

He proceeded with his sermon, now bringing the expectant people to the verge of the last period, now letting them slip back as if he were giving them a "breathing spell" to brace them for a still stronger stage in the argument. It was wonderful how this simple preacher, without education or training, managed to keep the interest of the congregation at boiling point for more than an hour before he pronounced the two magical words that would unlock the whole mystery of the discourse. Before him sat old Whigs, Know-nothings and Democrats, Republicans, militant Abolitionists, and outspoken friends of slave-owners in the South. But the Load-Bearer was there, his eyes riveted on the speaker, every nerve strung to the utmost pitch, assuming by moral compact the actual responsibility of the sermon. If the preacher failed Elihu Gest would assume his loads; if the sermon was a triumph he would share in the preacher's triumph.

As the sermon drew to a close it became evident that by some queer, roundabout way, by some process of reasoning and persuasion that grew upon the people like a spell, they were listening, and had all along been listening, to a philippic against slavery.

At last the preacher's face lost its timorous look. With great vehemence he repeated the last part of his text:

" 'Fer they shell *cry* unto the Lord bekase of the oppressors, en he shell send them a saviour, en a *great* one,' "—here he struck the table a violent blow—"en he shell *deliver them!* "

There was a moment of bewilderment and suspense, during which Lem Stephens was preparing for the worst. His mouth, usually compressed to a thin, straight slit, was now stiffened by a bull-dog jaw which he forced forward till the upper lip had almost disappeared; Minerva Wagner sat rigid, her mummy-like figure encased in whalebone wrapped in linsey-woolsey.

The preacher gave them no rest:

"Now right here I want ye all te ask yerselves who it air thet's a-cryin' fer deliverance. Who air it?" he shouted. "Why, thar ain't but one people a-cryin' fer deliverance, en they air the slaves down thar in Egypt!"

The words fell like a muffled blow in the silence. Lem Stephens sat forward, breathless; Uriah Busby heaved a long sigh; fire flashed from Mrs. Wagner's grey, faded eyes; Ebenezer Hicks turned in his seat, his bushy eyebrows lowering to a threatening frown; while the face of Socrates wore a look of calm and neutral curiosity.

But hardly had the meeting realised the full force of the last words when the preacher put the final questions:

"En *who* shell deliver them? Do any o' ye know? Brethering, thar ain't but one human creatur' ekil to it, en thet air Abraham Lincoln. The Lord hez called him!"

An electrical thrill passed through the meeting. A subtle, permeating power took possession of the congregation, for the preacher had pronounced the first half of the name, Abraham, in such a way that it seemed as if the patriarch of Israel was coming once more in person to lead the people. An extraordinary influence had been evoked; a living investment of might and mystery, never at any time very distant, was now close at hand.

Ebenezer Hicks rose, and casting a fierce glance about him hurried out; Minerva Wagner sprang from her seat like an automaton suddenly moved by some invisible force and left the meeting, followed by her two tall, lank sons; Lem Stephens hurried after them, and with each step gave vent to his feelings by a loud thump on the bare floor with his wooden leg. When he got to the door he cast one last withering look at the preacher.

But Uriah Busby's voice rang out loud and sonorous:

> "How tedious and tasteless the hours
> When Jesus no longer I see."

The old hymn was taken up by Kezia Jordan in the next line. Once more her voice filled the meeting-house with golden waves, once more every heart beat in unison, and every soul communed in an indescribable outpouring of religious melody.

The whole congregation was singing now. With Kezia's voice a balm of Gilead came pouring over the troubled waters created by the strange, prophetic and menacing sermon. The Load-Bearer, with hardly voice enough to speak aloud, was singing; the preacher sang even louder than he had preached; Serena Busby sang as I never heard her sing again; and while those who had left the meeting were about to depart they heard what they would never hear repeated. The opportunity to join hands with the coming power had passed, and as they set out for home they must have been haunted by the matchless magic and simplicity of the words and music, and more than ever would the coming hours seem "tedious and tasteless" to them.

THE LOAD-BEARER

We had been four months in the Log-House and my mother was just beginning to feel at home when one afternoon, as I was sauntering along the road near the gate, I saw a man on foot coming from the south.

As he approached I noticed that his features had a peculiar cast, his hair was rather long, his movements somewhat slow, and when he arrived in front of the gate he squared about and stopped with a sort of jerk, as if he had been dreaming but was now awake and conscious that this was the place he had come to visit. He peered at the Log-House as though awaiting some interior impulse to move him to further action; then he opened the gate, and, walking through the yard to the front door, rapped lightly.

I had followed him in, and when my mother opened the door and the stranger said, in a listless sort of way, "I jes' called to see how ye're gettin' on," I saw it was Elihu Gest, the Load-Bearer.

My mother thanked him, invited him in, and offered him a chair.

"I 'low ye're not long settled in this 'ere section," he said, taking a seat.

"Not long," she answered; "we are quite settled in the house, but on the farm my husband has so much to do he hardly knows where to begin."

She placed the kettle on the stove for coffee, and busied herself about getting the strange visitor some substantial refreshment. I thought I had never seen a face more inscrutable. He eyed my mother with grave interest, and after a silence that lasted some considerable time he said:

"If yer loads is too heavy jes' cast 'em off; the Lord is willin' en I ain't noways contrary."

Not till now did she realise that this was the man she had heard so much about; but not knowing just what to say, she gave no answer.

As he sat and stared at my mother his presence diffused a mysterious influence. My mind was busy with queries: Who sent him? What are his loads? Why does he take such an interest in my mother? And I thought she must be giving him coffee and eatables the better to enable him to support his loads, whatever they might be. She placed the coffee and other good things on the table and cordially invited the stranger to make himself at home. After pouring out a cup of coffee she sat down with folded hands, her pale face more pensive than usual, making some remarks about the weather and the good prospects for the new settlers.

Elihu Gest sat, a veritable sphinx of the prairie, wrapped in his own meditations. She almost feared that his visit might be a portent of some coming calamity, and that he had come to warn her and help her to gather force and courage for the ordeal.

Yet there was something in his look which inspired confidence and even cheerfulness, and she concluded it was good to have him sitting there. He began to sip his coffee, and at last, as if waking from a reverie, he put the question:

"How air ye feelin' in sperit?"

"The Lord has been merciful," she replied, the question having come as an immediate challenge to her religious faith and courage.

"Yer coffee is mos' appetizin'," he said, with a slight sniff.

"I am glad you like it, and I hope you are feeling rested, for you seem to have come a long way."

"They's a powerful difference a-twixt a mile and what a man's thinkin'. When yer mind is sot on one thing the distance a-twixt two places ain't much noways."

"Do you always walk?" she asked sympathetically.

"It's accordin' te how the hoss is feelin'. If the beast's anyways contrary he gives a snort, ez much ez te say, 'Mebbe I'll carry ye en mebbe I won't; but when he snorts and kicks both te oncet thet means he'll kick the hind sights off all creation if I try te ride him. I've seen him when Joshua en his trumpet couldn't git him outen the barn door. I don't believe in workin' dumb critters when their sperits air droopin'. I'm allers more contented when I'm 'bleeged te walk; en hosses air powerful skase."

"Necessity compels us to do many things that seem impossible, but we learn to accept them as the best things for us. Won't you have some more coffee?"

"Yer coffee is mos' appetizin', it is so."

"And won't you eat something?"

"I'm much obleeged, but I don't feel no cravin' fer vittles. Accordin' te Sister Jordan, yer cakes en pies beats all she ever see."

"Mrs. Jordan is a very good woman."

"She is so; I've knowed her from away back."

There came another pause, during which the visitor looked straight before him, lost in thought. Presently he began:

"Thet comet's convicted a good many folks. Ebenezer Hicks war skeered half te death when he see it a-comin', makin' the loads mos' heavy fer his pore wife."

Then, addressing my mother, he continued:

"The night he war 'flicted, I couldn't git te sleep nohow. I sez to myself, 'Thar's an axle-tree wants ilein', en I'll be blamed if it ain't over te Ebenezer Hicks's.' I went te the barn te see how the hoss war feelin', en I sez, 'Kin ye carry me over te Ebenezer Hicks's if I saddle ye?' But Henry Clay give a kick thet sot me wonderin' how I war ever goin' te git thar."

"Many people think the end of the world is at hand," said my mother.

"They do, fer a fact."

He paused a moment, then went on:

"But them thet's skeered air folks without faith. I ain't got no call fer te take loads from folks what's skeered. Summow I cain't carry 'em."

"The burdens of life are, indeed, hard to bear alone."

"They air so; en 'twixt you and me, marm, I'm jest a might onsartin 'bout what it air 'flicts some folks. 'Pears like Satan skeers more folks 'n is ever won over by the Lord's goodness en mercy. Them thet's allers a-tremblin' ain't much account when it comes te strappin' the belly-band real hard; they don't never set tight in the saddle when they're called on te go plumb through a wilderness o' thistles."

After meditating again for a time, he resumed:

"But Ebenezer Hicks warn't a patchin' on Uriah Busby what lives yander at Black B'ar Creek. He war so skeered he sot to weepin' when he see me come in, en I never see a woman ez hoppin' mad ez Sereny

Busby! I couldn't take no loads from Brother Busby; accordin' te my notion, he warn't settin' up under none, en jest ez soon ez I sot eyes on Sister Busby I see *she* hedn't hitched up to nothin' of any heft neither. She don't set still long enough. I 'low I war some dis'p'inted."

He laughed faintly; perhaps he wished to convey the impression that the burdens of life were not so dreadful, after all.

"I fear you had your trouble all for nothing," said my mother.

"Ye see, Brother Busby war skeered, en Sister Busby got her dander up. I never knowed a woman with red hair that war afeared of man or beast."

"Mr. Busby must have been very much frightened," remarked my mother, smiling.

"Not so skeered but what he could talk. Si Jordan had his speech tuck plumb away, en I never see Sister Jordan so flustered. But she don't say much nohow. Sereny Busby she keeps the top a-spinnin' the livelong day. But I hev seen Uriah Busby caved in more'n oncet. I knowed 'em both afore they war married. If I wanted a woman, sprightly with her tongue ez well ez with her hands, I'd take Sereny Busby fer fust ch'ice; if I wanted a woman what knows a heap en sez mos' nothin', I'd take Kezia Jordan. Human natur' ain't allers the same. I 'low Sister Busby's got the most eddication."

"But education never helps much if the heart is not in the right place."

"Thet thar's what I've allers said. 'Pears like sometimes Sereny Busby's heart's jest a leetle lopsided en wants re-settin', ez ye might say. But thar's a sight o' difference atwixt one load en another. When I set with some folks what's in a heap o' trouble, I go away ez happy ez kin be, but when I hev te go away without ary a load, I feel mos' empty."

Here there was another spell of silence, but after a few sips from a third cup of coffee he continued:

" 'Pears like thar warn't never no heft te Sereny Busby's troubles. She don't give 'em no chance te set; en jest ez a duck's back goes agin water, her'n is set agin loads."

"The Lord has given her a cheerful mind; I think she has much to be thankful for."

"She hez, fer a fact. But I never kin tell jes' how her mind is a-workin'. She steps roun' ez spry ez kin be, hummin' fiddle tunes mos'ly; en when Brother Busby tuck te bed with thet fever what's mos' killed him, she kept on a-hummin', en some folks would a-said she war triflin', but she warn't. She give Uriah his med'cine mos' reg'lar, en mopped his head with cold water from the well, en made him appetizin' rabbit soup. The

Bible sez the sperit's willin' but the flesh is weak, but I don't see no failin'
in a woman thet kin hum all day like a spinnin'-top. . . . But I allers
kin tell what Kezia Jordan is a-thinkin', en thar ain't no two ways 'bout
it; Sister Jordan kin sing hymns so ye want te give right up en die, ye
feel so happy."

"She has something wonderful in her voice when she sings," said my
mother; "I felt that when I heard her sing 'in meeting.'"

"I 'low Si Jordan ain't pertickler benev'lent, but Kezia Jordan counts
fer more'n one in that 'ar house."

"I fear she has had a life of much care and trouble, and perhaps that
is one reason why she is so good."

"Folks is born like we find 'em, marm. I've been nigh on thirty year
wrastlin' with the sorrows o' life, en I ain't seen ary critter change his
spots. A wolf don't look like a wild cat, en I never see a fox with a
bob tail; en folks air like varmints: God Almighty hez marked 'em with
His seal."

He looked round the room abstractedly, and then said:

"It's looks thet tells when a man's in trouble; en a heap o' tribulation
keeps folks from hollerin'. Sister Jordan hez knowed trouble from away
back. But thar's a tremenjous difference a-twixt her en Si Jordan. He kin
talk en pray when he gits a-goin', en I've heared him when it looked like
his flow o' words would swamp the hull endurin' meetin'; but when the
risin' settled, thar warn't much harm done no way. But jes' let Sister
Jordan sing a hymn, en ye feel like the hull yearth war sot in tune."

"That is because she is so sincere," observed my mother, gravely.

"Thet's a fact. I ain't never forgot the time when I hed thet spell o'
sickness en felt ez if thar war nothin' wuth a-livin' fer. What with sickness,
en the defeat o' Fremont, en them desperadoes cuttin' up over in Kansas,
en the goin's on o' them Demicrats in Springfield, 'peared like I never
would be good fer nothin' more. All te oncet the feelin' come over me te
go over te Kezia Jordan's. Thet ud be 'bout ez much ez I could do, seein'
I war like a chicken what's jes' pecked its way through the shell. I hedn't
got ez fur ez the kitchen door when I heared her a-singin':

> " 'Come thou Fount of every blessin',
> Tune my heart te sing Thy praise.'

"Thet voice o' her'n set me a-cryin', en I sot right down on the door-
steps, en thanked God fer all His goodness. Arter a while, she come out
fer a bucket o' water.

" 'Good Land!' she sez; 'I'm right glad te see ye. Go right in; ye're jest in time fer dinner; I've got some real nice prairie chicken en pum'kin pie; everything's 'mos' ready.'

"Soon as I went in she sez:

"'Mercy on us, Elihu! I never see ye look so! Set right down, en tell me what ails ye; ye ain't been sick 'thout lettin' me know, hev ye?'"

"I like to have such a good Christian as my nearest neighbour," said my mother, with much feeling.

"I allow she warn't allers a Christian. I war over at Carlinville when she heard Pete Cartwright fer the fust time, en the meetin'-house warn't big enough te hold the people. Sister Jordan warn't moved te sing any durin' the fust hymn, but she j'ined in the second, en arter thet Brother Cartwright tuck right holt, ez ye might say, en swung 'em till their feet tetched perdition.

"'Yo're ripe,' he sez, holdin' out his fist, 'yo're ripe, like grain waitin' fer the reaper! Ye'll be mowed down, en the grain 'll be plumb divided from the chaff, en the Christians 'll be parted from the sinners.'

"The hull meetin' began to move like wheat a-wavin' in the wind. The preacher knowed Kezia Jordan fer a nat'ral-born Christian by her singin', fer he p'inted straight, en sez:

"'Ye're at the cross-roads, sister; ye'll hev te choose one or t'other; en the years en the months air gone fer most o' ye, en thar's on'y this here hour left fer te choose. Which will it be? Will it be the road thet leads up yander, or the one thet leads down by the dark river whar the willers air weepin' night en day?'

"This war the turnin' p'int fer a good many; but the preacher warn't satisfied yet. He rolled up en went te work in dead arnest. He told 'bout the fust coon hunt he ever see:

"'Sinners,' he sez, 'is jes' like the coon asleep in thet tree—never dreamin' o' danger. But the varmint war waked all on a sudden by a thunderin' smell o' smoke, en hed te take te the branches. Someone climbs up the tree en shakes the branch whar the coon is holdin' on.' En' right here Pete Cartwright slung his handkerchief over his left arm en sez, 'A leetle more, a leetle more, a l-e-e-e-tle more en the varmint's bound te drap squar' on the dogs.' He shuck his arm three times—down, down, down, he sez, lettin' the handkerchief drap, 'down te whar the wailin' en gnashin' air a million times more terrible 'n the sufferin's o' thet coon.'"

The Load-Bearer bent forward and his face assumed a look of tragic intensity as he continued:

"A veil o' mournin' war a-bein' pulled down over the meetin'. He war takin' the people straight te jedgment, like a flock o' sheep, with the goats a-followin', usin' no dividin' line, for he put it to 'em:

" 'Whar would ye all be if this here floor war te slide right from under ye, leavin' ye settin' on the brink, with Time on one side en Etarnity on t'other?'

"The hull meetin' war shuck te pieces, some hollerin', some too 'flicted te set up; en I see nigh on twenty plumb fainted en gone."

Elihu Gest sighed as he sat back in his chair, and proceeded in his usual way:

"When the meetin' war over I sez te Sister Jordan, 'How air ye feelin' in sperit?' En she sez, 'I've had more'n enough o' this world's goods!'

" 'I want te know!' sez I.

" 'Yes,' she sez, 'I don't never want no more.' En I see it war for everlastin'."

No one spoke for a long time.

At last he rose from his chair and moved towards the door like one in a dream, his face wearing a look of almost superhuman detachment.

Then, just before passing out, he turned and said,

"I'll bid ye good-day, fer the present."

This visit made the day a memorable one for me, for I saw in Elihu Gest a human wonder; he opened up a world of things and influences about which I had never dreamed. And when he had disappeared down the road to the south, the way he had come, I wondered how he was carrying his loads, what they could be, and whether my mother felt relieved of any of her burdens. But I held my peace, while she simply remarked:

"A very strange but very good man. I wonder if we shall ever see him again?"

Here was a man who did everything by signs, tokens, impressions; who was moved by some power hidden from the understanding of everyone else—a power which none could define, concerning which people had long since ceased to question. He came and went, influenced by signs in harmony with his own feelings and moods, by natural laws shut off from our understanding by the imperative rules of conventional religion and society. Things which were sealed mysteries to us were finger-posts to him, pointing the way across the prairies, in this direction or in that. Is it time to go forth? He would look up at the heavens, sense the state of Nature by the touch of the breeze, sound the humour of the hour with a plumb-line of his own, then set out to follow where it led.

The Load-Bearer's presence, his odd appearance, his descriptions and peculiar phases, his spells of silence, his sudden enthusiasms, the paradox of humour and religious feeling displayed, brought to our home the fervour and candour of the meeting-house—honest pioneer courage and frankness, and, above all, an influence that left on me an impression never to be effaced. How far, how very far, we were from the episcopal rector, with his chosen words, studied phrases, and polite and dignified sympathy! How far it all was from anything my parents had ever dreamed of even in so remote a country! The prairie was inhabited by a people as new and strange as the country itself.

Selected Bibliography

Barnes, Gilbert H. • *The Anti-Slavery Impulse, 1830-1844.* New York, 1933.

Blau, Joseph T., ed. • *Social Theories of Jacksonian Democracy.* New York, 1947.

Bode, Carl • *The American Lyceum.* New York, 1956.

Branch, E. Douglas • *The Sentimental Years, 1836-1860.* New York, 1934.

Cash, Wilbur J. • *The Mind of the South. New York,* 1941.

Cross, Whitney R. • *The Burned-Over District.* Ithaca, New York, 1950.

Daniels, George H. • *American Science in the Age of Jackson.* New York, 1968.

Duberman, Martin B. • *The Anti-Slavery Vanguard: New Essays on the Abolitionists.* Princeton, New Jersey, 1965.

Elson, Ruth Miller • *Guardians of Tradition: American Schoolbooks of the Nineteenth Century.* Lincoln, Nebraska, 1964.

Flexner, James T. • *That Wilder Image: The Painting of America's Native School from Thomas Cole to Winslow Homer.* Boston, 1962.

Gabriel, Ralph H. • *The Course of American Democratic Thought.* New York, 1956.

Ekirch, Arthur A. • *The Idea of Progress in America 1815-1860.* New York, 1944.

Griffin, Clifford S. • *Their Brother's Keeper: Moral Stewardship in the United States 1800-1865.* New Brunswick, New Jersey, 1960.

Grimsted, David • *Melodrama Unveiled: American Theater and Culture, 1800-1850.* Chicago, 1968.

Hamlin, Talbot • *Greek Revival Architecture in America.* New York, 1944.

Harris, Neil • *The Artist in American Society; The Formative Years, 1790-1860.* New York, 1966.

Hurst, J. Willard • *Law and the Conditions of Freedom in the Nineteenth-Century United States*. Madison, 1956.

Jaffa, Harry V. • *Crisis of the House Divided: An Interpretation on the Lincoln-Douglas Debates*. New York, 1959.

Johnson, Charles A. • *The Frontier Camp Meeting*. Dallas, Texas, 1955.

Kouwenhoven, John • *Made In America: The Arts in Modern Civilization*. New York, 1948.

Larkin, Oliver W. • *Art and Life in America*. New York, 1949.

Lawrence, D. H. • *Studies in Classic American Literature*. New York, 1923.

Lewis, R. W. B. • *The American Adam: Innocence, Tragedy and Tradition in the Nineteenth-Century*. Chicago, 1958.

McMaster, John Bach • *A History of the People of the United States, from the Revolution to the Civil War*. New York, 1883–1923. 8 vols.

Marx, Leo • *The Machine in the Garden: Technology and the Pastoral Ideal In America*. New York, 1964.

Matthiessen, F. O. • *American Renaissance: Art and Expression in the Age of Emerson and Whitman*. New York, 1941.

Meyers, Marvin • *The Jacksonian Persuasion: Politics and Belief*. Stanford, 1957.

Miller, Perry • *The Life of the Mind in America, from the Revolution to the Civil War*. New York, 1965.

Newhall, Beaumont • *The Daguerreotype in America*. New York, 1961.

O'Dea, Thomas • *The Mormons*. Chicago, 1957.

Olmsted, Frederick Law • *The Cotton Kingdom*. New York, 1861–1862.

Parrington, Vernon • *The Romantic Revolution in America, 1800–1860*. New York, 1927.

Pessen, Edward • *Most Uncommon Jacksonians: The Radical Leaders of the Early Labor Movement*. Albany, New York, 1967.

Rourke, Constance • *American Humor: A Study of the National Character*. New York, 1931.

Rusk, Ralph L. • *The Literature of the Middle Western Frontier*. New York, 1925. 2 vols.

Sanford, Charles L. • *The Quest for Paradise: Europe and the American Moral Imagination*. Urbana, Illinois, 1961.

Smith, Henry Nash • *Virgin Land: The American West as Symbol and Myth*. Cambridge, Massachusetts, 1950.

Smith, Timothy L. • *Revivalism and Social Reform: American Protestantism On the Eve of the Civil War*. New York, 1957.

Somkin, Fred • *Unquiet Eagle: Memory and Desire in the Idea of American Freedom, 1815–1860*. Ithaca, New York, 1967.

Taylor, William R. • *Cavalier and Yankee: The Old South and the American National Character*. New York, 1961.

Tocqueville, Alexis de • *Democracy in America.* New York, 1946. 2 vols.

Tyler, Alice Felt • *Freedom's Ferment.* Minneapolis, 1944.

Ward, John William • *Andrew Jackson, Symbol for an Age.* New York, 1955.

Williams, William Appleman • *The Contours of American History.* Cleveland, 1961.

Wishey, Bernard W. • *The Child and the Republic: The Dawn of Modern American Child Nurture.* Philadelphia, 1967.